"RAILS ACROSS THE C
THE STORY OF THE BIRMINGHAM CROSS CIT

A Class 100 dmu crosses the Worcester & Birmingham Canal at Withybed Green just north of Alvechurch, with a train for Redditch on th December 1980.

(P.J.Shoesmith)

written and compiled by

JOHN BOYNTON

– to the memory of my father, Leslie Boynton, with grateful thanks for the happy hours we spent at Bescot station when I was very small.

The Birmingham Cross City Line today

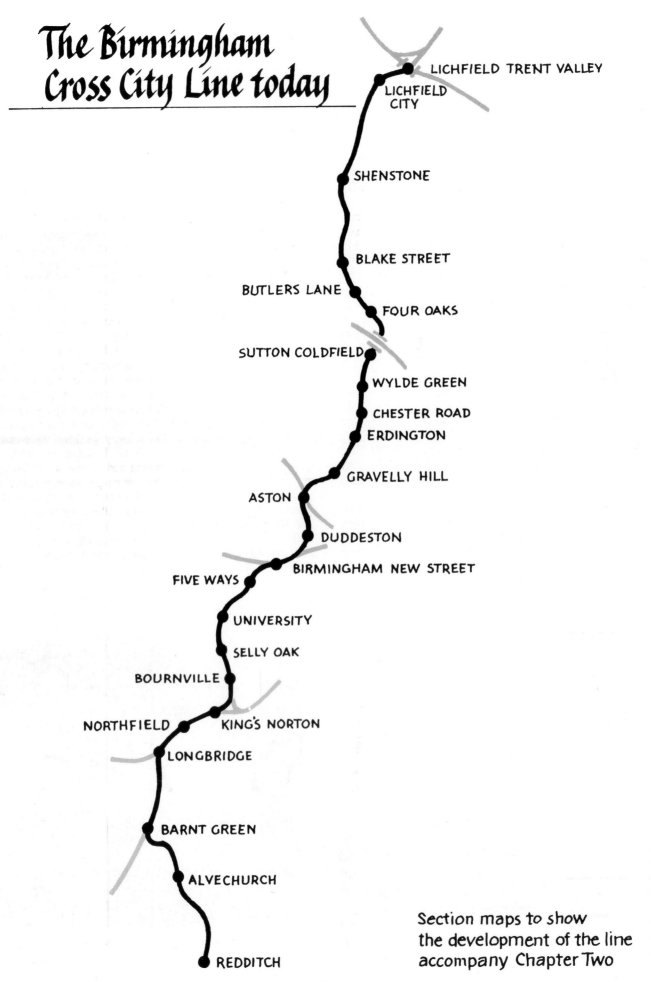

LICHFIELD TRENT VALLEY
LICHFIELD CITY

SHENSTONE

BLAKE STREET

BUTLERS LANE
FOUR OAKS

SUTTON COLDFIELD

WYLDE GREEN

CHESTER ROAD
ERDINGTON

GRAVELLY HILL

ASTON

DUDDESTON

BIRMINGHAM NEW STREET

FIVE WAYS

UNIVERSITY

SELLY OAK

BOURNVILLE

NORTHFIELD
KING'S NORTON

LONGBRIDGE

BARNT GREEN

ALVECHURCH

REDDITCH

Section maps to show
the development of the line
accompany Chapter Two

INTRODUCTION

Many railways have a fascinating history. No line ever ran in isolation or merely for the amusement of its operators. They all began life as commercial ventures, even those that were built mainly to thwart the ambitions of rivals. Every line has had some impact on the lives of the people it has claimed to serve.

The Birmingham Cross City Line, between Lichfield, Birmingham New Street and Redditch, is no exception. Every step forward and each setback in its development has been the result of some human interest; co-operation, conflict, generosity, bureaucratic wrangling, or whatever.

The first of this book's three chapters, "At The Very Centre", puts the line in its context, as the busiest commuter route outside London. It is seen in its role as the single most important public transport corridor in the West Midlands, and in relation to the other lines which focus on Birmingham. The chapter concludes with a journey along the line.

The middle chapter, "Growth and Struggle", covers the history of the line from the 1830s until the end of the diesel era. It begins with the development of the lines that would one day become the southern half of the Cross City Line, pausing to look at the birth pangs and growing pains of New Street station before charting twentieth century development and decline.

The northern half of the route, the earliest part of which dates from 1837, had a relatively uneventful existence until the 1950s. The tragedy of the 1955 Sutton Coldfield crash, the introduction of the new diesels, the World Scout Jamboree and the beginning of the Motorail service, were four important events that happened in as many years. The chapter concludes with the Cross City service, from the birth of the idea, the early days of operation in 1978 and through to the eve of electrification.

The text includes memories and recollections of people who have had close associations with the line, some going back more than seventy years. There are certain to be readers who will finish this chapter having found no reference to some event which they can remember. No account of any railway can hope to offer a complete detailed history, which would be exhaustive to compile and dreary to read, but any disappointment may be lessened by the discovery of new and unfamiliar parts of the story of this line.

The final chapter, "Under The Wires", deals with electrification, from submission of the scheme to the beginning of the train service. It is set out largely as a diary of the main events and also includes less obvious and less direct parts of the programme, such as rail safety talks to local schools, customer relations etc. The book concludes with thoughts on possible developments for the future.

The line has enjoyed a colourful history and looks toward an optimistic future, despite the fact that it has often had its back to the wall. Development and investment have frequently been slow, or absent altogether. This is not merely a twentieth century phenomenon; the northern terminus was fixed at Sutton for over twenty years before the Lichfield extension was built, and the original route into Birmingham from the south was hardly a proper railway at all. During the Beeching years the Redditch branch escaped closure by a whisker, and went on to endure a twilight service of three trains per day for over ten years. By the 1970s the Lichfield line showed increasing signs of decay and neglect, with ever scruffier stations served by late, decrepit and worn-out trains. Freight traffic had earlier dwindled and was entirely lost to the overcrowded roads with hardly a whimper.

Throughout all the difficulties, both recent and historical, the hard work and commitment of railway workers, not to mention the patience and general goodwill of the travelling public, have ensured that the line has survived and is now set to prosper as never before. Today it carries more people more efficiently than at any time in its history. As the century draws to a close it seems certain that, at long last, other ill-equipped urban lines in the West Midlands and elsewhere outside the London area will follow in the wake of Cross City, being allowed to modernise, upgrade, electrify and develop further, so that they too can play a fuller role within their communities.

A southbound Class 116 dmu approaches Longbridge on the evening of 24th July 1989. The boundary between the railway and Daffodil Park is the River Rea, here confined to an inconspicuous ditch. *(P.J.Shoesmith)*

CHAPTER ONE : AT THE VERY CENTRE
The line as part of today's railway

(The Hub of the Network : Local Lines : The Most Important Spoke in the Wheel : New Street Station : Cross City Journeys, North & South)

THE HUB OF THE NETWORK

Birmingham's New Street Station would never win a glamour contest. The visual appeal of stations such as York, Bristol Temple Meads, St.Pancras or even Coventry is completely absent here. This is a long low concrete world, at least at platform level, that ought never to be described as architecture. Nevertheless, it scores over all other stations in one vital respect; it is the hub of the British Rail network. Through services connect with almost all corners of the country; Penzance, Cardiff; Aberystwyth, Liverpool, Glasgow, Aberdeen, Edinburgh, Norwich, Euston, Brighton, Southampton, and most important places in between, with just a few exceptions, most notably Hull and Swindon. The opening of the Channel Tunnel holds out the prospect of through services to Europe, in particular Paris and Brussels. Because so many through services meet here, and because much of BR's long distance time-table is structured round New Street, it is a very significant interchange station. It has been deliberate policy, since at least the 1960s, for pairs of long distance trains to arrive and depart within minutes of each other, at either face of an island platform whenever possible, to allow easy transfer from one to the other. A glance at Table 51 in the BR Passenger Timetable will confirm this.

Most types of passenger locomotives and multiple units can be seen here on a regular basis, excluding those normally confined to the former Southern Region. New electric locomotives of the Class 90 series can be found working the intensive InterCity service to Euston, which operates every half hour. At the other end of the spectrum those elderly and reliable diesel workhorses, the Class 47s, still appear on some important services. For many long distance trains this is the change over point between diesel and electric traction, all adding to the bustle, congestion and potential for delay. The most obvious multiple units, both in size and sound, are the High Speed Trains (HSTs), dating from the 1970s and now the backbone of InterCity's North-East/South-West Cross-Country route, the core of which lies between Newcastle and Bristol. Up-market Sprinter dmus, the Regional Railways Class 158 "Express" units, link Birmingham with the East Midlands, East Anglia, South Wales and Shrewsbury. Earlier Sprinters, generally Class 150s in the smart green livery of Centro, or Class 156s with their 23 metre long cars, serve such places as the Stourbridge line, Hereford and Hednesford. Older electric multiple units, Class 310 or earlier, are common on the local trains to Walsall, Wolverhampton and Coventry, with Class 321s of Network SouthEast working the hourly semi-fast trains to Euston. The start of the full electric Cross City service, using Class 323 emus, has meant that the remaining 1950s dmus stabled at Tyseley have largely disappeared from New Street.

LOCAL LINES

Centro, the West Midlands Transport Authority on whose behalf and with whose financial support BR run local rail services, has an area bounded, clockwise from the north, by stations at Blake Street, Coventry, Dorridge, Earlswood, Longbridge, Stourbridge Junction, Wolverhampton and Hednesford. Within this area, in 1989, 11.1% of commuters came into Birmingham by rail. This was a total of 25.9 million passenger journeys, generating an income of £11.45 million. Centro's aim, stated when the figures were released, was to increase rail's share of the commuter market by 5%, making a total of 38 million passenger journeys per annum. This must be seen in perspective when 25.9 million passenger journeys represent less than one journey per week for the population of the Centro area. The hoped for increase is desirable, but is likely in the short term to impose more strain on underfunded rolling stock and have little real effect on overall travel patterns within the conurbation. Those travelling by the most cost-effective, efficient and least polluting means of transport will still be a small minority.

However, if these figures are read in conjunction with those for buses, as they should be, the picture is much more encouraging. Statistics released in November 1991 showed that:-
> "More than half the 120,000 commuters who travel into Birmingham city centre daily use buses and trains instead of cars - making public transport dominant for the first time in ten years.

The count, taken in November 1990, showed a 14% increase in the number of morning rush hour passengers .. averaging 62,190 a day. The number of light vehicles .. fell by 11% to a daily 58,009.
> It was a remarkable turnabout on 1989 when 55,000 (46%) used buses and trains, but 65,000 (54%) favoured cars."
> ("Birmingham Post" November 16th 1991)

A report in the same paper nine days earlier showed that the trend had continued during 1991:-
> "Another 4,000 travellers were using local trains as services became more prompt and reliable, according to Centro. ... 80% of rush hour trains arrived on time in the four weeks to October 11th ....in the same period last year it was only 70%.
> Mr.Michael Parker, head of operations for Centro, said: 'More people are travelling at peak time, which is a sign of reliability'..... He said the number of train journeys had risen by 8% to nearly 60,000 a day.
> Sales of monthly rail travel cards increased 75% and the combined bus and rail ticket by a quarter."
> ("Birmingham Post, 7th November 1991)

The Centro area (1993) contains 96.4 route miles of passenger-carrying railway, with 60 Centro supported stations, 29 of which have car parks offering 3,230 free places. Approximately 800 personnel are sponsored by Centro through an agreement with British Rail.

At the time of writing, 1993, local services operate out of New Street as follows:

** - Cross City:-
Cross City North, four per hour, all trains go to Lichfield Trent Valley.
Cross City South, four per hour to Longbridge, alternate trains continue to Redditch.
North and South are one through electric service as from July 1993, calling at all stations, all day, seven days per week.

** - Electric service to Coventry, half-hourly.
Serves all stations (Berkswell and Canley alternate trains only), all day, six days per week. In practice this service operates through New Street in conjunction with the stopping trains to Wolverhampton, although this second unofficial cross-city line is not actively promoted as such.

** - Three per hour service to Walsall.
Two serve all stations (except Duddeston) and one of them goes through to Hednesford. The third is a fast electric service via the Soho Loop. Operates six days per week.

** - Electric all stations service to Wolverhampton, half-hourly. All stations, six days per week.

** - Diesel service on the Stourbridge line, four per hour, two all stations to Stourbridge, two semi-fast to Worcester and beyond. Only the semi-fasts run on Sundays.

** - Diesel service to Shrewsbury, served by hourly semi-fast 158 Sprinters, which continue through to Chester or Aberystwyth.

** - Sprinter service to East Midlands and beyond, some trains calling at Water Orton and Wilnecote. These stations are outside the Centro area but local to Birmingham.

Centro published "Keeping the West Midlands Moving" in 1992, outlining a twenty year strategy for public transport development. This document confirmed that use of the local rail network doubled between 1974 and 1984 and a further growth of 36% was likely by the end of the century. Most lines would have more trains and be considered for electrification, many station car parks would be expanded, and consideration would be given for the construction of at least 22 new stations, seven of them on the Cross City Line.

These have not all been given names yet, but they would be located as follows:-

1) between Northfield and King's Norton
2) Selly Oak Hospital, north of Bournville
3) Edgbaston, between University and Five Ways
4) between Gravelly Hill and Erdington
5) Boldmere, north of Wylde Green
6) Tamworth Road, north of Sutton Coldfield
7) Mere Green, north of Four Oaks.

THE MOST IMPORTANT SPOKE IN THE WHEEL

The Cross City Line serves a natural travel corridor through the heart of Birmingham, with certain key stations well placed for the daily travel needs of thousands of people. Apart from New Street itself, other important stations are the Sutton group - Sutton Coldfield, Four Oaks, Butlers Lane and Blake Street - serving a population of about 100,000; Five Ways, close to a large area of office developments; University, lying between Birmingham University (11,000 students) and the Queen Elizabeth and maternity hospitals (800 beds); Bournville, next to Cadbury's factory and its 8,000 employees; and Longbridge, near the Rover car works. These all combine to ensure that the line has a two way flow during each peak, especially south of the city. Shift work and other regular travel patterns, particularly at University and Five Ways, means buoyant off peak use.

For commercial reasons there are no figures available for local rail services in the West Midlands area, on a line by line basis, for any financial year more recent than 1985/6, but even these elderly statistics highlight the importance of the Cross City Line in the local network; an importance it has retained since the figures were issued, despite increasingly unreliable diesel trains, followed by inevitable further disruption during electrification engineering works.

Annual passenger journeys (millions)			
	1978/9	1981/2	1985/6
CROSS CITY NORTH	3.75	4.15	5.47
CROSS CITY SOUTH	4.64	4.49	6.11
CROSS CITY TOTAL	8.39	8.64	11.58
STOURBRIDGE	2.42	3.24	4.21
NETWORK TOTAL	21.11	22.50	27.17
CROSS CITY as % of total	39.75%	38.4%	42.62%

Almost lost in a world of urban motorway clutter, a Class 116 dmu heads south under Spaghetti Junction on 20th December 1979.

(P.J.Shoesmith)

Despite welcome growth on other routes since 1990, notably the lines to Stourbridge and Hednesford, the Cross City Line remains the most important spoke in the wheel of local services which focus on the centre of Birmingham.

NEW STREET STATION

The names of all the main stations in Birmingham are under periodic review, and one suggestion is that New Street could become 'Central', a name as full of character and individuality as cold custard. To the people of Birmingham it will always be New Street. Its history and development are discussed in the next chapter, this section is concerned only with the modern station.

It emerged out of the demolished ruins of the Victorian station as Birmingham was linked to the original West Coast Main Line Electrification Scheme, begun in 1957 and involving over four hundred route miles (1,480 track miles) between Euston, Manchester and Liverpool. The concrete raft over the platforms covers 250,000 square feet. All twelve new platforms were complete and all overhead wiring was in place by 11th October 1966, with full electric services beginning on 6th March 1967. As "Railway Magazine" for April 1967 put it:-

> "Because 300 - 400 diesel trains will still pass through daily, an elaborate ventilation system for the platform areas has been designed, providing for the removal of diesel exhaust fumes on all tracks, using the 'induced extraction' method - the fumes are blown away from the platform areas towards extract ducts situated at high level above the tracks and centrally between the platforms."

..... if only theory had worked out in practice! Brummies were soon deciding that they did not like the new station, complaining about the fumes, delays at the booking office and the absence of waiting rooms and toilets at platform level, and the lack of direct access to and from the city centre ("Railway Magazine", March 1968).

Let me declare an interest here. New Street is all the bad things they say about it; the diesel fumes are sometimes sickening, the dark, dirty and low overall roof gives the platforms a squashed claustrophobic feel, platform level facilities are inadequate and there is still no straightforward access to the city centre. And yet I like the place because, despite all its disadvantages and the sheer volume of people and trains, most of the time it actually works!

Since 1967, when the people of Birmingham awoke to the realities of their new station, there have been improvements. Attempts were made to brighten up the platform environment with waiting rooms, refreshment areas, brighter tiling, paintwork and improved lighting. Even the brash illuminated advertisement panels were a step forward. The attempts have not really succeeded, large areas at platform level are still gloomy and will remain so, but this and other shortcomings are the fault of the original design.

Following the King's Cross tragedy New Street was designated as an underground station by the fire service, where the safety rules in force on the London Underground apply. All wooden doors and frames at platform level were to be replaced by metal ones. On platform 12, little used by passengers when trains were fewer in the 1960s, passengers and parcels traffic are now physically segregated. There is a total ban on smoking and fire safety doors have been installed at the foot of each staircase. There has been a big improvement in the environment of each stair well but not, regrettably, the addition of expensive but necessary down escalators. New Street's escalators, just one per island platform, stubbornly continue to move in the up direction only.

An enclosed footbridge, beyond the concrete raft at the Wolverhampton end, serves all island platforms. It was opened in 1993 and although built primarily as an escape route in the event of fire, it is a convenient direct link between the station and the city centre. Its Navigation Street exit is open between 9.00am and 7.00pm, Sundays excepted. This is arguably the biggest single improvement at the station since 1967, at least for the able-bodied and those without heavy luggage. It is a useful alternative to the long overcrowded route between the trains and the sweaty concrete ramp leading down to the corner of New Street and Corporation Street. There was furious opposition from commuters when direct access to the outside world was blocked during rebuilding, but the commercial interests of the developers were allowed to triumph over common sense. They retained the right of way across the station previously marked by the famous footbridge but gave it so many compulsory twists, turns and changes in level past their retail outlets that a simple route was changed into an obstacle strewn maze.

It is easy to criticise New Street, especially when waiting for a delayed train, but history cannot be denied. Ever since it opened in 1854 the station has always operated a busy time-table in an overcrowded space. When it doubled in size in 1885 the number of trains and passengers expanded accordingly. Again the modern station, with the intensive service to London, the easy interchange for long distance passengers and the expanding local services, is a victim of its own success. It now handles over 630 trains each weekday, about 50% more than it was designed for, all of them entering and leaving by just two pairs of tracks at either end. The numerous manual signal boxes are history, but the confined site still hampers train movement as much as congestion. The pointwork is so complicated at both the throats, where the platform tracks converge on the tunnels, that there is not always space to insert the desired number of check rails inside the running rails to minimise the risk of derailment. This - and the fact that platforms have signals halfway along so as to accomodate two trains at once - means that there is a blanket speed restriction of 10 mph within the whole station area, a vital safety factor which does nothing to help the speedy arrival or departure of late running trains.

The table below shows the evening weekday departures from New Street, 17.00 to 18.00, between July and September 1993, following the introduction of the full electric service on the Cross City Line. It gives some slight insight into the problems of operating this hyperactive station. It does not show arrivals, empty stock workings, movements associated with locomotive changes etc. The potential for time keeping to disintegrate, given the volatile mix of diesel and electric, old and new, InterCity, semi-fast and all-stations trains, is easy to see.

Departures via the West Suburban Line (XC = Cross City)
(The West Suburban is the main line to Bristol and the South West)

Time	Destination	Type
17.05	Redditch	XC
17.10	Hereford via Bromsgrove	(XC)
17.15	Longbridge	XC
17.20	Redditch	XC
17.35	Longbridge	XC
17.45	Plymouth	InterCity
17.50	Redditch	XC

Departures via the Wolverhampton Line

17.00	Chester	
17.03	Great Malvern	
17.08	Stoke-on-Trent	
17.11	Kidderminster	
17.14	Hednesford via Soho Loop	
17.19	Wolverhampton	InterCity
17.24	Wolverhampton	all stations
17.30	Hereford	
17.35	Liverpool	InterCity
17.38	Wolverhampton	all stations
17.41	Kidderminster	
17.44	Manchester	InterCity
17.53	Wolverhampton	InterCity
17.56	Aberystwyth	

* Departures via the Euston end of the station

(No trains shown for East Midlands & East Anglia - direct service suspended throughout 1993 summer time-table due to closure of Arley Tunnel for repairs)

17.00	Walsall	
17.03	Lichfield	XC
17.06	Poole	InterCity
17.11	Birmingham International	
17.15	Blake Street	XC
17.17	Cleethorpes	
17.18	Euston	InterCity
17.21	Coventry	all stations
17.24	Lichfield	XC
17.28	Blake Street	XC
17.33	Walsall	
17.35	Nottingham	
17.36	Euston	NSE semi-fast (all stn.to B'ham Int.)
17.39	Lichfield	XC
17.44	Blake Street	XC
17.48	Euston	InterCity
17.51	Coventry	all stations
17.54	Lichfield	XC
17.58	York	InterCity
18.00	Lichfield	XC

* NOTE:- Many books refer to the Euston end as the 'south end' but in reality it faces north and many of its trains head north. There are crossovers between the two pairs of tracks at both ends of the station, although at the Wolverhampton end there is normally less lateral movement than at the Euston end. Trains using the Wolverhampton line have access to all platforms, but those using the West Suburban line have access only to the southern half of the station.

It may seem perverse to like New Street, but it does have compensations, not the least being that over 80% of trains manage run on time. Announcements are clear, frequent and unobtrusive, there are two 'next train' monitors on every platform, duplicated at the top of platform staircases and in my experience station staff are generally visible, numerous and helpful. The station areas above platform level are kept bright, clean and functional. The constant bustle throughout the day - the sheer volume of people and the incessant train movements - is what helps the total character of this station to add up to far more than the sum of its rather forlorn parts.

A Class 117 dmu heads towards New Street from Five Ways, past the ramparts of the cutting retaining walls. Former access to the Midland Railway's Central Goods Depot is visible on the right. 15th November 1982. *(P.J.Shoesmith)*

A JOURNEY NORTH TO SUTTON COLDFIELD AND LICHFIELD

The first three miles of a journey on the northern half of the Cross City Line, until the train passes under Spaghetti Junction, achieve the almost impossible; they manage to be shabby and interesting.

Leaving New Street by the 'south' tunnel, the train encounters two sections of rising gradient, at 1:51 and 1:60, each preceeded by a shorter section of falling gradient (1:58 and 1:80), to give a switchback effect as speed increases. At the top of the rise, in a street to the right and with its roof at track level, is the Birmingham Proof House, complete with multi-coloured crest above the main entrance. The train is at Proof House Junction, less of a bottleneck since remodelling a few years ago, but still prone to congestion and delay at busy times. The Proof House itself is a reminder of one of Birmingham's many traditional industries. Guns have been made and tested (proofed) here for over two centuries and the building still fulfils its original purpose.

The stone building with Greek pillars, below on the left, is the entrance to Curzon Street station. This original terminus of the London & Birmingham Railway dates from 1837. It was in use for regular passenger traffic until 1854, for Bank Holiday excursion trains to Sutton Coldfield until 1893, and for goods traffic until 1990. The original train sheds and platforms have long since vanished, but as this last important remnant is a listed building it is safe from demolition.

The train crosses the blue brick viaduct opened in 1893 to eliminate conflict on the level with Curzon Street goods traffic. Between here and Aston the route followed is that of the Grand Junction Railway, dating from 1837.

As the train slows for the stop at Duddeston, the small power box on the right is a former manual signal box dating from the 1950s. It now controls the Cross City Line between Aston and Lichfield Trent Valley. Duddeston station has been known as 'Vauxhall' at various times during its existence; at other times bets have been hedged and it has been known as 'Vauxhall & Duddeston'.

To the left of the station is an old brick building of no obvious interest to the casual traveller. The openings in the wall for the rail tracks are lined in bright warning yellow. This is a civil link depot, with a staff of about thirty who repair and maintain British Rail's civil engineering fleet, which consists of vehicles such as breakdown cranes, inspection saloons and stock used to install and maintain overhead electrification equipment. Originally the depot was the Birmingham engine shed for the Grand Junction Railway, which reached Vauxhall from the north in July 1837. Though of no great architectural merit, it is one of the oldest engine sheds in the world, and it could be argued that in railway terms it is as important as Curzon Street station.

Just as the train slows for Aston, on the right, is the junction with the electrified freight line to Stechford, on the main line to Euston, one of several avoiding lines and spurs which ensure that New Street is a 'freight-free zone'. It is also used by diverted passenger trains and by some specials serving the National Exhibition Centre, adjacent to Birmingham International station. It will assume much greater significance if the proposed InterCity station is ever built at Heartlands.

Grand Junction tracks fork left at Aston and carry passenger trains to Walsall and Hednesford, and freight trains to Bescot yard. The Cross City, Grand Junction and Stechford lines should eventually be joined at Aston by Line 2 of the Midland Metro. This is the route that will have termini at Five Ways and Birmingham International Airport, serving New Street and the city centre inbetween. It will have its own stop adjacent to Aston station at street level.

Leaving Aston station the train bears right and is soon sucked into the jumble of flyovers and concrete pillars that is Spaghetti Junction, the biggest motorway interchange in Europe.

The train emerges from under the motorway into a cutting and runs into Gravelly Hill station, the main building of 1884 sitting on the embankment high above the up platform, and new access ramps for disabled travellers much in evidence.

On a steadily rising gradient the line continues virtually straight and in cutting to Erdington, with its Edwardian terraces, and on to Chester Road. There is a left curve past allotments and scrub, then a steady straight climb to Wylde Green, the highest point on the line occuring just south of the station. The original station masters' houses survive at Chester Road and Wylde Green. These two stations were modernised in the autumn of 1990, with new brick built ticket offices and corrugated metal platform shelters painted blue and grey. Their shape and style echoes and updates those between Five Ways and Longbridge, on the southern half of the route. Erdington has suffered from arson attacks over the years, most recently in 1989 when remaining platform buildings were gutted. This station was modernised during the summer of 1993.

The housing starts to look expensive and the train gathers speed downhill into a deep cutting, emerging suddenly onto an embankment above the rooftops and into Sutton Coldfield, which is on a sharp curve. This redbrick LNWR station lost its down platform canopy as a result of severe damage in the 1955 accident, when a diverted York to Bristol express failed to take the curve, with the loss of seventeen lives. Much of the rest of the station, including the distinctive enclosed stairway from the street to the down platform, known locally as the 'wooden hill', is substantially as it has always been. Architecturally this is an important station, which was opened with the extension of the line to Lichfield in 1884. The glass and iron entrance canopy, to shelter waiting horse cabs, has gone, but much good quality brick and plaster work remains, including the two fine ceiling roses in the entrance hall, from which gas chandeliers - gasoliers - once hung. The large amount of wood in the station no longer exudes that certain indefinable smell that came from prolonged contact with steam locomotives; gone too is the thin film of smut and engine oil that used to coat every outdoor surface.

The line from Birmingham reached Sutton Coldfield in the summer of 1862 and the station was a terminus until the extension to Lichfield was opened in December 1884. Sutton's curved platforms form the beginning of that extension because they are alongside the site of the original platforms, to the left. Traces of the original station can still be seen fronting the car park.

The route continues via a short tunnel under the town centre, then it is immediately bridged by the Sutton Park line. This important freight link joins Bescot and Walsall with the Birmingham - Derby main line at Castle Bromwich. There was an outcry from the ordinary people of Sutton when building of this line had been sanctioned in 1872, when they realised that it would cut through their beloved park, 2,400 acres of open uncultivated land, given to the town by Bishop Vesey in 1528. This can be seen as an early example of environmental awareness, but objections quickly evaporated once people were told by its builders, the Midland Railway, that the new line would bring them cheaper coal direct from the Nottinghamshire coalfield, which also happened to be served by the Midland. In the few summers before the end of the passenger service (1965) on the Sutton Park line, when car owning families were thinner on the ground than they are now, it was at its busiest on Sundays, with an all-day shuttle service from Walsall. Its finest hour, as many ex-Guides and Scouts will have cause to remember with fond nostalgia, occurred in the summer of 1957. Sutton Park was the site of the World Scouting Jamboree and most of the full length special trains run in connection with that event used the line.

The park was also the home of a 15" gauge steam railway, built as a tourist attraction near the Town Gate. Rolling stock included two 4-4-2 locos, which each hauled a rake of four maroon carriages, which had roofs but no doors. The locos and their brasswork were always spotless, with a livery which was virtual LMS. The line closed in 1962, although the stock and some of the track is rumoured to still be in store 'somewhere in Oldbury'....

Having passed under the Sutton Park Line, the Cross City Line continues round a long leftward curve, past much good quality detached housing. This is one of the most desirable areas of the West Midlands in which to live, its appeal obvious from the train window. At Four Oaks, another well-kept 1884 station, there is a large commuter car park and a bus interchange.

North of Four Oaks the line continues through pleasant suburbia to Butlers Lane, formerly Butlers Lane Halt, which was a well maintained little station built entirely of wood. It was constructed as cheaply as possible and opened as a temporary structure in September 1957 to serve Sutton's expanding northern hinterland. Severe rot, and a rather quaint appearance at odds with the image of a modern electric railway meant complete demolition and replacement of the 'temporary' platforms in the winter of 1991/2, followed by the original ticket office in 1993.

Blake Street, with connecting buses, large car park and modern well-kept buildings, is everything a small station should be. The original station, with it low wooden platforms, oil lamps and what seemed like dozens of advertisements for Virol, was a victim of dry rot.

Blake Street sits almost on top of the West Midlands' county boundary with Staffordshire, and suddenly the housing vanishes, giving way to open countryside with expansive views all round. It is two miles to Shenstone, where the station still has its original stylish buildings that were carefully renovated prior to electrification.

North of Shenstone the train crosses over a rare dual-carriageway section of the A5, the modern successor to Watling Street and Telford's London-Holyhead mail coach road.

There remains a three mile sprint to Lichfield and the three spires of the cathedral can be glimpsed briefly between the hills for those who know where to look. Just before Lichfield City station a remnant of the South Staffordshire line joins from the left. This now serves only Charringtons works at Brownhills, but at one time it was a direct link with Walsall, which could boast some through passenger trains to Derby, via Lichfield. Reinstatement of the four mile gap in this line, costed in 1990 at £4.5 million, would provide a direct freight route north from Bescot and take some pressure off the Sutton Park line, which is heavily graded, very busy and indirect. Several local authorities have also expressed interest in a restored passenger service, probably between Wolverhampton and

The pleasant setting of Gravelly Hill, less than a mile from Spaghetti Junction, is evident as a Class 116 dmu bound for Longbridge enters the up platform on 13th April 1982.
(P.J.Shoesmith)

Derby, which would open up extra travel opportunities for the people of Lichfield, amongst others.

City station itself is a good LNWR period piece, with a redbrick frontage and a white tiled subway giving access to the island platform, which contains robust wooden buildings with an overall roof which survived electrification unscathed. The goods loops within the station area were removed at electrification, the masts stand in the middle of the trackbed.

The mile and a quarter journey to Lichfield Trent Valley, mostly in a shallow cutting and through a light industrial estate is made by few people outside the peak hours. Numbers are slowly growing, thanks to new housing nearby and a car park with room to spare, a luxury unknown at the City station. It proved a simple task to refurbish the concrete platforms on the high level, closed in 1965, prior to re-opening for Cross City trains in November 1988. Only the rebuilt and extended down platform is now in use. It sits on the bridge over the low level station on the West Coast Main Line. Beyond the high level platform is the single track connection down to the main line, little-used but strategically useful. The line north from the high level is open for freight trains to Wichnor Junction, five miles away, on the Birmingham-Derby main line.

Midwinter dusk, 8th December 1988. A Class 117 unit from Longbridge has just arrived at Lichfield Trent Valley, and is about to work as empty stock and cross over north of the station. The '1', denoting first class, is surplus to requirements. The high level platforms at Trent Valley had been re-opened for just eleven days when this picture was taken.

(P.J.Shoesmith)

A JOURNEY SOUTH TO REDDITCH

This is by far the most attractive rail route out of Birmingham, although the beginning shows little promise. The four miles between here and King's Norton can be vulnerable to congestion and delay, as Cross City trains share the tracks with InterCity traffic to the South-West and Regional Railways' services to Worcester and Cardiff. This calls for considerable skill by time-table planners so that the different types of trains do not delay each other. The situation is eased south of King's Norton, where the two tracks become four.

Every exit from New Street involves tunnelling on a rising gradient, virtually from the platform ends. Here there is just time to notice, on the left, the New Street signal box, dating from 1966, with grimy concertina walls that were once white. New Street and Saltley are the two power boxes jointly covering the Birmingham area. Plans to replace them with one 'megabox', probably at Saltley, are in their early stages. The line curves to the south west, on a rising gradient of 1:77, and plunges into a series of five tunnels. Modern building development has bridged the gap between the first two tunnels, so now there seem to be just four, which are linked by brief deep cuttings lined with dark blue brick. Their ridges and buttresses make them look like nothing so much as the lower ramparts of some sinister castle, gloomy even in bright weather.

At the end of the fifth tunnel lies Five Ways, a busy commuter station serving many office blocks on the fringes of Edgbaston, the city's wealthiest suburb. Line 2 of the Midland Metro is due to have one terminus here and the other at the airport, reached via the city centre and a direct connection with New Street. The nature of the station site at Five Ways, in a deep cutting, prevents any direct link between railway and Metro, though it should only be a short walk away, as are many bus routes serving most parts of the city.

The station at Five Ways, closed in 1944 and built afresh on the same site in 1978, is the first of a series of seven between here and Longbridge that were either built or rebuilt at that latter date. The architecture is most definitely of its time, with metal and clear plastic platform canopies, all fluted and curved and with few edges and corners.

The original station may have closed in 1944, but for many years afterwards the platforms remained intact and Five Ways, though absent from the time-tables, became a ticket platform. Prior to rebuilding in the 1960s Birmingham New Street was one of the very few open stations (ie; without ticket barriers) in the country, thanks to the public right of way along the footbridge which served all its platforms. To deter fraudulent travel, trains were stopped and tickets checked at minor suburban stations, a time-consuming and irritating process that would not be tolerated today. Five Ways was the ticket platform on this south-western approach, and Duddeston served the same purpose on what is now the northern part of the Cross City Line. Nowadays the wheel has turned full circle, and New Street remains a closed station - in the ticket barrier sense - whilst others of comparable size, such as Glasgow Central and York, have become open.

Leaving Five Ways, the derelict land on the left marks the abandoned junction with the freight lines that used to penetrate to Suffolk Street in the city centre. Soon the Birmingham and Worcester Canal joins the railway on the left, or rather the railway joins it, as the canal was first on the scene in 1815. Here, at the top of a 1:80 gradient and just before a brief tunnel, there used to be a station at Church Road, closed in 1925, although the platforms remained in situ for almost half a century longer. The line gently curves and twists - there is nothing straight about this railway for several miles yet - past more gloomy brick retaining walls on the right, but not so high this time. Beyond is Harborne, another attractive suburb known to rail historians for the Harborne line, a single track branch which carried passengers from 1874 to 1934, clinging on to freight traffic until 1963. Prosperous at first, it was killed by bus competition and by rail congestion into New Street. It joined the main line from Wolverhampton, and its trains were frequently delayed, having a very low priority with the junction signalmen.

On through more gentle curves alongside the canal, under the bridge carrying Somerset Road, the site of another long dead station, and soon the train stops on a sharp curve at University station.

It takes less than two minutes to reach the next station, at Selly Oak, and as the train slows, just before it crosses the Bristol Road, the quick eye will notice, to the right, the remnant of an old viaduct at an angle to the present line. It looks strangely fragile and narrow, and that is because it once carried but a single track. It was the original railway on this busy route, the Birmingham West Suburban line, opened in 1876. Even at that date it is odd to think that its promoters thought they could adequately approach the heart of Birmingham with a single track byway.

So on to Bournville, which, thanks to chocolate sponsorship, must surely be the only purple station on British Rail. It is on a confined site, with the canal at rail level very close on the left. On the right the Cadbury's factory is adjacent to the railway.

South from Bournville, on through more greenery and the train slows on the approach to King's Norton. The triangular junction with the Camp Hill line lies just north of the station. The top of the triangle, the Lifford Curve, veers away so sharply to the left that the very few trains using it are limited to 10 mph. Soon the junction proper is reached, and two running lines expand to four. The Camp Hill line was the original southern approach to the city, being part of the Birmingham and Gloucester Railway of 1840. It had its own suburban stations in south Birmingham at Lifford, Hazelwell, King's Heath, Moseley, Brighton Road and Camp Hill, but they were closed as a wartime economy measure in 1941, never to be re-opened.

The platform building on the left, at the country end of King's Norton station, is original, dating from 1849. Beyond the footbridge is the station master's house, built at the same time. A terrace of cottages built by the Midland Railway for its workers falls gently down the hill here.

As the train leaves King's Norton the site on the left was originally occupied by carriage sidings. Later, British Leyland vehicles were loaded onto trains here. Most recently this has been the site of the Cross City Electrification Depot.

A long sweeping curve through suburbia connects King's Norton with Northfield. Between these stations are two sets of ladder crossings connecting all four tracks; their simple but effective layout is in sharp contrast to the complex pointwork of steam days, especially for those who, as boys, saved their pocket money up for weeks to buy items like a 'diamond crossing with slips' for their own model railway. Northfield's outer platforms and their buildings date from 1978. The island platform was made unusable during 1993 when the edge paving was removed, yet at the same time it was smartened up. The sculptures are old wooden sleepers, carved to make them look like small totem poles. The hundred space car park is always full to overflowing, although the same cannot be said for the thirty place cycle rack, a rare feature at a modern station, almost as rare as proper provision for cycles aboard a modern train.

A sprint through allotments and tower blocks brings the train to Longbridge, a two platform station built on a new site, and the last of the 1978 series which began at Five Ways. Half the Cross City trains terminate here. The station is within easy walking distance of the British Leyland factory and hundreds of homes, but the difficult location means that there is no space for a car park, which can cause problems in surrounding streets. The trackwork is also inconvenient, as the first leg of a ladder crossing is sited halfway along the down platform. Trains from Birmingham have to stop before using the crossing, entailing a long walk for all passengers, which is not good news in wet weather, or for the disabled, mums with small children, etc. The redundant half of the platform faces what is a freight only line, so it cannot be used by passenger trains even when it is not occupied by a freight train. The ladder crossing, spanning all four tracks, gives rail access to the branch on the right into the Rover car complex.

This branch originally meandered through deepest countryside to Halesowen, and on to a junction at Old Hill, on the Birmingham-Stourbridge line. It closed to regular passengers as long ago as 1919, but remained open for workmen's trains until 1964. There has been sporadic talk, ever since the early 1970s, of reviving a short part of the line beyond the Rover works to serve the vast housing estate at Frankley, but the talk has remained talk and no authority appears willing to invest in such a service and the benefits it would bring.

After Longbridge the city is left behind, with the Lickey Hills on the right and beautiful rolling countryside on the left. The train is now on the fast line, the freight only track soon merges

A train bound for Four Oaks, alongside the canal near University, in WMPTE white livery, December 1980. *(P.J.Shoesmith)*

from the left, and from here until Barnt Green there is an unusual stretch of three-track railway; one line down from Birmingham and two up. Now might be a good time to notice the cast-iron mileposts on the right, black numerals on a yellow background. There are also sub-posts every quarter of a mile. In the days before most locomotives were fitted with speedometers, anytime before the early 1960s, these posts supplemented the driver's experience when he needed to measure the speed of the train.

The Birmingham & Gloucester Railway built this stretch in 1840, it soon became part of the Midland Railway, and these posts still mark out the distance to Derby, where the Midland had its headquarters, even though that company ceased to exist at the end of 1922.

By now three tracks have reduced to two, just in time to split again for the four platform junction station at Barnt Green. The main line continues straight ahead, soon to dip sharply down the 1:37 Lickey Incline to Bromsgrove, the steepest gradient on any British main line. The Cross City platforms at Barnt Green are at the start of a very sharp curve.

From here the line is single track for the remaining five miles to Redditch. Here is English countryside at its most typical and best, perhaps undervalued because there still seems to be so much of it. The line passes under the M42 before briefly teaming up once more with the Birmingham & Worcester Canal. A left curve on an embankment gives a panoramic view of Alvechurch, an expanded commuter village, with St.Lawrence's Church, surrounded by trees, rising gently above the mottled friendly roofscape. The original derelict station, dating from 1859, was replaced by the present simple platform in the spring of 1993.

The approach to Redditch is on an embankment through one of the pre-war districts of this New Town, which mushroomed in the 1960s and 70s. There follows a cutting, then curves to right and left up a rising gradient of 1:130, and line's end at the station platform. A busy ticket and parcels office here was erected as a temporary structure, with a planned life of five years, in 1977. It was replaced by permanent buildings early in 1993, the fourth station at Redditch on the third site. Beyond the country end of the platform is a natural wilderness that was the town's goods yard in more enlightened times; beyond the town end of the platform, through a bridge which once carried the line on to Alcester and Evesham, is the site of the second station where now there is pedestrian access to the adjacent bus station, multi-storey car park and indoor Kingfisher Shopping Centre. The planning lesson of locating the amenities close to the transport facilities was learnt well at Redditch.

Journey's end at Longbridge, December 8th 1980. The unit is signalled to cross over to the stabling siding prior to its next duty. 'SY' denotes signals controlled from Saltley Power Box, on the Midland main line north of New Street. *(P.J.Shoesmith)*

CHAPTER TWO : "GROWTH AND STRUGGLE"
A history of the line

CROSS CITY SOUTH, between Birmingham and Redditch
(Early Days on the Birmingham & Gloucester Railway : Rails to Redditch : A Grand Central Station : Chocolates & Memories at Bournville : A Four-Track Main Line : Barnt Green, A Railway Village : Slow Decline at Redditch)

Early Days on the Birmingham & Gloucester Railway

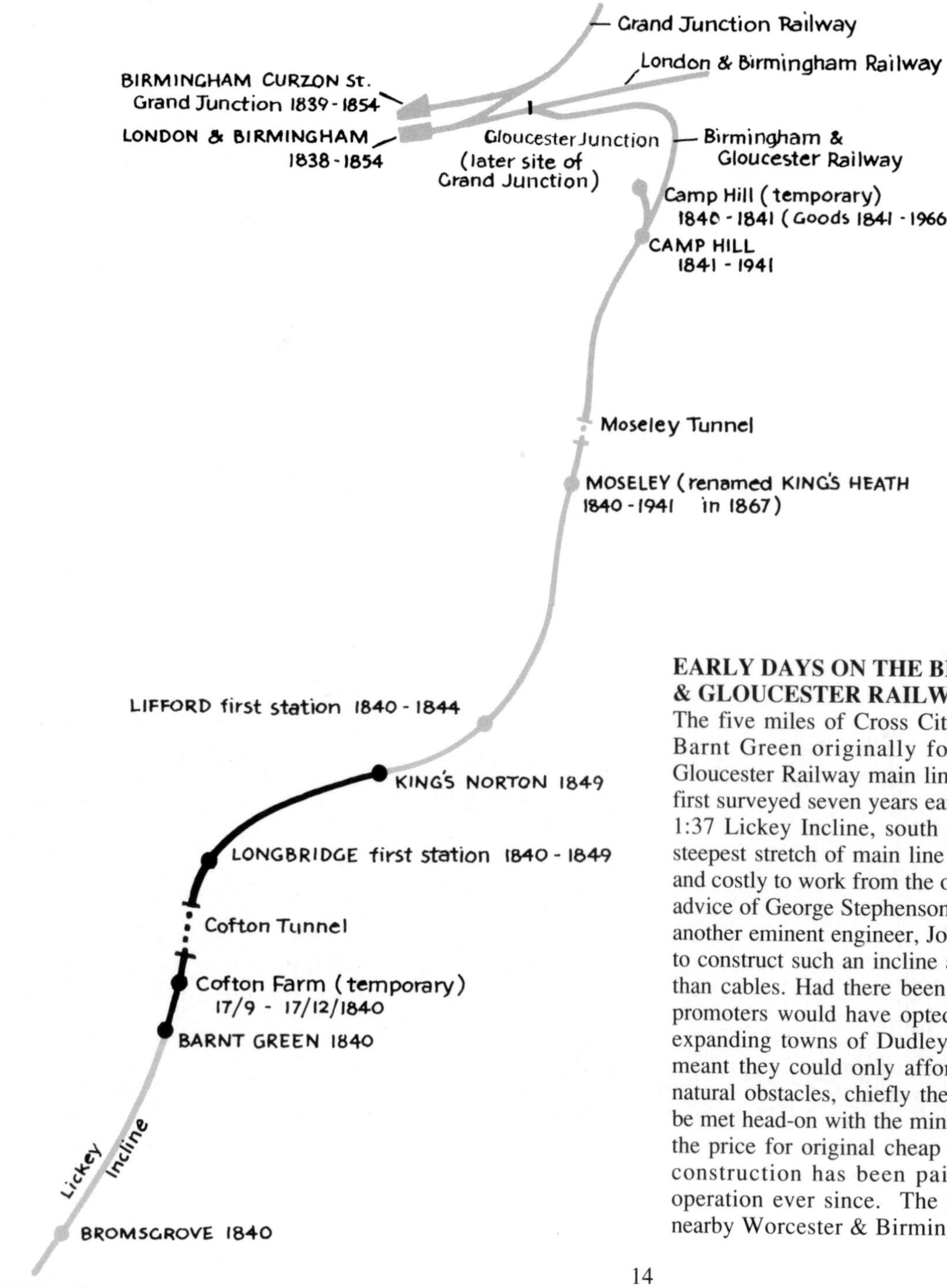

— Grand Junction Railway

London & Birmingham Railway

BIRMINGHAM CURZON St.
Grand Junction 1839 - 1854

LONDON & BIRMINGHAM
1838 - 1854

Gloucester Junction
(later site of
Grand Junction)

Birmingham &
Gloucester Railway

Camp Hill (temporary)
1840 - 1841 (Goods 1841 - 1966)

CAMP HILL
1841 - 1941

Moseley Tunnel

MOSELEY (renamed KING'S HEATH
1840 - 1941 in 1867)

LIFFORD first station 1840 - 1844

KING'S NORTON 1849

LONGBRIDGE first station 1840 - 1849

Cofton Tunnel

Cofton Farm (temporary)
17/9 - 17/12/1840

BARNT GREEN 1840

Lickey Incline

BROMSGROVE 1840

EARLY DAYS ON THE BIRMINGHAM & GLOUCESTER RAILWAY

The five miles of Cross City Line between King's Norton and Barnt Green originally formed part of the Birmingham & Gloucester Railway main line dating from 1840. The route was first surveyed seven years earlier, and included the two mile long 1:37 Lickey Incline, south of Barnt Green. This remains the steepest stretch of main line in the country, and proved difficult and costly to work from the outset. It was built against the expert advice of George Stephenson and Isambard Kingdom Brunel, but another eminent engineer, Joseph Locke, said that it was feasible to construct such an incline and work it with locomotives rather than cables. Had there been more money available the original promoters would have opted for a longer route via the rapidly expanding towns of Dudley and Stourbridge, but lack of cash meant they could only afford to buy cheaper rural land. Any natural obstacles, chiefly the Lickey escarpment, would have to be met head-on with the minimum of engineering or earthworks; the price for original cheap land purchase and relatively cheap construction has been paid for in difficult and expensive operation ever since. The promoters chose not to notice the nearby Worcester & Birmingham Canal, which was beset with operational difficulties of its own, caused by the 30 consecutive locks at Tardebigge which were necessary to take the waterway over the same rising land. Had a more easily graded railway route been chosen neither the Bristol main line nor the southern half of the Cross City Line would exist in their present form.

The resident engineer was Captain W.S.Moorsom, who let separate contracts for the construction of specific sections of the line rather than one contract for the whole. This concept was a logical economy measure and the captain's way of keeping a close eye on the progress and quality of the work, and it was revolutionary for the time. The line may have been called the Birmingham & Gloucester, but it was built the other way round, reaching Cofton Farm from the south in September 1840. At this temporary station, just south of Longbridge, passengers transferred to road coach for the remaining eight miles into the centre of Birmingham until the railway opened to Camp Hill in December.

Stations were then at Longbridge, Lifford, Moseley and Camp Hill, itself a terminus until the line was opened throughout to Birmingham Curzon Street in August 1841.

Few vestiges of the 1840 railway now remain. Cofton Tunnel, of which more later, was demolished with some difficulty in the 1920s, and even the lesser earthworks, with their associated bridges etc., were altered when the double track was quadrupled in stages, between 1892 and 1930. The only important original structures still extant are at King's Norton station, which was not opened until 1849, by which time the Birmingham & Gloucester had been absorbed by the ever expanding Midland Railway. Here the old ticket office and waiting room can be found on the down platform, out of passenger use and looking rather forlorn as a Signalling & Telecommunications office. Nearby, almost hidden under the footbridge, is the squat and solid stationmaster's cottage.

North of King's Norton the 1840 railway approached Birmingham on what is now the freight only 'direct' line, the so-called Camp Hill route, named after a road which it bridges on the approach to Birmingham. By a connection known as Gloucester Junction - a logical name from a railwayman's point of view but confusing to anyone else - the line joined the tracks into the London & Birmingham Railway's terminus at Curzon Street, on the northern fringe of the town centre. In this way Curzon Street became one of the earliest important stations to be shared between two railway companies. The large stone entrance building, originally the station's hotel and a smaller echo of the famous Doric Arch at Euston, has survived more or less intact, despite closure of Curzon Street to regular passenger trains since 1854.

Early in the railway age a certain George Bradshaw (1801-1853) spotted what today might be described as a 'market opportunity'. Although the railway network was expanding rapidly, and longer journeys were becoming practical, every important line was worked by its own company, largely independent of other railways, with frequent open hostilities between rival concerns. Little thought was given to co-operation and co-ordination. This may have stimulated competition on occasion, but it did nothing for integration, the arrangement at Curzon Street being a rare exception. Travellers using the services of more than one company were too often left to their own devices. Bradshaw helped considerably when he issued the first of his famous railway guides in 1839. Despite being full of all manner of advertisements, it was not a travel guide in the modern sense, simply an all-line time-table, the forerunner of that issued by British Rail today. As the network generated more travellers, those travellers could now plan their longer journeys with confidence, although by today's standards the presentation and layout of a typically Victorian 'Bradshaw' often made it difficult to decypher.

The Camp Hill Line, the original main line between King's Norton and Birmingham, has not had its own passenger service since 1941. Those lucky enough to travel over it on diverted trains can enjoy superb distant views of the city centre. A northbound Class 116 dmu approaches Camp Hill on Saturday 21st November 1981. The mixture of small industrial premises, terraced houses, corner shops and pubs, glimpsed through the bridge, is typical of much of inner Birmingham.   *(P.J.Shoesmith)*

The early Bradshaws were published monthly, and the January 1845 issue makes fascinating reading. The entire passenger service for the Birmingham & Gloucester Railway occupies a single page. At first glance it appears that there are seven through trains between Birmingham and Gloucester, but a look at the arrival and departure times, not to mention the eccentric mileages in the left hand margin, shows that all is not what it seems. Worcester appears to have a train service, but in fact rails did not reach that city until 1850, and the times shown are for road coach connections. The lack of such basic information, combined with the excruciatingly small print, must have turned a simple train enquiry into a nightmare for both passengers and the semi-literate staff at all the lesser stations en route; nevertheless it was a start. Half hidden in this time-table are the early ancestors of two of today's Cross City Line stations, at Barnt Green and Longbridge. The down main line platform at Barnt Green is still in its original position and the short-lived first station at Longbridge was a little to the south of the present one. There were no stations yet at the ancient Worcestershire villages of Northfield and King's Norton, though the few residents of the latter place who needed to travel any distance could easily walk to the station at Lifford - but only for four brief years.

Lifford does not feature in this 1845 time-table. It did not prosper and so was closed without fuss in 1844. Station closures are not just a twentieth century phenomenon; a surprising number passed into oblivion in Victorian times, all without the benefit of a proper closure procedure. If people suffered hardship that was simply their misfortune. Two other stations were built at Lifford, spanning the years 1876 to 1941.

The temporary terminus at Camp Hill closed to passengers when the line reached Curzon Street, but Camp Hill goods station survived on the site until the 1960s. For almost a century, from August 1841 to January 1941, Camp Hill had a station on the main line. At first it was designated 'third class', served only by third class trains, which were mixed, a collection of waggons and vans behind the locomotive being followed by a ragbag assortment of passenger stock. Not safe, not fast, hardly a train at all in the eyes of those lucky enough to afford a first or second class ticket.

Gladstone's Railway Act of 1844 compelled all railway companies to provide enclosed carriages for third class passengers at 1d per mile on at least one train daily, calling at all stations and having a minimum speed of 12 mph. Not content merely to promote useful laws like this one William Gladstone actually travelled by train, often third class, incognito, as a way of keeping in touch with ordinary people; modern politicians please note! Some companies complied with Gladstone's act by running the one 'Parliamentary' train at the legal minimum speed in the middle of the night, so by providing two at reasonable hours the Birmingham & Gloucester was quite progressive.

The 1845 Bradshaw shows that Barnt Green third class passengers bound for Birmingham had to travel in a train which took fifty minutes for the eleven miles (9.25 miles by today's route), paying one shilling (5p) for the single journey at a time when labourers and agricultural workers were lucky to earn £1 per week. The equivalent single fare in modern times, assuming the passenger concerned had earnings of about £12,000 per year, would be at least £12.

BIRMINGHAM & GLOUCESTER.

Miles	DOWN TRAINS.	1½	2	3	4	5	6	7	8	9	10	11	Fares. 1 Cls. s. d.	Fares. 2 Cls. s. d.	Fares. 3 Cls. s. d.
	DEPARTURE FROM	a. m.	a. m.	a. m.	a. m.	noon	a. m.	p. m.	p. m.	p. m.	p. m.	p. m.			
	BIRMINGHAM......	1 0	..	6 30	8 50	..	11 45	..	2 45	5 0	..	7 0			
2	Camp Hill............	..	..	6 40	..	..	..	..	..	..	..	7 10	..	..	..
4	Moseley............	..	..	6 45	..	..	..	..	..	..	..	7 15	..	..	..
9	Longbridge.........	..	..	7 10	9 10	..	..	..	..	..	..	7 30	..	..	..
11	Barnt Green	..	..	7 25	9 15	..	..	..	..	5 30	..	7 35	3 0	2 6	1 0
13	Blackwell	..	..	7 35	9 20	..	12 18	..	3 20	5 40	..	7 50	3 0	2 6	1 0
15	BROMSGROVE	1 45	..	7 45	9 30	..	12 28	..	3 30	5 50	..	8 0	3 6	2 6	1 6
17	Stoke Works	..	..	7 52	..	..	..	..	3 37	..	..	8 6	4 6	3 0	2 0
20	DROITWICH	1 59	..	8 0	9 40	..	12 40	..	3 44	6 5	..	8 16	5 6	4 0	2 0
22	Dunhampstead	..	..	8 5	..	..	..	..	..	..	..	8 20	..	..	..
26	SPETCHLEY	2 17	..	8 25	10 0	..	12 56	..	4 0	6 18	..	8 40	..	..	..
30	WORCESTER {arriv. {dep.	2 47 / 1 41	..	9 0 / 7 45	10 35 / 9 20	..	1 30 / 12 15	..	4 35 / 3 20	6 53 / 5 38	..	9 15 / 8 0	7 0	4 6	2 6
28	Norton	..	..	8 30	..	..	..	..	..	..	..	8 45	..	..	..
29	WADBOROUGH ...	..	..	8 36	..	..	..	..	..	..	..	8 50	7 0	4 6	3 0
32	Besford	..	..	8 40	..	..	..	..	..	..	..	8 54	..	..	..
33	Defford	..	..	8 55	..	..	1 18	..	4 20	6 40	..	9 5	8 6	5 6	3 6
34	Eckington	..	..	9 2	10 22	..	..	..	..	..	..	9 10	9 0	6 0	3 6
37	Bredon	..	..	9 15	..	..	..	..	4 30	..	..	9 25	9 6	6 6	4 0
39	ASHCHURCH	2 54	..	9 25	10 37	..	1 36	..	4 38	7 5	..	9 34	10 0	7 0	4 6
41	TEWKESBURY {arr {dp.	3 9 / 2 34	..	9 35 / 9 18	10 47 / 10 30	..	1 46 / 1 30	..	4 48 / 4 31	7 15 / 6 58	..	9 40 / 9 20	10 6	7 6	4 6
	Cleeve	..	..	9 30	..	..	..	..	..	..	..	9 46			
46	CHELTENHAM	3 12	8 45	9 50	11 0	12 30	1 55	4 20	5 0	7 30	8 30	10 6	12 0	9 0	5 0
48	Badgworth	..	8 50	..	..	12 35	..	4 25	..	..	8 35	..			
53	GLOUCESTER .. arr.	3 30	9 0	10 15	11 25	12 45	2 10	4 35	5 20	7 45	8 45	10 30	14 0	10 0	5 6

Miles	UP TRAINS.	1	2	3	4	5	6	7	8	9	10	11½	Fares. 1 Cls. s. d.	Fares. 2 Cls. s. d.	Fares. 3 Cls. s. d.
	DEPARTURE FROM	a. m.	a. m.	a. m.	a. m.	a. m.	a. m.	p. m.	p. m.	p. m.	p. m.	p. m.			
	GLOUCESTER	5 15	7 45	8 15	10 30	11 30	12 45	3 10	3 40	6 0	7 30	8 50			
5	Badgworth	..	..	8 25	..	11 40	..	..	3 50	..	7 40	..	..	..	..
7	CHELTENHAM	5 35	8 3	8 35	10 48	11 50	1 3	3 29	4 0	6 20	7 50	9 10	1 6	1 0	0 6
0	Cleeve	5 45	..	..	..	..	..	..	..	6 25	..	..			
14	ASHCHURCH	6 0	8 20	..	11 5	..	1 21	3 47	..	6 38	..	9 26	3 0	2 6	1 6
16	TEWKESBURY {arr {dp.	6 10 / 5 52	8 30 / 8 10	..	11 15 / 10 58	..	1 31 / 1 15	3 57 / 3 40	..	6 48 / 6 30	..	9 40 / 9 20	3 0	2 6	1 6
16	Bredon	6 8	8 27	..	..	..	..	..	..	6 43	..	..	4 0	3 0	1 6
19	Eckington	6 20	8 35	..	..	..	1 30	..	..	6 50	..	..	5 0	3 0	2 0
20	Defford	6 25	8 40	..	11 20	..	..	..	..	6 55	..	..	5 0	3 6	2 0
21	Besford	6 29	..	..	..	..	..	..	..	7 0	..	..	..	..	..
24	Wadborough........	6 35	4 48	..	..	..	..	..	..	7 5	..	..	6 0	4 0	2 6
25	Norton	6 40	..	..	..	..	..	..	..	7 15	..	..	..	..	..
27	SPETCHLEY	6 50	8 58	..	11 40	..	1 55	4 20	..	7 35	..	10 6	..	..	..
31	WORCESTER {arriv. {dep.	7 25 / 6 10	9 33 / 8 20	..	12 15 / 11 0	..	2 30 / 1 15	4 55 / 3 40	..	8 10 / 6 55	..	10 36 / 9 26	7 6	5 0	3 6
31	Dunhampstead	7 10	..	..	..	..	..	..	..	7 45	..	..			
33	DROITWICH	7 20	9 15	..	11 55	..	2 15	4 38	..	7 55	..	10 23	9 0	6 0	3 6
36	Stoke Works	7 35	..	..	..	..	2 25	..	..	8 5	..	..	9 0	6 0	3 6
38	BROMSGROVE	7 45	9 35	..	12 10	..	2 31	5 0	..	8 15	..	10 35	9 6	6 6	4 0
40	Blackwell	8 0	9 50	..	..	..	2 43	..	..	8 30	..	..	10 6	7 0	4 6
42	Barnt Green	8 10	9 58	..	..	..	2 50	..	..	8 36	..	..	12 0	8 0	5 0
44	Longbridge	8 20	..	..	..	..	..	..	..	8 46	..	..	..	..	..
49	Moseley	8 36	..	..	..	..	..	..	..	9 0	..	..	..	..	..
51	Camp Hill	8 45	..	..	..	..	..	..	..	9 5	..	..	..	..	..
53	BIRMINGHAM .. arr.	9 0	10 30	..	1 0	..	3 25	5 45	..	9 15	..	11 20	14 0	10 6	5 6

First and second class carriages with all the trains. Third class carriages with trains Nos. 1 and 9 from Gloucester, and 3 and 11 from Birmingham.

Only the mail trains run on Sundays.

DAY TICKETS from Cheltenham to Gloucester,

First Class, 2s.

Second Class, 1s. 6d.

Birmingham & Gloucester Railway Time-Table, January 1845, as shown in Bradshaw's Railway Guide. This illustration is the same size as the original
(British Rail)

The services each railway company offered, whether slow, infrequent or expensive, were always better and usually cheaper than those of the road coaches. People scraped and saved to travel by train, first for the sheer novelty of doing so and then because it was so much more convenient than anything else. The volume of rail traffic soon grew. Receipts from passenger fares on the B&G rose from £65,730 in 1841 to £139,387 in 1846. Goods receipts over the same period more than tripled, from £20,054 to £68,679.

The trains were rudimentary in the extreme. Railways were still so new that a recognisable house style had not properly developed, which is why prints of the period show trains of 'carriages' or 'coaches' almost identical to the road vehicles they were forcing out of business. Guards and luggage were still carried on the roof, and the carriage interiors were often so low that passengers could not stand upright, just as in road coaches. Before 1844 most companies conveyed third class passengers in trucks.

Such early travelling conditions are familiar to most people interested in railways; they were universal and not confined just to the Birmingham & Gloucester Railway. What is unusual about the B&G trains of the period is the upstart little locomotives that pulled them. At a time when Britain was the greatest industrial nation on earth, had given birth to railways and was now starting to create a huge railway industry and a national railway network, it is quite staggering to find that some of the first B&G locomotives were American imports! The company needed some engines for the sole purpose of working the Lickey Incline, and no British loco builder felt able to tender for the order, because it specified that each machine should routinely be able to haul 100 tons up the incline at 20mph, a task on the outer edge of the possible with the technology then available. This did not deter William Norris of Philadelphia, whose locomotives soon began to arrive, via Liverpool. They proved to be inadequate to their task from the start, wheezing and leaking steam as they crept up and down the Lickey like weary asthmatic cats. The best three were put to work assisting trains up the incline from the front (they never banked from behind because buffer heights were not yet properly standardised), and the remaining twelve were given general duties, to which they were better suited, *including working trains through to Birmingham*. As such they were capable of hauling four coaches and two trucks, a total weight of 45 tons, at a respectable 35mph on level track, slowing to 25mph on a rising gradient of 1:300.

All the early B&G locomotives had names; none were numbered. A few were even British. One of these, an unreliable curiosity named "Eclipse", had been built about 1836 for the London & Birmingham, soon transferring to the Grand Junction at Vauxhall, before that company was glad to sell it cheaply to the B&G. This machine had never worked well, and although only four years old it was already past its 'sell-by' date. On November 11th 1840, without warning, it blew up whilst at Bromsgrove shed, killing two railway men. The artist who designed their tombstones visited the station and sketched the first engine he saw, one of the Norris Americans. Its likeness appears on both graves in St.John's churchyard, as an inaccurate but apt memorial to the tragedy, as well as an illustration of an early form of Cross City motive power.

January 10th 1840 saw the introduction of the penny post and there was a sudden upsurge in letter writing. A staggering 112,000 letters were posted in London on the first day alone. This new cheap prepaid system, as opposed to the expensive and much abused payment-on-delivery system which it replaced, was given further impetus when gummed labels - the Penny Black stamps - came into use in May. Although the first mail train had run on the Grand Junction Railway in 1837, while the penny post was still just a gleam in Rowland Hill's eye, here now was lucrative nationwide traffic for the railways to win. So it was on January 14th 1841 that the 7pm departure north from Gloucester carried Her Victorian Majesty's mails for the first time; triple headed to combat the deep drifted snow. The sound of the three exhausts as these decidedly low-tech engines spat out showers of sparks in their best efforts to keep to time must have been impressive to people living near the Lickey Incline, or in villages such as Longbridge and King's Norton, who until a few months earlier had heard nothing more exciting than a galloping horse. Carriage of the mails, and completion of the line to Curzon Street saw revenue on the B&G exceed £1,000 per week.

In the hurly-burly rail politiking typical of that time, when the network was beginning to take on a shape recognisable today, the small Birmingham & Gloucester Railway clearly had excellent potential for development and was ripe for absorption by a larger concern. An attempted take over by the broad gauge Great Western, which had already reached Gloucester from Swindon, was thwarted by the Midland Railway. In February 1845 George Hudson, the larger-than-life chairman of the newly-formed Midland Railway, signed an agreement with the B&G and the Bristol & Gloucester, which included an option to purchase. Hudson made this take-over bid, "under the conviction of the absolute necessity of a uniformity of gauge between the northern manufacturing districts and the Port of Bristol". He had an unattractive personality, money-grubbing and unscrupulous, but his assessment of the situation was, as usual, deadly accurate. The agreement was effective from 1846, the enlarged Midland Railway prospered and the Great Western was denied a direct broad gauge link between Bristol and Birmingham.

Within Birmingham the intimate shared station at Curzon Street, set alongside the equally small Grand Junction terminus for trains to the north, rapidly became inadequate. A new station, briefly one of the largest in the world, was opened at New Street in 1854. The old B&G had had running rights into Curzon Street, and the Midland Railway inherited these rights, which were now valid for New Street. However the track layout meant that Midland main line expresses were effectively barred from New Street, with portions having to be attached/detached at minor stations on the fringes of the town - hardly satisfactory for a railway that prided itself on being one of the most progressive in the country. This clumsy arrangement was the direct cause of the completion of the southern section of the Cross City Line, from King's Norton through to New Street. Meanwhile, things were stirring in deepest Worcestershire....

Rails to Redditch

also showing the strategic importance of the Gloucester Loop when Redditch was the most significant station on this through route.

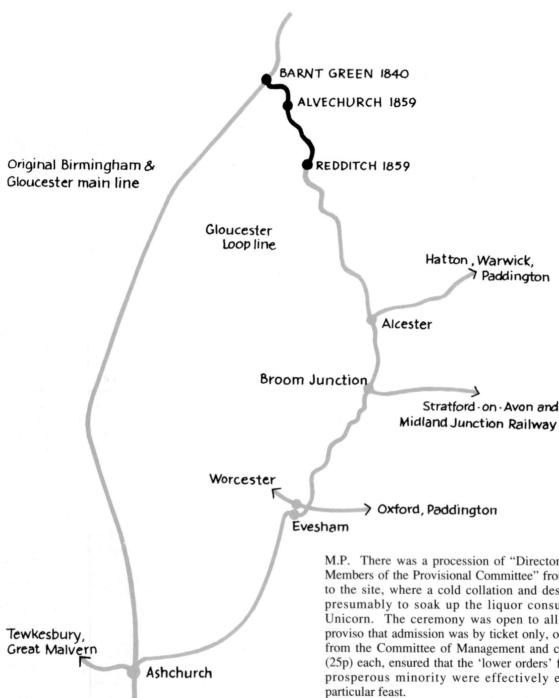

BARNT GREEN 1840

ALVECHURCH 1859

REDDITCH 1859

Original Birmingham & Gloucester main line

Gloucester Loop line

Hatton, Warwick, Paddington

Alcester

Broom Junction

Stratford-on-Avon and Midland Junction Railway

Worcester

Oxford, Paddington

Evesham

Tewkesbury, Great Malvern

Ashchurch

Bristol

M.P. There was a procession of "Directors, Shareholders and Members of the Provisional Committee" from the Unicorn Hotel to the site, where a cold collation and dessert were provided, presumably to soak up the liquor consumed earlier at the Unicorn. The ceremony was open to all, in theory; but the proviso that admission was by ticket only, obtainable in advance from the Committee of Management and costing five shillings (25p) each, ensured that the 'lower orders' frowned upon by the prosperous minority were effectively excluded from this particular feast.

The single track between Redditch and Barnt Green, the junction with the main line, was due to open less than thirteen months later, on September 1st 1859. Unfortunately the works were behind schedule, and as the date approached a heavy ballast train traversed the branch several times a day, testing the strength of the bridges and culverts. All was well, and the line was passed by the Government Inspector on September 9th. The passenger service began ten days later, and it generated a fever of excitement in the town. By the time the first train arrived at 8am - one polished and decorated engine, eight carriages and 70 V.I.P. passengers - two thousand people were crammed onto and around the station. Two hours later the crowd had almost doubled to

RAILS TO REDDITCH

On 5th August 1858 the first sod of the Redditch Railway was turned at the site of the town station. This ceremony was performed by The Honourable Robert Windsor Clive, the local cheer off the first public train from Redditch, which consisted of 18 first and second class carriages filled with four hundred people on a free excursion to Cheltenham. On arrival back in the town at six in the evening this train was greeted by Bromsgrove Band and a peal of bells from St.Stephen's. The excursionists mingled with the crowds, and the Unicorn - not to mention all the other inns - did a very brisk business. Even the next day there were crowds at the station, gawping at the novelty of it all, and every train was full, most passengers simply out for the ride. The arrival of the railway was an excuse for a celebration by ordinary people who led hard monotonous lives. They instinctively knew that it represented progress; today we are more used to celebrating all sorts of events but shy away from being enthusiastic when new motorways or link roads are opened, perhaps because our instincts tell us otherwise.

The first edition of the "Redditch Indicator" appeared five days after the opening, and the coming of the railway was the main front page story. The paper also predicted a drop in the price of coal, as vital to the ordinary householder then as electricity is now. Coal and other freight traffic began on 1st October.

The line, like so many other small concerns, was independent in name only, as it was operated by the Midland Railway from the start and formally absorbed at the beginning of 1865. A free time-table was distributed with the "Redditch Indicator" on July 1st 1861. As with the Birmingham & Gloucester time-table in the 1845 'Bradshaw', there was a minimum of basic information; no list of fares, and nothing to indicate, for example, that a change of train was necessary at Barnt Green. At least there was an even spread of daytime trains, and a Sunday service, although this was axed a few years later. Third class passengers had access to all the branch trains, which is more than could yet be said for those on the main line! There was even a horse bus connection to Alcester and Studley, which became redundant when the line reached those villages in 1868. The time of 15 minutes each way between Redditch and Barnt Green compares

with an average of 12 minutes during the final years of diesel operation and 10 minutes by electric train.

The change from main line to lightly engineered branch remains obvious, even before the train has left Barnt Green. The branch platforms are at the start of a sharp eastward curve. Just beyond the double track becomes single. This was the site of the old Barnt Green Single Line signal box, which controlled the section to Redditch North box, on the approaches to the station. This has always been a single track railway and there was never a passing loop between these two points. The continous curvature of the line, like a lazy worm, can be seen merely by looking at a map. There is a falling gradient of 1:74 for over a mile out of Barnt Green, which used to cause problems in steam days as heavy north-bound freight trains struggled with greasy rails or autumn leaves. The gradient eases through Alvechurch, apart from a short section at 1:67, before rising more gently than it fell, approaching the town on a mile long stretch at 1:130.

The first Redditch station, a small cottage-like structure in Clive Road, proved adequate for only nine years. The second station, a grander affair with typical Midland buildings and ornate platform canopies, opened in 1868 at the same time as the section of track between Redditch and Alcester. Redditch was no longer a branch terminus, but on a line through Evesham to Ashchurch, where it joined the original Birmingham & Gloucester main line. It was known to railwaymen as the "Gloucester Loop" and conceived as an alternative to the direct line via the Lickey Incline. Whilst the incline was an operational nightmare, the loop had drawbacks of its own; it was indirect, meandering and partly single track. It never really prospered in its own right as a through passenger route although for almost a century it provided an important service for the towns and remote villages south of Redditch, places like Studley, Alcester and Ashton-under-Hill. There were junctions with three other lines, at Alcester, Broom and Ashchurch. There was also easy interchange with the Great Western at Evesham. The Gloucester Loop was *really* useful in the scheme of things as an alternative through freight line. It also

Alvechurch, a neat country station, seen in 1962. A new station was built on the site of the coal sidings at electrification.

(Lens of Sutton)

generated specialised traffic of its own, such as needles and fishing tackle from Redditch, and seasonal fruit from the Vale of Evesham. It was a strategic diversionary route for express passenger trains too, should there be engineering work or a mishap on the Lickey.

All the remote wayside stations south of Redditch were staffed, and most had sidings served by that symbol of the Victorian rural railway, the daily pick-up goods train.

Some traffic was generated by local industries, such as the flour mill at Broom, or Bomford's steam rollers and a jam factory, both at Salford Priors.

Alvechurch too, fitted into this pattern. The station was well cared for and there was a coal siding. (Local folklore has it that the stationmaster could tell when rain was due because the whistles of trains at Barnt Green, two miles away, sounded very clear.)

By the 1960s closure of a line such as the Gloucester Loop was inevitable under the Beeching Plan; non-bulk freight traffic and alternative routes between two given points were outside his understanding or tolerance. South of Redditch the end came in three stages; Alcester-Evesham succumbed suddenly in October 1962 because the track was supposed to be unsafe, Redditch-Alcester closed to passengers eight months later and to freight in July 1964. Redditch became a terminus once more and soon had to endure its own closure threat.

Meanwhile, in 1872 the Midland Railway struck a blow for greater social equality and the health of its own bank balance when it became the first company to provide third class accommodation on all its trains. Three years later it abolished second class travel, but kept some second class carriages and re-classified them as '3rds'. The 'artisan classes' had never had it so good!

During the 1870s the Midland was progressive in other matters as well. It was rightly proud of its own new main line into London, complete with high Gothic wedding cake terminus at St.Pancras. It had failed to agree with the London & North Western about running rights to Carlisle for access to Scotland, so it built the Leeds-Settle-Carlisle line; surely the most courageous, awe-inspiring and expensive raspberry ever aimed by one railway company at another?

However, when the Directors of the Midland cast their eyes over Birmingham all was not well. The main line from the south was indirect and it was very difficult for Midland trains to operate a fast efficient service. The Bristol - Birmingham - Derby line was second only to St.Pancras in importance. Because Midland trains could only enter or leave New Street at the Derby end there was a stark choice for the prestige expresses that operated the route. Birmingham portions had to be attached/detached and suffer mandatory ticket inspections at the minor stations of Camp Hill or Saltley while the main train by-passed the town altogether, using the short direct link line which had been completed in 1864. This was an expensive and wasteful use of manpower and locomotives, it was inconvenient and slow for passengers and - most important - it hurt the pride of the Midland Railway. The situation would only improve if Midland trains were able to operate through New Street. Help was at hand in the unlikely guise of a piffling little single-track suburban line, which ran through territory where suburbs hardly existed as yet.

The second station at Redditch, with a dmu recently arrived from Birmingham, 5th April 1963, a year before the Beeching closure attempt.
(M.A.King)

The West Suburban and Camp Hill Lines

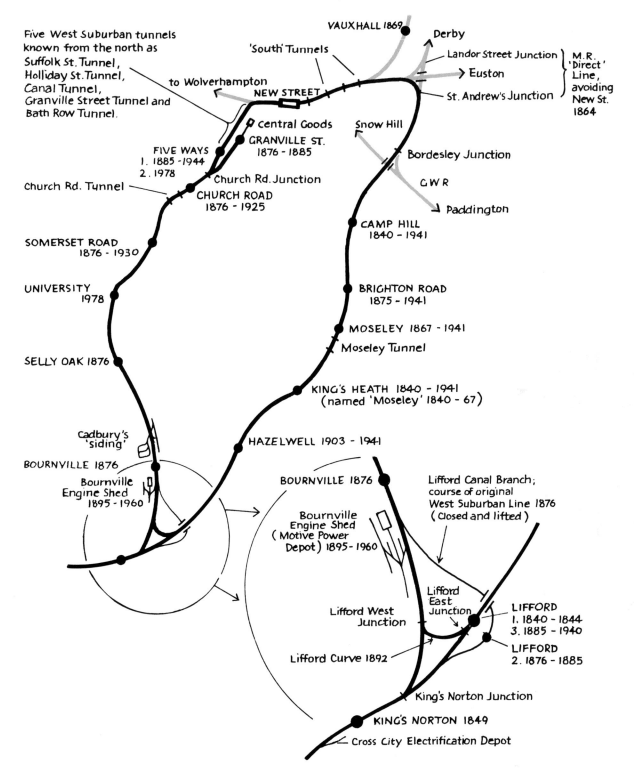

Five West Suburban tunnels known from the north as Suffolk St. Tunnel, Holliday St. Tunnel, Canal Tunnel, Granville Street Tunnel and Bath Row Tunnel.

'South' Tunnels

VAUXHALL 1869

Derby

Landor Street Junction

Euston

St. Andrew's Junction

M.R. 'Direct' Line, avoiding New St. 1864

to Wolverhampton

NEW STREET

Central Goods

GRANVILLE ST. 1876 - 1885

Snow Hill

Bordesley Junction

G W R

Paddington

FIVE WAYS
1. 1885 - 1944
2. 1978

Church Rd. Junction

Church Rd. Tunnel

CHURCH ROAD 1876 - 1925

CAMP HILL 1840 - 1941

SOMERSET ROAD 1876 - 1930

BRIGHTON ROAD 1875 - 1941

UNIVERSITY 1978

MOSELEY 1867 - 1941

Moseley Tunnel

SELLY OAK 1876

KING'S HEATH 1840 - 1941
(named 'Moseley' 1840 - 67)

Cadbury's 'siding'

BOURNVILLE 1876

Bournville Engine Shed 1895 - 1960

HAZELWELL 1903 - 1941

BOURNVILLE 1876

Lifford Canal Branch; course of original West Suburban Line 1876 (Closed and lifted)

Bournville Engine Shed (Motive Power Depot) 1895 - 1960

Lifford East Junction

LIFFORD
1. 1840 - 1844
3. 1885 - 1940

Lifford West Junction

LIFFORD
2. 1876 - 1885

Lifford Curve 1892

King's Norton Junction

KING'S NORTON 1849

Cross City Electrification Depot

THE BIRMINGHAM WEST SUBURBAN RAILWAY

The coming of the railways helped to secure an improved standard of living for most people, but it was not realistic to expect coach or canal owners to appreciate that. For over twenty years after the opening of the Birmingham & Gloucester Railway in 1840, the Worcester & Birmingham Canal made strenuous but unsuccessful attempts to halt the decline in its traffic by promoting various schemes to work with a railway. In 1864, for instance, it had an idea for a West Birmingham Railway & Canal Company, which was to build a line, from a site near to but separate from New Street station, along the canal bank to join up with the main railway at King's Norton. There was also to be a branch to Harborne. The idea was not supported by the necessary cash, due to the state of the stock market, and it was dropped.

However, in 1870 a group of Birmingham businessmen revived the scheme, suggesting that the railway would pay an annual rent of £1 400 for use of the canal company's land, and that the Midland Railway would work the line. In this form it met with success and the Birmingham West Suburban Railway Act was passed on 31st July 1871. It included provisions for the canal company to participate in the management and profits of the railway. The terminus was to be at Albion Wharf, at the rear of what is now the Central Television building. No provision was made for the branch to Harborne. During construction it was decided to build the Birmingham terminus at Granville Street, short of Albion Wharf and saving the expense of crossing the canal. Plans still exist for the Albion Wharf terminus that never was, to be known as Suffolk Street Station. As originally envisaged there would have been a simple single platform station at the end of a brick viaduct. An alternative more costly plan shows a two platform station, with a long ramp approach from the street, giving it the faintly ridiculous air of a pier stranded miles away from the sea. Granville Street as built was much more modest, a single short platform with basic wooden buildings and a run-round loop. The Midland Railway obtained powers to take the company over in 1875. These powers were exercised from the beginning.

This basic little upstart of a railway, a simple single-track branch line that slavishly followed every curve in the canal, opened on April 3rd 1876, with a service of nine trains a day between King's Norton and Granville Street. There were stations at Stirchley Street (Bournville), Selly Oak (which had the luxury of the line's only passing loop), Somerset Road and Church Road. Lifford station opened two months later. Granville Street station was inconveniently sited outside the central area, off Broad Street, and without connections to any other railway.

The "Birmingham Gazette" gave it a rather low key welcome:-

"Opening of the Birmingham West Suburban Railway"
    The Midland Railway Company commenced running trains on this line between Granville Street Station and Breedon Cross, King's Norton, for the first time yesterday. The first passenger train left Granville Street at 7.30am and so great was the crowd of passsengers that it was with great difficulty that they could all be accommodated. During the day the number of passengers by each train was equally large. The whole of the arrangements were very satisfactory. Mr.Needham, of the Midland Company, visited Granville Street during the day, and Mr.Pearson, district superintendent, directed the traffic of the line."

The Midland soon took the line in hand. This was the missing link in their urgent need for a route through Birmingham New Street, and they wasted little time before acting, obtaining Parliamentary powers to double the track and build an extension into New Street in 1881.

Upgrading began in 1883 and was completed in under two years. Doubling of the track was accompanied by easing of the curves near most of the bends in the canal.

Standard Midland Railway signal boxes were built at Church Road, Selly Oak, Stirchley Street & Bournville, and Lifford. Despite this standardisation there were some signalling curiosities, notably at Somerset Road station. Here there was a

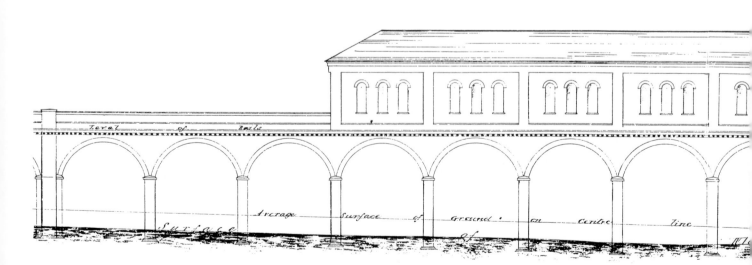

Not a seaside pier stranded many miles inland, but an elevation of Suffolk Street Station, the proposed Birmingham terminus of the West Suburban Railway. The rail approach would have been on a long single-track viaduct, eventually crossing the Worcester & Birmingham Canal and ending in this two track station. Economies meant that the line finished short at Granville Street, without the expense of crossing the canal. With its 1:10 ramp to street level - ideal for skateboard enthusiasts - this was the de-luxe version; alternative plans lever frame on the down platform which was controlled by station staff. The levers operated a home signal at the Birmingham end of the platform and its related distant signal, nearer Church Road. The signals were supposed to protect the rear of stopping trains but they were ill-fitted for this purpose. Passengers at Somerset Road were so few that by the time a porter had put the signals to danger behind a train it was ready to go again. At least one driver, assisted by Fred Jenkins of Bournville, who was a fireman on the route in the 1920s, conspired to see whether it was possible to have the train moving again before the signals could be operated - frequently it was.

The stations were also standardised by the Midland. The primitive structure at Bournville was in stark contrast to the later station, and draughtsman's plans for Selly Oak, dated July 7th 1885, are works of art in their own right (see inside covers). The careful pleasing design and attention to detail are much in evidence, as is the corporate image of the company by the use of standard fittings. The glass canopies over the up platform, with accompanying brackets, finials and ornamentation, were of a type that still survives at some former Midland stations, most notably Kettering. The dark wooden bench seating, fixed to the waiting room walls, the discreet and modest ladies' toilet, which could only be reached via a lobby within the ladies' waiting room, the stark contrast of the outdoor urinal well removed from the gentlemen's waiting room, the porters room with its cold unyielding blue brick floor - all these and more were daily accessories to nineteenth century rail travel.

Transformation of the West Suburban Line was total, and the only vestiges of original route now remaining are the remnants of a single track viaduct just north of Selly Oak station, and a section alongside the canal at Lifford which has been converted into a road.

Church Road Junction signal box, its days numbered, 1966. This was a Midland Railway standard box, but with a slimline base for use in a confined space, in this case with its back against the canal wall. The tracks to the Central Goods Depot have already been lifted and cabling troughs for power box signals are being installed. A similar box at Ilkley was demolished in 1992 in preparation for electrification of Leeds/Bradford local lines, also to be operated by Class 323 emus. *(M.A.King)*

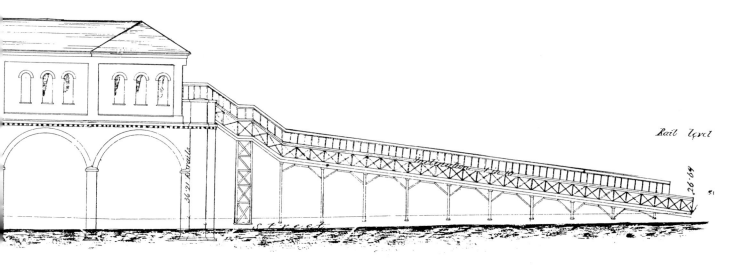

substituted a formidable looking staircase. Platforms would have been 36 feet above street level. These plans for the city centre station that never was have been in library archives for over a century. Virtually unknown and unseen, they degenerated over the years and were carefully repaired so that this copy could be made."
(courtesy of Birmingham Central Library)

A basic railway, Victorian style. Stirchley Street (Bournville) in 1879. This view, looking south, shows the bridge carrying Mary Vale Road and the distant signal for Selly Oak, the only passing place. Would you dare to ask for a ticket from the formidable looking station staff? This station suffered an acute identity crisis in early years. It began life as "Stirchley Street", was renamed "Stirchley Street & Bournville" in 1880, "Bournville & Stirchley Street" in 1888 and finally just plain "Bournville" in 1904.   *(courtesy of Cadbury's Ltd.)*

A much improved Bournville looking north, about 1908. The signal post has arms for the spur into the engine shed, the main line and the Lifford canal branch. The angled nameboard is a standard Midland design but the painting of alternative boards on the platform awning in a dark and light colour is unusual. It illustrates well, however, that the area painting foreman was allowed a certain amount of discretion, as long as he used the two basic colours of stone and brown.
(Lens of Sutton)

An Ordnance Survey map of 1884 is remarkable in showing the new double track and station at Selly Oak, abruptly ending south of the station. The old single track is still extant. By this time Selly Oak had been served by a standard gauge horse tramway along the Bristol Road from Birmingham for eight years. This line had an interesting career, worth outlining briefly as it poached many passengers from the railway in its later years. In 1890 it was converted to Birmingham's narrow gauge of 3'6" and operated by battery electric cars. These were cumbersome and slow, and dissipated much of their energy by the sheer effort of dragging their own weight around. The line was extended into the centre of Selly Oak and converted to conventional overhead power in 1901; the arrival of faster, lighter more modern cars, offering a cheap frequent service to the city, became a serious challenge to the local train service. After the First World War, in an imaginative move that was tragically short-lived, Birmingham Corporation embarked on an ambitious programme of constructing dual carriageways along main roads radiating from the city, using the central reservations for fast traffic-free tramways. The Bristol Road received this treatment, with trams reaching the famous Rednal terminus within spitting distance of the Lickey Hills, in April 1924. Between 1924 and 1931 some 48,000 new houses were built in the city, 70% were municipally owned, many replaced slums and most were near the new tram routes. In order not to penalise the former inner city slum dwellers tram fares were kept very low; the workman's return fare from Rednal to the city in 1931 was 5d (2p) for 16 miles. The railways could not compete with the trams for frequency and economy of travel, but fought back for the leisure market, with special cheap excursion trains to Barnt Green at a fare of just 6d (2.5p) return from New Street. Excursion trains and trams both eventually succumbed to the status symbol of the car and the more modern image of the bus. The tramway received no further investment - the city's newest tram was a unique vehicle dating from 1930 - and the Bristol Road route, much loved by Brummies and many others living further afield, saw its last tram in July 1952. The pleasure of travelling this route, prior to a ramble on the Lickeys, remains fresh in the minds of many older people, yet it comes as something of a shock to realise that the route in its final form (1924-52) had a shorter life than the diesel trains that operated the Cross City Line before electrification! To return to the nineteenth century ....

Between Bournville and King's Norton the improved West Suburban Line left the canal side completely and took a short cut, known rather grandly as the Stirchley Street & Bournville to King's Norton Deviation Line. This was the last section to be completed, opening on September 26th 1885. It left the original single track to be worked as a loop siding which became known as the Lifford Canal branch. Lifford station was stranded on this loop, so it closed. Thus Lifford had been served by two stations for a total of only thirteen years. The third station, on the Camp Hill line, opened as soon as the second closed and lasted until 1940. The canal branch itself closed in the early 1960s, one of the last trains over it being a Stephenson Locomotive Society dmu special on Saturday June 2nd 1962, which was touring much of the local network to celebrate the centenary of the opening of the line to Sutton Coldfield.

Ordnance Survey map of Selly Oak, 1884, clearly showing the upgrading of the West Suburban Line in progress. The original single track hugs the canal almost like a towpath, but the double track line enters the new station from the north, stopping abruptly at the signal box. The copper and metal works had its own self-contained railway; with curvature like that it must have been narrow gauge.

(courtesy of Birmingham Central Library)

A Class 116 dmu, sporting 'whiskers' in the days before overall yellow end panels, negotiates the last surviving part of the original West Suburban Line, the Lifford Canal loop, with a Stephenson Locomotive Society special on 17th March 1962. The site of Lifford's short-lived second station (1876-1885) is just to the rear of the train. The Lifford Canal Branch was a useful interchange point between rail and water-borne freight traffic. One of the last trains over this line, another SLS special, which toured many freight lines and spurs in the West Midlands, ran to mark the centenary of the line to Sutton Coldfield on 2nd June 1962. *(P.J.Shoesmith)*

The promoters of the original West Suburban Railway had not been able to raise money for a bridge over the canal at the Birmingham end of the line; the Midland had the motivation and resources to meet the more expensive challenge of tunnelling under this waterway on a gradient of 1:80. It had to opt for the tunnel solution in order to gain access to New Street.

The expansion of New Street, virtually doubling its area and capacity, was the only common sense solution, and the work was concurrent with the upgrading and extension of the West Suburban line. The enlarged station came into use in February 1885, just five months before the extension into New Street was opened. This latter involved much heavy engineering and earthworks, and the employment of eleven hundred men, not to mention seven contractor's locomotives and sixty horses. The five tunnels - which now appear as four thanks to modern building development overhead - are approached by retaining walls sometimes over fifty feet high, which consumed over 30 million tough and expensive blue bricks that have hardly a scratch on them over a century later. The tunnels themselves conceal the fact that the Worcester & Birmingham Canal crosses overhead. The West Suburban extension, the associated freight line to Worcester Wharf and the new Holliday Street (which was built at Midland Railway expense because rail construction had caused disruption and severance of other local streets) all tunnelled under the canal within a distance of 80 yards! Achieving this feat caused the greatest difficulty of all, as the canal had to be carried in huge wooden troughs, with minimum disruption to water-borne traffic, while the tunnels were being built. The absorbing story is outlined in the biography of the line's contractor, "The Life & Work of Joseph Firbank J.P., D.L., Railway Contractor", published by Frederick McDermott in 1887:-

"Tunnelling under the canal would have proved a sufficiently delicate operation under the most favourable circumstances, but in this case the difficulty was greatly increased by the fact that the canal is, at this point, carried at a height of 70 feet above the level of New Street Station, on an embankment of loose material. Whilst, therefore, the tunnelling operations were in progress, the waterway had to be carried in wooden troughs, large enough to allow the free passage of canal boats. These troughs were necessarily of immense strength, and when the tunnels - one of which is for a road, another for the West Suburban line, and the third for the approach to the Midland Company's new goods yard - were completed, and the water at this part of the canal was pumped out, for ten days over 100 men were engaged, night and day, in removing the massive timbering, in 'puddling' the bottom of the canal near the tunnels, and in rebuilding the canal walls where interfered with. It is difficult to realise the administrative skill and grasp of details required in planning and carrying out such a work as this: it could, indeed, only be executed by the help of tried assistants, and a reliable staff. In return for such services, Mr. Firbank did all in his power, on this as on other contracts, for the comfort and welfare of his men, many of whom had worked for him for twenty years - some could, indeed, at the time of his death, claim to have been associated with him for forty years of active service."

A classic shot of the West Suburban approach to New Street showing the first station at Five Ways, many years after closure, 25th May 1957. The track on the left, with ex-Midland Railway signals, leads to the Central Goods Depot. The road vehicle beyond the wall carried Kunzle's chocolates, as much a symbol of the 1950s as 'Vimto' and 'Tizer' *(Lens of Sutton)*

West Suburban trains began running into New Street on July 1st 1885. (From that date it can be said that the route of today's Cross City line was complete because, by coincidence, the London & North Western Railway's extension from Sutton Coldfield to Lichfield had opened a few months earlier, in December 1884.) Granville Street closed on the same day and Five Ways opened. On October 1st Midland expresses at last began running through New Street.

In the final phase of the development the Granville Street line was extended into a new Midland Railway goods depot at Worcester Wharf, on a site now occupied by Stanier House, British Rail's principal administrative block in the city. It branched off the new main line at Church Road Junction, just north of that station, and the trackbed can still be seen at Five Ways. Thus the Midland had a spanking new extension into New Street and a new freight terminus on the southern side of town. "Worcester Wharf" opened for business in 1887 but was not completed until July 1st 1892, when it was renamed Birmingham Central Goods Station. That same day saw the opening of Lifford Curve. Freight trains could now reach Central Goods from the Derby direction without reversal, as useful in freight

terms as the ability to run passenger trains through New Street. The opening of the curve also saw the start of a new 'Circle' passenger service, New Street to New Street, via the Camp Hill and West Suburban lines. It did not flourish, ran mainly at peak hours and avoided King's Norton. The Circle service ended in 1941 as a wartime economy, and the passenger stations on the Camp Hill line closed at the same time.

The enlarged station at New Street consisted of two distinct parts, the 'North Western' side and the 'Midland' side. The trains of one company almost never strayed onto the tracks of the other and New Street was, for most operational purposes, two adjacent but separate stations. This way of working persisted until the rebuilding of the 1960s, when the station became a more unified whole, thanks largely to the abolition of Queen's Drive, a road which had run through the middle, parallel to and level with the platforms, separating the North Western side from the Midland. Having said that, it may come as a surprise to learn that for the first four years of through running northbound Midland trains always used the North Western side. So, what were the characteristics of this unique station, and how had they come about?

The Development of New Street and its approaches

Aston

Bloomsbury & Nechels 1856-69

Derby

Grand Junction Engine Shed 1840

(VAUXHALL) AND DUDDESTON 1869

Saltley Junction

Landor Street Junction

Vauxhall (G.J. temporary terminus) 1837-40

1.

2.

3.

2a

Euston

4.

3a

G.J. 1839

Curzon Street L & B

1838

Grand Junction

St. Andrew's Junction

Proof House Junction

Bristol - Derby 'direct' line, 1864, a New-St. by-pass for Midland Railway Expresses

Bristol

BIRMINGHAM NEW STREET

3b

1854

1885

Wolverhampton

1851

West Sub. Rly. 1885

W.S.R. 1876

Central Goods

Granville Street

1. Lawley Street Station. In use for passengers 1842-51.

2. M.R. curve of 1851, leading to Derby Junction (2a) a poorly-signalled bottleneck. Sutton trains would have used this junction had a Midland sponsored line to the town been built.

3. This burrowing curve, via a re-sited Gloucester Junction (3a) eliminated traffic conflict at Derby Junction, which was redundant. (2) was lifted 1897. An extra pair of tracks into New Street, via a widened tunnel (3b) opened on the same day as (3), May 17th. 1896.

4. Lawley Street Viaduct, opened in 1893, carried Walsall / Lichfield / G.J. trains clear of the goods neck at Curzon Street. Two years earlier, the section north from Curzon Street almost to Aston Station had been quadrupled

A GRAND CENTRAL STATION

No history of any non-Great Western line in the Birmingham area can be properly considered without reference to New Street, so this section is a thumbnail sketch of some aspects of that most fascinating station. Although it opened in 1854 it is necessary to look further back to understand its origins, together with some of the problems that it inherited and passed on, in turn, to today's railway.

By 1841 Curzon Street was the focus of three main lines, the Grand Junction, London & Birmingham and Birmingham & Gloucester. These gained a near neighbour in 1842 when the Birmingham & Derby Junction Railway opened its own pokey inconvenient terminus at Lawley Street, between the other lines but 40 feet below them.

From the very beginning the railways converging on Birmingham often tried to adopt a policy of co-operation. As early as 1838 the Grand Junction completely recast its service so as to provide good connections and through carriages with the London & Birmingham. In addition it was possible, by the autumn of 1842, to travel direct - in the loosest sense - in a through carriage from Euston (dep.09.45) to Gloucester (arr.17.15) via Curzon St. The growth of all forms of rail traffic and the rapid expansion of the national network was the most important feature of English life in the 1840s. In Birmingham this led to congestion which soon threatened to overwhelm the small termini. However, a proposed line to Wolverhampton, as described in an Act of Parliament of 1846, was to have a junction near Curzon Street, branching *away* from the line leading into that station and gaining access to an excellent site for a large new through station in the town centre via a tunnel. This Birmingham, Wolverhampton and Stour Valley Railway was to be worked by the LNWR from the outset.

The new station, briefly called Navigation Street, was partially opened for services to Wolverhampton at the end of 1851, but a dispute with the Shrewsbury & Birmingham Railway over running rights, and an almost paranoid anxiety by the LNWR to keep the Great Western off its tracks, resulted in legal battles which delayed full opening until July 1st 1854. The overall roof was constructed during this time, without interruption to the train service and without a single accident. Special wooden stagings were used during construction. They occupied the whole width of the station, measured 200 feet by 22 feet, had a height of 50 feet and were moved on cast iron rollers. Groups of men worked on the roof from on top of the stagings.

Significantly, New Street was one of the first centrally sited through stations in any large British town, and this "grand central station" as the 'Illustrated London News' called it, occupied about half the site of today's station. E.A.Cowper, who designed the roof, had worked on the Crystal Palace as Joseph Paxton's junior partner. His immense iron and glass roof, 840 feet long, (1,100 feet counting the extension covering the awkward triangular area at the Wolverhampton end) 75 feet above rail level at the apex and with a single shallow curve spanning 212 feet, was then the largest in the world. The glass alone, in sheets measuring 6 feet by 16 inches, weighed 115 tons; the iron weighed almost ten times that amount and cost £32,274. Barlow's train shed at St.Pancras, dating from the 1870s, was 150 feet shorter and only 30 feet wider. If the roof was spectacular the main passenger entrance was absurd, consisting of a small opening at the side of the LNWR Queen's Hotel, which faced New Street. The station and its hotel were not actually in New Street, because the whole site was separate and set back, under the terms of the Act of Parliament, from King Edward VI Grammar School, which was in New Street. The passenger entrance was cramped at the outset and so were the running lines, as there was just one double track into and out of the station. The problem of congestion, for both people and trains, remains unsolved.

There were four through platforms and four bays, plus two extra through loop lines. Platform numbering followed what was then normal practice; any island platform had the same number for both its faces. So it was that the world's largest roof span sheltered a station whose eight platforms were only numbered up to three; bays 1, 2, 1A, 2A, and platforms 1, 2 (two faces) and 3. All this must have been confusing to the unwary. The trains to Sutton, and later to Lichfield, normally used 1A and 2A, known as the South Staffs bays.

The platform layout, though not the numbering, survived until the rebuilding of the 1960s, which is more than can be said for the small turntables which straddled almost every line, the purpose of which was to marshal carriages onto traverser lines at right angles to the through lines, so that they could be stored in cramped sidings at the south side of the station. Longer rolling stock soon committed these quaint working practices to history.

The station doubled in size in 1885, with the arrival of the Midland sponsored West Suburban Railway from the south west. There were now two double tracks serving that end of the station, but the single pair of tracks at the Euston end persisted for a while longer. Indeed, the potential for congestion at the Euston end was far greater than it is today, despite what southbound Cross City travellers and others may think as their trains queue to gain access to the platforms. The three major bottlenecks were all eliminated, as a matter of urgency, within the space of as many years. The marshalling of Curzon Street's many and lengthy goods trains often fouled the Lichfield line, but Lawley Street Viaduct, which carried that line clear of the nuisance, was opened in May 1893. The so-called 'south' tunnel was widened to take four running lines and came into use on May 17th 1896, giving the Midland Railway its own pair of tracks at that end of the station. These tracks were extended out so that on the same day Midland trains on the Derby line were able to use the new Landor Street Curve passing under the LNWR Euston line. A physical connection was retained between the Derby and Euston lines at Grand Junction, but it was not normally used by Midland or LNWR expresses.

The station extension, the 'Midland' side, cost half a million pounds to construct and had four through platforms, spanned by a curved double arched roof. The original numbering system was perpetuated, the new platforms were 4, 5 (two faces) and 6 (through line and bay). Suburban trains going south via Camp Hill normally left from Platform 4 and arrived at Platform 6; this arrangement was reversed by stopping trains using the West Suburban Line.

Once again New Street was briefly the largest station in the world, and the many photographs taken between 1885 and 1920 show just how well proportioned it was. The enlargement caused the demolition of some of Birmingham's most squalid slums and rookeries, but it also ruptured the street plan. Great Queen Street was buried under building works, only to re-emerge as Queen's Drive, a road separating the LNWR and Midland halves of the station. This was not a right of way, and the gates at each end were closed briefly every Christmas Day to prove the point. The pedestrian right of way, the footbridge spanning the original platforms, which followed the route formerly taken by King Street, was extended across the whole station and became its most famous single feature. There is evidence that this bridge had for some time been a kind of linear red light district, attracting Birmingham's prostitutes like moths to a flame. A letter writer to the "Birmingham Daily Mail" in 1870, who signed himself as "A Friend to Public Morality" wrote of the 'ladies of the pavement':-

> "Surely they must select some more retired spot
> for the carrying on of their disgraceful traffic than
> New Street Station? No sooner does it begin to get
> dark than they begin to haunt the place, the
> platforms and bridge in particular."

The footbridge gave direct access to all platforms, as well as an excellent view of the signalmen in No.3 cabin, which straddled the footbridge and had outside levers. It also meant that New Street was an 'open' station from the beginning. This was expensive in manpower and time, as there were ticket barriers at some platforms, manned 'as required'. In the late nineteenth century there were as many as seven ticket offices around the station and most incoming trains, from the 1850s through to the 1960s, were required to stop for lengthy ticket inspections at an inner suburban station. These took place at Five Ways on the West Suburban, and Banbury Street Ticket Platform near the Proof House (later at Vauxhall) on the Sutton line. Five Ways remained open as a ticket platform for several years after it closed as a passenger station. On rebuilding in the 1960s New Street bucked the national trend because the new fully enclosed footbridge could only be entered via the ticket barrier; the station ceased to be 'open' and off-train ticket checks could be carried out on all passengers for the first time in its history. The public right of way across the station was retained but awkwardly re-routed through the shopping precinct on a higher level.

What of the train services, especially on the pre-Cross City lines? When New Street was in its Edwardian heyday - rail was king, manpower was still cheap enough for the station roof to be kept clean and the car was still only a gleam in rich men's eyes - the time-table for April 1909 was as follows:-

"Cross City" South

Departures from New Street to King's Norton and beyond via CAMP HILL

Weekdays

06.25	10.34	15.45	21.08
08.02	10.50	16.41	21.40
08.20 H	12.05 H	17.06	22.15
08.37	13.00	18.00(SO)	23.20
09.25	13.20	18.45	
09.55	14.30	19.40	

Sundays

08.15	12.55	16.40	20.35

via FIVE WAYS

Weekdays only

07.20	12.30(SX)	17.50 H	21.45
08.20	12.48	18.40 F	23.05
09.40	14.18 H	19.00(SX) H	
11.00	14.50	19.55	
12.18(SO)	17.20	20.35	

(SX) Saturdays excepted : (SO) Saturdays only
L limited stop
H connection at King's Norton for Halesowen

Departures from New Street for the CIRCLE service

Weekdays only
New Street - Camp Hill-Lifford Curve-Five Ways - New Street

07.00	17.13	19.08
08.16	18.18	20.15

New Street - Five Ways-Lifford Curve-Camp Hill - New Street

07.03	08.00	08.55	18.22

Perhaps the most striking feature of these services to modern eyes is the apparent haphazardness of it all; the frenzied activity during the rush hours and the long intervals between off-peak trains. Sometimes trains bunched, as with the two mid-morning services along the Camp Hill line only 16 minutes apart, followed by a gap of 75 minutes and two lunchtime trains 20 minutes apart. There are similar self-evident curiosities in the Sutton line time-table. With services like this the railway was not properly alerted to the tram, bus and car competition that was coming. And why should it be? It is true that by this date most people had deserted the trains for the superior tram service at a few stations such as Selly Oak, but passenger carryings at Bournville were growing with Cadbury's factory and, north of Birmingham, Four Oaks was beginning to expand as a desirable commuter dormitory. And yet as early as 1881 some local lines had services operating at more or less regular intervals. Walsall, Wolverhampton and Harborne were all served by hourly local trains and all experienced a growth in traffic as a result; by comparison the West Suburban and Sutton lines were neglected.

On the eve of the First World War the station handled 20 million passengers per year, an average of almost 55,000 per day, providing employment for about 560 men.

"Cross City" North

Departures from New Street for the SUTTON line

Weekdays

06.40 FO	12.35 FO	17.20 FO	20.20 FO(SX)
07.05 FO	13.07 FO	17.40 FO	20.40 FO
07.55 LD	13.26 FO(SO)	18.00 LD	21.10 FO
08.10 SC	13.53 LD	18.15 FO	21.50 FO
08.48 FO	14.15 FO	18.33 FO	22.35 FO
09.08 LD	15.10 LD	18.55 L	22.48 FO(SO)
09.50 FO	16.15 FO	19.17 FO	22.55 L
10.48 FO	16.30 FO	19.45 SC	23.15 FO
11.50 LD	17.05 FO(SX)	20.10 LD	

Sundays

09.00 SC	14.30 SC	20.35 SC
13.00 SC	16.15 SC	21.30 SC

(SX) Saturdays excepted : (SO) Saturdays only
FO - to Four Oaks : SC - to Sutton Coldfield
L - to Lichfield
LD - to Lichfield and Derby, non-stop between New Street and Sutton Coldfield

After that war the character of New Street changed imperceptibly. Trams, buses and cars made increasing inroads into the suburban traffic, stations began to close (Church Road was an early casualty in 1925) and neglect set in. The glass roofs were no longer cleaned properly, so New Street became dingy and unwelcoming. As early as 1920 one commentator was already writing "the lavatories proclaim their presence by the awful smell".

Worse was to come, courtesy of Hitler's Luftwaffe. There were four serious incidents in October and November 1940, when bombs damaged the station and signalling. There were no train movements for two days on 19th-21st November. One high explosive bomb known to have hit the station and thought to have gone off in the general chaos was excavated eighteen months later with its fuse intact! More enemy action on 10th April 1941 closed the West Suburban tunnels for eight days, the longest single disruption to services.

New Street emerged from the war fully functioning but tattered, with Cowper's bomb damaged LNWR roof needing urgent attention. It was soon declared unsafe, removed and replaced by individual platform canopies in 1948. Colour light signals began to replace the semaphores in 1946 (apart from platforms 7 & 8 on the Midland side, which had been treated in 1924 following an accident which claimed three lives in 1921), though the last of the pre-Grouping semaphores lingered until the complete rebuilding of the station during the 1960s. The present signal box opened in 1966, replacing six manual boxes within the station area.

A book issued by British Railways in 1954 ("The Story of New Street" by F.W.Grocott, price 1/-) outlined the improvements, many of them merely cosmetic, already taking place. It still required over six hundred staff to run the station, as in 1914, but the figures of 370 daily train movements and three million passengers a year (8 220 per day) show just how much rail had succumbed to competition.

The Lichfield line was about to be dieselised, and all other lines would follow. Nevertheless, it would still be some years before the quality and frequency of most local train services could again be taken seriously. From this time until the early 1970s only 4% of local commuters travelled into Birmingham by rail.

Birmingham New Street, LNWR side, September 1885. Platform 1 is to the left, the 'South Staffs' bays 1A and 1B to the right. Labour is sufficiently cheap and plentiful to ensure that the overall roof remains clean. Trains to Sutton and Lichfield departed from these bays, although the one shown is believed to be a stopping service to Worcester and Bristol. The footbridge is topped by the famous No.3 signal cabin. Everyone is watching the photographer, except for the man on the standard LNWR bench, who must have been persuaded or bribed to adopt such a nonchalant pose. The indifferent blur is his dog. The rolling stock design has still not quite outgrown the appearance of the stage coach. *(National Railway Museum)*

A magnificent portrait of the Midland side of New Street, platforms 4 and 5, in pristine condition seven months after opening, September 1885. Queen's Drive is on the left. The train is bound for King's Norton via Camp Hill and will leave New Street by the LNWR tracks, as the Midland did not have its own tracks at the Euston/Derby end of the station until 1896. The lighting is interesting, both the side lamps at the rear of the train and the lamps within the station, less ornate and more modern that their counterparts on the LNWR platforms. *(National Railway Museum)*

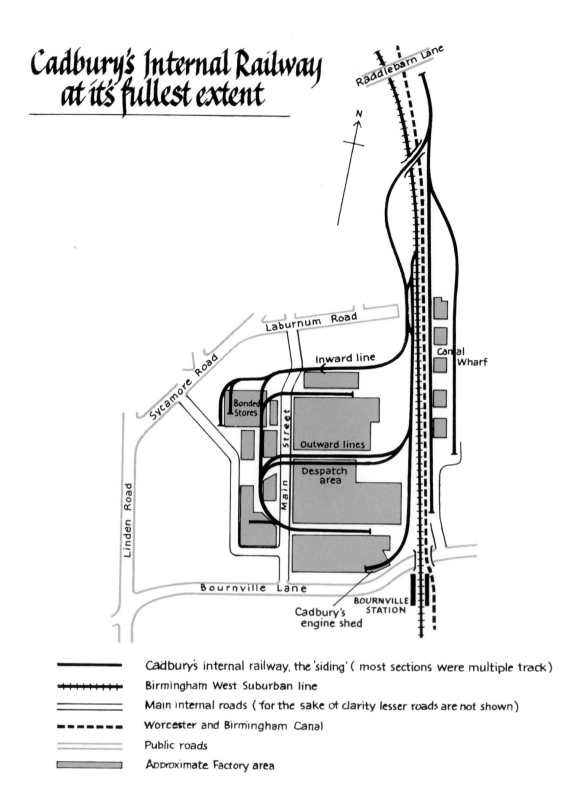

Cadbury's Internal Railway at it's fullest extent

Raddlebarn Lane

N

Inward line

Canal Wharf

Laburnum Road

Sycamore Road

Bonded Stores

Main Street

Outward lines

Despatch area

Linden Road

Bournville Lane

Cadbury's engine shed

BOURNVILLE STATION

———————— Cadbury's internal railway, the 'siding' (most sections were multiple track)

+++++++++ Birmingham West Suburban line

———————— Main internal roads (for the sake of clarity lesser roads are not shown)

- - - - - - - Worcester and Birmingham Canal

———————— Public roads

▨ Approximate Factory area

CHOCOLATES AND MEMORIES AT BOURNVILLE

When the Birmingham West Suburban Railway opened in 1876 Bournville as such did not exist. The station began life as "Stirchley Street". Three years later George and Richard Cadbury moved out from the town centre and opened their new chocolate factory here. The 'Bourn' in their chosen name recognised the proximity of the Bourne Brook and the 'ville' was a declaration that this was to be the site of a new town, a model village to serve the factory. The brothers picked the area in order to improve conditions for their workers and because of the excellent transport potential. The railway and the Worcester & Birmingham Canal were both on the doorstep, while the main road into Birmingham was less than a quarter of a mile away. Today warehouses and distribution centres often cluster round motorway junctions, even on green field sites; this was a nineteenth century equivalent. Homes for a few key workers were built along with the factory, followed by a lull until 1895, when construction of the village began in earnest. In the early years most employees travelled out from their existing homes. True to their nature, the Cadbury brothers quickly negotiated bargain rail fares for their workforce to offset the cost of the longer journey to work.

Two rakes of Midland Railway wagons, each with a loco at the head, in readiness for loading inside Cadbury's despatch shed. About 1920, the year is uncertain but the time is definitely 11.15. *(courtesy of Cadbury's Ltd.)*

The first station at Bournville had no facilities capable of handling Cadbury's goods traffic, all of which had to be trans-shipped by horse drawn van between the factory and Lifford station, one mile away. As the West Suburban line was upgraded, so Cadbury's invested in the construction of their own internal railway system. Work began in 1883 and trains began operating the following year. The completed network, which grew as the factory expanded, eventually consisted of four and a half miles of track serving all parts of the works. Despite its length and complexity, it was always referred to in official company documents as 'the siding'. The layout was almost circular, designed for speedy and efficient reception and despatch. Connection with the main line was made to the north of the factory, and a bridge which still exists spanned the main line tracks nearby. This gave Cadbury's trains access to the company's canal wharf opposite the main factory block and on the far side of the railway and canal. As an article in "Bournville Transport 1925 (Cadbury's)" noted -

"The method of working allows for all traffic to come in at one point ... and to leave at another ... this circular motion being so devised to facilitate the working of traffic and to minimize congestion delays, and also reduce factory shunting costs. It is thus possible for full trains to be received from the railway company at practically any time of the day, and without interference with outgoing traffic. For shunting purposes within the siding four steam locomotives are used. ..... The work of the packing and despatch sections is co-ordinated and carried out simultaneously. It has been found possible to organize the working so that only one handling of packages is necessary from the packer into the railway vehicle. ... By the use of this system, handling in transit is minimized, with a consequent reduction in delays and claims for damage and pilferage. It is also possible to hand the railway company a number of full loads two or three times a day, a fact which enables early transit connections to be made. The usual practice is to despatch at least two trains per day, each of from 30 to 35 wagons, one of these being sent at mid-day."

....and at the point of transfer the crew of the main line locomotive would, if they were lucky, share in a cup of 'hot chocolate crumb' with the Cadbury enginemen, a pleasant change from cold tea.

At various points in the company's history up to six locomotives were used on its own rail system. Veterans were withdrawn in time, and replaced. The locos were invariably sturdy little 0-4-0 tank engines, weighing up to 40 tons and purchased new from the maker, not some hand-me-downs from elsewhere. Their short wheelbases were essential for negotiating the curves on the system, the tightest of which had a radius of only 55ft. They had their own shed on site and their reign lasted from 1884 until 1963. The last steam loco to be bought was No.10, a 39 ton 0-4-0 saddle tank built by Peckett & Son of Bristol, taken into stock in September 1955. It ran on coke, minimising smoke pullution, and had steel tubes, not copper. The other locos were converted to this greener way of running during the 1950s. The first diesel arrived in 1957 and six years later steam was ousted. Steam loco No.9 was kept in reserve before being scrapped in March 1966. The reign of the diesels was indecently brief, because the entire system closed in May 1976, by which time barely 10% of Cadbury's traffic arrived or departed by rail.

Cadbury's incoming rail traffic consisted chiefly of cocoa beans direct from Liverpool docks. Sugar from Gloucester docks and chocolate crumb from a branch factory at Knighton, in the

Potteries, arrived at Bournville by canal. Cadbury's were operating their own fleet of motorised canal narrow boats as early as 1911. Delivery of goods by canal ceased in 1963.

The number of employees at Bournville increased as follows-

    1879 - 230; 1889 - 1,193; 1899 - 2,689;
    1909 - 4,923; 1919 - 7,500; 1931 - 8,381

After the Great War Cadbury's prospered as never before, with a steady increase in goods despatched, coupled with a corresponding decrease in costs -

	nett tons	no.of trucks	av.cost/ton
1921	29,523	9,718	£3..5..3d
1922	31,674	12,199	£2.19..7d
1923	36,522	14,977	£2..9..0d

Over the same period the tonnage despatched by road vehicles increased from 4,178 to 5,111; canal tonnage despatches declined from 5,774 to 3,239.

The total gross tonnage of all freight movements at Bournville and Cadbury's satellite factories for 1923 show that rail accounted for 81.6%, road 3.7%, canal 11.5% and internal movements within each factory totalled 3.1%

Times were such that the company even operated, in 1924, a sort of Red Star Easter Egg service as -

"The Committee agreed for special arrangements to be made for deliveries to Health Resorts by Passenger Train for a few days prior to Easter, in order that customers can have goods in stock to meet requirements ......this arrangement will only apply to chocolate orders."

(Transport Committee Minutes, 10th April 1924)

As well as freight traffic, the period between the wars saw a boom in excursion trains, as organised parties from all over the country visited Bournville, to see the 'Factory in a Garden' and to share in the generous free samples that were an essential highlight of every trip.

Nowadays Cadbury's receive raw materials and deliver all their products by road via a huge computerised distribution depot at Oldbury, adjacent to the M5. The road collection and delivery network is very efficient, though in most developed countries it would be unusual for such a large potential bulk customer to have no rail borne traffic. There seems little prospect of any in the near future, although more government incentives to encourage companies to switch to rail where practicable, particularly the development of simple company based road/rail freight interchange points (as pioneered by Pedigree Petfoods of Melton Mowbray through "Charterail", now sadly defunct) may make simplified rail facilities at Cadbury's viable again. Any future installation would not, of course, extend to four miles of track with its own locomotive fleet. This time it could accurately be described as 'the siding'!

Cadbury's wharf in its last years, 12th November 1962. Locomotive No.1 was the last Cadbury's steam engine in service. It was withdrawn by the end of that year and saved from the scrapheap, initially bought by the Dowty Railway Preservation Society and stabled at Dowty's Ashchurch work.

(P.J.Shoesmith)

Excursion train at Bournville, summer 1930. The three carriages are of a design standardised for the LMS by the former Midland carriage superintendent R.W.Reid and built at Derby. The immaculate vehicle nearest the camera appears to be numbered 17166. The crowd is leaving the down platform by a route which no longer exists. Cadbury's hospitality, and their generous supply of free samples, was legendary, which explains the eager smiles. This apart, only two people have ventured out hatless.

(courtesy of Cadbury's Ltd.)

MEMORIES ....

The Bournville engine shed was a roundhouse and, if older readers who remember the days of steam will forgive me, that term needs some explanation. These large brick buildings were once a familiar sight at many places where steam locomotives were stabled. Some early examples, as at Chalk Farm and Curzon Street on the London and Birmingham line, were indeed circular, and the name persisted even when square sheds, as at Bournville, were built later. One, two or maybe three tracks into the shed converged on a central turntable, which acted as a hub and gave access to stubs of track spread round it like the spokes of a wheel. Each stub was long enough for at least one locomotive, and most contained a pit between the track, six feet deep, for ease of inspection, emptying the ashpan and doing all the other flithy jobs associated with the entrails of steam engines. It was not always easy to operate even moderately powerful engines gently enough for the confines of a roundhouse. Sooner or later someone would be too energetic or too careless for a moment, causing a tender to bash a large new unofficial exit in the side wall, or a loco with brakes half-heartedly applied would roll slowly off the turning turntable, jamming it and marooning all the engines that were 'on shed'. The roundhouse is now extinct on British Rail. The last working example was at Barrow Hill in Derbyshire, on the freight only line between Chesterfield and Rotherham, and it survived until 1991.

Bournville was a standard Midland Railway roundhouse, dating from 1895. It stood opposite the junction with the Lifford Canal branch, which had been part of the original West Suburban line. Originally coded 3a (re-coded 21B in 1935) it was provided with a 50 foot turntable and a single coaling stage It was built to house twenty-five locomotives and was a sub-shed of the much more important establishment at Saltley, two miles north of New Street on the main line to Derby. Bournville was meant primarily to cater for an expected increase in local passenger traffic which failed to occur. Most important freight and passenger services were handled by Saltley locomotives and Bournville played a relatively minor non-strategic role throughout its existence. Whilst there were long distance freight workings, some from Cadbury's, and a few significant passenger duties, such as semi-fast workings between New Street and Leicester/Peterborough, its engines were called upon chiefly to haul slow freight trains on secondary routes, such as the 'Gloucester Loop' through Redditch, or to operate the local passenger trains on the West Suburban, Camp Hill, Circle and Halesowen services.

This undemanding work could be safely left to older locomotives, and as the work began to dwindle the locomotives grew older and less numerous. By the end of the 1920s the local services were languishing. The Halesowen trains were now only workmen's specials, the Circle service remained confined to the

Two views of Deeley 'Flatiron' No.2015 come to grief at Halesowen Junction, February 1922. In disgrace, shrouded from public view, then re-railed by the Derby and Saltley cranes. *(W.L.Good : Tom King collection)*

peak hours, and on the West Suburban line Church Road had closed in 1925. By 1929 there were only fifteen engines on shed; four 2-4-0s, two 4-4-0s and six 0-6-0s all designed by Matthew Kirtley, three Deeley 0-6-4 Tanks and two Johnson 1F tanks. The Deeley tanks, engaged on local passenger duties and nicknamed 'Flatirons', suffered a series of mishaps. They were reckoned to be unstable when driven chimney first. This is commonly thought to have been caused by water swishing about in the side tanks, which ran the full length of the boiler, thus causing the locomotive to oscillate from side to side in a severe manner, occasionally bouncing off the track. No.2015 did just that at Halesowen Junction in February 1922! First it was hidden from public view by a tarpaulin, then re-railed with the aid of two steam cranes. The Derby crane, dating from 1916 and with a lifting capacity of 40 tons, was assisted at the rear by the 1893 15 ton capacity Saltley crane. The Flatirons continued to haul the Birmingham-Leicester expresses for two more years, then put on lesser duties, but following further mishaps in the early 1930s they were all withdrawn from service and stored in the yard beside the roundhouse.

Bournville's decline continued after the closure of the Camp Hill and Circle passenger services in 1941. It remained untouched by the extensive programme of upgradings and improvements which affected every important shed on the LMS system from 1933 onwards. It was not considered necessary, for example, to install any mechanical aids to 'coal up' the locomotives.

The length of the turntable was increased to 57' in 1948, but this extra room to manoeuvre did not prevent an engine from falling into the pit in 1956, damaging the turntable, which was sent to Swindon for repair. Locos used Saltley or Bromsgrove for boiler inspections and wash-outs while this took place.

In 1945 there were twenty-eight engines on shed, of which fifteen were of Midland Railway pre-1922 vintage. No fewer than twelve locos were abandoned here 'in store' on closure in January 1960. This was symptomatic of the fact that the shed was a forgotten backwater for much of its history, a retirement home for elderly engines, the sort of place that could feature in the 'Thomas the Tank Engine' stories of Rev.W.Awdry; "Kevin the Kirtley Engine" perhaps?

The remarkable collection of ancient Kirtleys, which survived until after the Second World War, ensured that in its final years Bournville was a place of pilgrimage for enthusiasts anxious to glimpse motive power that had been modern when their great-grandfathers were boys! Matthew Kirtley had learnt his craft from Robert Stephenson and was Chief Mechanical Engineer of the Midland Railway until his death in 1873, having been appointed Locomotive Superintendent at the age of 28 when the Midland was formed in 1844. He invented the brick-arched firebox which increased the draw of the fire, causing it to burn with a more intense heat than had been previously possible. When new, in the 1860s and 70s, his locomotives were the last word in efficient technology, although it is hard to believe, this far removed in time, that they were ever considered modern. The half cabs offered minimal protection to the crew and the Kirtley trademarks of outside leaf springs and outside connecting rods conspired to make them look quaint. In appearance they were difficult to take seriously, but in practice they were robust, smooth-riding, reliable and well-built. They performed their duties at Bournville for over sixty years. The class of 0-6-0 Kirtley goods engines, first constructed in 1863, once had 470 members, spread throughout the Midland Railway system. The last few locos found their way to the Bournville retirement home, where they undertook light passenger duties and were specially retained for the Halesowen Branch, which had a frail viaduct at Dowery Dell, unable to cope with most younger and heavier engines. The last member of this class, the only one to carry a British Railways number (58110) was finally withdrawn in 1951 after a working life of eighty-one years!

Some visits to this shed were more unofficial than others. Don Coleman sent me a description of expeditions with his mates, in their early teens, around 1945:-

> "A visit to Bournville shed on a Sunday could be rewarding, there being no one about. The entrance by foot was through a gate just over the bridge in Maryvale Road and down a long path. One could stand in the middle of the turntable, get all the numbers and sheds then run round and cab the lot!"

They appear to have done no harm, as their trespass was motivated by a liking for trains rather than a wish to create

Kevin the Kirtley Engine. In LMS days Bournville housed many pre-grouping locomotives in their declining years. Typical of this is the scene on 2nd March 1935 as ex-Midland Railway Kirtley 2-4-0, No. 20002, with a well stacked tender, stands ready for the road. *(H.C.Casserley : Don Powell collection)*

Kirtley 0-6-0 No.2336 leaving King's Norton sidings on a southbound slow freight during the summer of 1920.
(Tom King collection)

mischief, and Don grew up to spend thirty years of his life working on the railway.

The site of Bournville shed is now occupied by housing and light industry. One brief stretch of wall is still visible on the right, shortly after leaving the station on a south-bound train, but without any other points of reference it looks just like any old wall, without betraying its history.

Whilst writing this book near the end of the century it was my good fortune to meet two ex-Bournville railwaymen, Tom King and Fred Jenkins, whose long clear memories went back to near its beginning.

Tom King went to Bournville shed in February 1916, aged 17, and he remained there until 1923. He began work as a passed cleaner, which meant that he was qualified as a fireman, despite his young age. He even did some unofficial driving, as on one occasion when his driver let him take charge of the train, a Sunday diversion, making out that he was doing the lad a favour, when in reality it was soon obvious that he (the driver) didn't know the road. For over a year Tom was a spare fireman, not teamed with a regular driver nor attached to a regular link, or group of enginemen, so he quickly learned how to work with all sorts of men. Many of the Bournville drivers were nearing the retirement age of seventy - which was then also the pensionable age - and, because they had been the well paid elite of working men for three generations, some regarded themselves as only on a slightly lower level than God himself. Tom experienced a week's duty firing the New Street pilot locomotive, during which time his driver never spoke to him! At the end of each shift, when they went back to Bournville by passenger train, he told Tom to travel in a separate compartment, not by words but with signs.

Sometimes Tom fired one of the five shunting engines at Central Goods. Drivers had often been put on shunting duties as a punishment for rule infringement, and their pay was reduced from 46/6d (£2.32) to 36/- (£1.80) per week. Their behaviour could reflect this loss of status and well-being. One man in

particular, known as Mad Jack, was liable to disappear at around 10am, returning 'well-oiled' around 2pm, leaving his luckless fireman to perform solo shunting duties and drive and fire back to Bournville while he slouched in a corner of the cab. Another such driver preferred to be alone with his thoughts while working, dismissing his fireman to the shunters' cabin at the start of the shift with instructions that he was not to be disturbed until he sent for a cup of warm water.

The ten hour working day was still in force, which meant that there were many longer distance 'double home' workings for engine crews, ie; a journey there and back with a night's/day's lodging inbetween. There were two regular double home links to London operated from Bournville at this time; the 6.50pm from Cadburys siding to Kentish Town, an express freight of about fifty loaded vans, which went non-stop through New Street and took on water at Wigston and Bedford; and the 8.00pm from the shed which formed the fast overnight freight from Central Goods to Cricklewood. Other Bournville double home runs were to Bristol via Redditch, to Manchester, Sheffield and Normanton. These were still the days when each crew formed a partnership which could last for years and they always had the same locomotive. This often applied to freight as well as prestige passenger expresses. As Tom said, "You knew who the crew were when you saw the engine number". The eight hour day, introduced nationally in 1919, meant an end to this, as the shorter hours led to more flexible and economical working practices for locos and crew. It also helped diminish Bournville's importance as a shed, with the removal of its allocation of double home workings.

The summer of 1916 saw some of the most savage slaughter in the Great War, centred on the killing fields of the Somme. The afternoon passenger shift at Bournville, tootling up and down the West Suburban and Camp Hill lines, could end unpleasantly. Having worked the last train of the day the engine travelled light to Selly Oak to await an ambulance train from Dover. Such specials were timed to arrive after midnight, in line with the government's general policy of shielding the public, as far as possible, from the full horrors of the war. The Bournville engine had to remove the ambulance train as empty stock after unloading. Inevitably some of the wounded had not survived the journey and their bodies were removed first. Tom King had to ensure that there was a good blaze in the firebox, because the orderlies brought large quantities of blood-soaked bandages and other refuse for him to burn. The driver, meanwhile, might have retreated to a remote corner of the yard, crying with despair because he had a son or sons fighting in France. "After seeing such things, I decided a life in khaki was not for me", said Tom.

On other occasions two Johnson 3F 0-6-0s would stand at Halesowen Junction, waiting to take an alternative ambulance train on the final leg of its journey to Rubery, the nearest station to Hollymoor Hospital, which had been renamed as the "Second Birmingham War Hospital". This was for troops from the Empire - Anzacs, Canadians, South Africans. As these men began to recover Tom recalled firing aboard Halesowen branch trains in the late summer evenings of 1916 and seeing, blatantly in the fields, dozens of soldiers dressed in hospital blue enjoying all sorts of sexual frolics with local women, some of whom had earlier come by train from several miles away.

At Bournville, as elsewhere, each engine crew was allowed only thirty-five minutes to prepare themselves and their loco for the road. This involved booking on, examining special notices, collecting cleaning materials which consisted of two cloths and supplies of brass paste and Vaseline for polishing and blacking the boiler front and footplate; then going to the engine to take stock of the steam, checking the water level, seeing that the necessary tools were all there, topping up the oil cans from store, filling the sand boxes from the sand oven, stoking up the fire, oiling the motion, taking the engine out of the roundhouse via the turntable and having it stacked to capacity with coal! This was recognised as an impossible task by the 1919 National Agreement, which increased the time allowance by ten minutes and stipulated that the engine should already have been coaled.

The quantity of fuel used was strictly regulated, but the system was abused by coal dodging. On completion of a day's work each driver had to write in his log the amounts of coal on board at the beginning and end of each shift. Each trip had a specified allowance, and drivers were anxious to avoid penalties by staying well within it. Locos were coaled up manually at Bournville from 10 ton trucks, and some drivers tipped the coalman 3d (1.25p) to book less coal than was actually taken. At the end of a shift a driver could often be involved in bitter argument with his successor over the amount of coal on board. Typical freight train allowances were 70cwt (3.5tons) for a Johnson Class 3 0-6-0 to London, half that for the more easily graded route to Bristol. Thus our notion of the romance of steam begins to wilt a little at the thought of the fireman shovelling a hundredweight (50 kilos) of coal, on the London run, every two miles or less. This was gruelling work even with the large Midland shovels, which after the Grouping were compared favourably to those of the LNWR, known with derision as 'spoons'.

It was not all war, hard graft and sharp practice. Some of Tom King's happiest memories concerned the early passenger train to Evesham, which left New Street around 8am. During 1916-17, on this turn of duty, he frequently had the same driver, a kindly grandfather figure aged about 70, one of the many then still working who had featured on an official photograph when the shed had opened more than twenty years earlier. The locomotive was a Kirtley 2-4-0 with outside rods and the sight of the signalman at Redditch North box, flailing his arms like a windmill as he tried to avoid these rods at the same time as exchanging the single line token was always cause for a wry

smile. The leisurely half hour pause at Redditch allowed enough time for a visit to a butcher who sold leek sausages, followed by a traditional engineman's breakfast on the shovel - which was cleaned with the driver's spit prior to heating just inside the firebox - washed down with cold tea out of a quart stone jar, or perhaps some illicit cider. So on south to Evesham, with few passengers and even fewer worries about a tight schedule, regular interval time-tables or rival bus services.

There were less leisurely runs for Bournville locos. In 1916 the shed was still home to three Johnson single wheeler fast passenger engines, Nos.665, 666 and 667, which saw service in their declining years on the semi-fast trains between New Street and Peterborough. These were amongst the most handsome locomotives to run in this country and Tom remembered them with affection as being, "smooth, steady and firm on the track, they could go like a greyhound".

A faster and more profitable run for Tom was as fireman of the pilot engine to a heavy Bristol express. The pilot worked the complete round trip to Bristol. Still aged 17 and only a few weeks into the job, never having strayed far from his native Walsall, this was high-speed adventure, made all the more enjoyable when he discovered that express passenger train crews and their pilots were paid for mileage covered rather than hours worked, which normally worked in their favour.

As a spare fireman, who reported for duty at 6am, Tom soon learnt how to handle dead engines on Monday mornings. These were freight locomotives that had not been used over the weekend and had been standing on the sidings by the coaling stage, there being no room for them in the roundhouse. Now they had to be taken into the shed to be made ready for work once more. Pushing each cold engine onto the turntable, using a loco already in steam of course, was the easy part; propelling it off the turntable onto a pit road was more difficult. The solution relied on compressed air. Before being removed from the siding the dead engine would have its regulator opened and be put into reverse gear. This had the effect of drawing outside air into the boiler; the air became compressed and by the time the loco reached the turntable a pressure of 100lb/sq.in. often registered on the cab gauge, easily enough to push it off the turntable onto the correct pit road without all the trouble of lighting a fire first!

Fred Jenkins started as a cleaner at Bournville, aged 17, on January 7th 1919. For being sweeper-up, tea boy and general dogsbody he was paid eighteen shillings (80p) for a sixty-eight hour week, finishing at 2pm on Saturdays. The implementation of the National Agreement, in March, saw his appointment as the shed's third storekeeper with an eight hour day. The agreement also meant the right to one week's annual paid holiday and the provision of a uniform.

Fred was soon passed as a fireman - a passed cleaner - at the post-war minimum age of 18, and because he helped organise the roster, the moment no regular fireman was available for a Sunday ballast train he was able to put his own name down.

Like Tom King, whom he knew in the early 1920s, Fred Jenkins had experience firing the Kirtleys. They needed a fireman who understood them, he claimed, as working them was definitely an art form. He fired them to Leicester and occasionally to Nottingham, "but they didn't really want to go that far".

He also fired the excursions to Barnt Green in the 1920s and 30s, offering a fare of only 6d (2.5p) return for a good day out and a picnic on the Lickey Hills. The trams along the Bristol Road carried thousands of people every summer weekend, and although there were fewer trains - and the low fares meant that the profit margins must have been wafer thin - they were always successful. Stock normally consisted of four non-corridor suburban carriages, from New Street via the Camp Hill line and, as Fred recalled, "it was a job to get in by the time you got to King's Norton". Some regular travellers had the best of both worlds, going out by train and back by tram.

In 1933 Fred Jenkins became a passed driver, drawing 66/- (£3.30) per week basic pay. Young passed drivers could not neccessarily expect to drive on a regular basis at first, only when a roster was available. By 1939, now a regular driver on the top rate and working overtime, he was often taking home more than £6 per week. Between 1933 and 1939, at a time when railway drivers were still respected as skilled aristocrats amongst manual workers and paid accordingly, he was able to support his wife and two young children, take out a mortgage, run a car and enjoy two week's holiday at the seaside every year. Workers who earned more than £5 per week on a regular basis did not pay National Insurance contributions as, "you were supposed to be above that sort of thing".

Prior to all this Fred had served over twelve years as a fireman, "not a bad apprenticeship". To qualify as a passed driver he spent two days with a locomotive inspector. On the first day it was his job to convince the inspector that he had a thorough knowledge of rules and regulations, the workings of a locomotive, how he would cope in the event of engine failure etc.. The second day was the practical test, on a line he knew

(Birmingham to Burton), driving a freight train out and a stopping passenger train back. The train's regular driver would seldom be warned before such an event and was always banished to the guard's van by the inspector. The outward run was completed successfully, whereupon the inspector disappeared for a lunchtime pint. He returned sober but late, just in time to have an agitated Fred show him the tail lamp of the stopping train to Birmingham as it receded from view. Several hours yawned ahead before the next stopper was due, but the 12 coach Leeds-Bristol express would soon arrive, probably hauled by a new Stanier Black 5. These engines already had a reputation among ex-Midland men, who called them 'bent-backed bastards' on account of their long and unfamiliar tapered fireboxes, ex-Midland locos having parallel ones. They also had left hand drive (M.R.locos were right hand) and Fred had never even set foot on one. "Now's your chance to learn", said the inspector as the train pulled in. The regular driver, aged about 60 and a proud relic of the Victorian age with a heavy West Country accent, was aghast when ordered to travel with the guard while this 'lad' attempted to drive his precious new locomotive! Once in the cab Fred's reasoning was straightforward; this train was tightly timed non-stop to New Street, passing Tamworth (13 miles) in 17 minutes, and as the fireman was no friend of his he was going to ensure that they both worked hard and fast. He did just that, passing Tamworth on time and arriving at New Street two

Inside the roundhouse at Bournville, 23rd May 1959, during the last full year of the shed's existence. Ex-Midland Johnson 0-6-0 2F No.58138 is nearest the camera. The smokey atmosphere is relieved only slightly by the sunny weather from outside; this was the beginning of a superb summer.

(P.J.Shoesmith)

minutes early. Here the fireman came in especially useful, having a clearer view of the calling-on signals in the cramped and smokey confines of the station than Fred, who was driving on what to him was the wrong side of the cab. No sooner had the train stopped when the inspector hastily bundled his successful pupil out of the cab and hustled him into the Post Office subway. He had caught a glimpse of a senior colleague and explained, "I don't want anyone to see me passing you for a driver on a crack express!"

As a new driver Fred soon gained experience of a wide variety of main line passenger locomotives, though it came in very short slices. Whenever a long distance Cadbury's special arrived at New Street - and they came from as far away as Newcastle - a Bournville crew who knew the road took over there for the final leg of the journey, delivering passengers to Bournville, taking the stock to King's Norton carriage sidings for cleaning, and turning the loco on the triangle formed by Lifford Curve. This last move was necessary because Bournville's nineteenth century turntable was too short to cope with most twentieth century engines.

The M.R. control office at Central Goods frequently rang the storekeeper at Bournville, making enquiries when freight trains were unduly late. It was Fred's duty, when he began in 1919, to find out the reason from the train crew and to report back to control. At first the things he was told seemed like weird and wonderful excuses. One long distance train had lost time heavily in the Peak District and it failed to recover any. Control demanded an explanation so the driver simply said, "Tell him we had the frost in the wagons". Fred refused to ring with what seemed like some flippant nonsense which he did not understand, but the driver offered him half a crown (12.5p) if control rebuffed his explanation. Control accepted it, the driver kept his money and explained that such a thing was quite common. It was a Monday, they had picked up a rake of fifteen wagons from Rowsley sidings which had been standing all weekend at that exposed spot north of Matlock, their axle boxes were lubricated with fat rather than oil, so they had frozen solid and had been almost impossible to move. On another occasion a late running driver said, "We had the wind in the wagons". Surely this had to be a joke at the young storekeeper's expense, but control again accepted it without quibble. It would not be long before Fred learnt at first hand the effect of high winds on a train. A gusting cross wind on fifty empty wagons would certainly cause delay, and even the twelve coach Bristol mail could be slowed noticeably, the decrease in speed matched only by an increase in coal consumption, providing more hard work for the luckless fireman.

A BOURNVILLE REQUIEM

After the demise of the last Kirtley locomotive in 1951, the Bournville based Johnson 2F 0-6-0s did duty over the Halesowen branch. An unidentified member of this class, all numbered by BR 581xx, is signalled to take the branch at Halesowen Junction, on the site of the present Longbridge station. Even this short train was only just within the maximum allowance for the branch and its unhealthy lattice viaduct at Dowery Dell. This picture was taken on January 9th 1960; Bournville shed and the Halesowen branch both closed shortly afterwards.

(P.J.Shoesmith)

A FOUR TRACK MAIN LINE

The 1880s was a time of expansion and high hopes for the Midland main line south of Birmingham. The upgrading of the West Suburban line, the establishment of Cadbury's and even the opening of the Halesowen branch all generated more traffic. From 1885 the Midland had, in effect, four tracks north of King's Norton into New Street, using the Camp Hill and West Suburban lines. The five miles south of King's Norton to Barnt Green were also to be provided with four tracks, yet despite the short mileage the work was done in three stages spanning almost forty years.

During 1892 a section just over a mile long was quadrupled, from a point immediately south of King's Norton station, through Northfield to Halesowen Junction, at the site of the present Longbridge station. "1892" is still picked out in metal studs set into the subway floor at Northfield.

The short two track section through King's Norton station was quadrupled in 1925. There exist some fine photographs of the station prior to and during this development. They clearly evoke something of the atmosphere of the railway of the time and provide good visual evidence for anyone with a general interest in railway history, even those who may never have been within a hundred miles of King's Norton.

The first picture, looking north, was taken about 1912. The original 1849 platforms are nearer the camera, the higher extensions were added in 1885. It is curious that the Midland spend huge sums on the extension of the West Suburban into New Street but did not, at the same time, undertake the trifling expense of raising the height of the original platforms. There was no Department of Transport or Health and Safety Executive in those days. The original brick waiting shelter was supplemented by the wooden structure, also dating from 1885, the one with the small subtle chimney stack. The high signal box, just beyond the bridge which carried the Redditch road, controlled the junction of the West Suburban and Camp Hill lines, just out of view, although the junction signals can be seen. The gas lamps, enamel advertisement signs and high telegraph poles were all furniture which no self-respecting railway used to be without. Note the large wicker baskets, the uncomfortable looking bicycle and the even more uncomfortable high stiff regulation collars worn by the juvenile station staff, who seem to be eyeing the ladies on the up platform.

King's Norton had been brought within the city boundary, from Worcestershire, in 1911. The station was served by West Suburban and Camp Hill line trains and was also the terminus of the service to Halesowen, a line which from 1905 was jointly owned by the Midland and Great Western, and which saw five passenger and four freight services in each direction daily.

The second photograph dates from 1924 and faces south. The train is an early morning Bristol to Derby express, hauled by a Johnson '483' Class 4-4-0 No.513, a locomotive rebuilt by John Fowler. To the left is the 1849 station building with the station master's house beyond, both still extant. The signal box, footbridge, level crossing and two houses on the right were all victims of the quadrupling. The milk churns, typical of the period, had a capacity of seventeen gallons; never mind the awkward non-metric measurement, feel the hernia! The carriage sidings beyond held rush hour stock, overspill from the overcrowded sidings nearer to New Street. Stock from all over the country, which had arrived at Bournville with Cadbury's specials, was also serviced here. Between the wars older carriages were held here to be used, as required, for excursion and holiday trains, some with headboards for east coast resorts such as Cromer. During the Second World War seaside holidays were still allowed, although choice of destination was very limited and trains were few and very overcrowded. Trains from New Street to Llandudno, for example, were marshalled in the sidings and called at King's Norton station. Those in the know came from several miles away so as to join the train there and get a seat. The practice of starting holiday excursions from King's Norton continued into the 1960s. Since that time the sidings at this site have served as a loading point for new British Leyland vehicles and, most recently, as the Cross City Electrification Depot.

The third illustration, taken on April 19th 1925, shows what is probably the Derby steam crane lifting a section of the new footbridge into position. The loco is 4F 0-6-0 No.4040 and the wagons in the foreground are of M.R. origin; 'ED' denotes 'Engineers Department' on the pair of trucks, and the bogie flat wagon was an ex-War Department vehicle used at one time to convey military equipment. Soon the demolition of the signal box would improve the station master's view of his territory,

King's Norton, looking towards Birmingham, c.1912

(Lens of Sutton)

King's Norton in early LMS days, 1924. The scene is still pure Midland Railway, as Johnson 4-4-0 No.513 hustles through with a Bristol-Derby express. An early type of telephone box lurks among the barrows on the up platform.

(W.L.Good : Roger Carpenter collection)

Installing the new footbridge, King's Norton, 19th April 1925.   *(W.L.Good : Roger Carpenter collection)*

though the abolition of the level crossing, replaced as a right of way by the footbridge, would split Station Road into two. The cottages on the right were built by the Midland Railway.

The 1925 station had four platform faces. From the south these were down Camp Hill (dating from 1849), a new island for up Camp Hill and down West Suburban, and a new platform for up West Suburban trains. The newer style of gas lamp on the new platforms was almost the only small concession to the twentieth century. The buildings were too solid and lavish for the relatively small number of trains even when built and they were not useful for long. Within sixteen years the original platform (No.1) and the island face opposite became redundant with closure of the Camp Hill service. All the 1925 buildings were demolished in 1971 and today the island platform is bare and forlorn, out of normal use. Platform 1 is used by all southbound Cross City trains. Since the start of the Cross City service in 1978 the station's centre of gravity has shifted from the original entrance on Station Road to that on the Redditch Road bridge, handy for the bus stops and the main entrance to the car park. Despite the obvious appeal of these old pictures, the whiff of steam, the hiss of gently glowing gas lights and the delight of a semi-rural location, King's Norton today enjoys a train service which is faster, cleaner, more frequent, quieter and more efficient than anything it has known before.

The two miles between Halesowen Junction and Barnt Green were quadrupled between 1926 and 1930. First proposals were put forward by the Midland Railway in 1922, detailed plans finalised by its successor, the LMS, in 1924 and the contract was then placed with Messrs. Logan & Hemingway of Doncaster. The scheme cost a quarter of a million pounds and employed over four hundred men, many based in temporary accommodation at Barnt Green. The new tracks were not to be laid on either side of the existing pair, but to their east, as this simplified the whole operation, taking less land and causing less disruption, particularly in Barnt Green.

The single most important task was the demolition of Cofton Tunnel. It had been in continuous use since December 1840, was a quarter of a mile long and had the narrowest bore of any on the Midland system. The conventional distance between two running lines is six feet, but within the tunnel this was compressed to five feet one inch. Had the line remained just double track today it is certain that progress would still have overtaken this tunnel. Modern rolling stock which makes the fullest use of the loading gauge - not to mention the sudden fluctuations in air pressure when two trains pass in a confined space at a closing speed around 150mph - would have made demolition inevitable.

Opening out involved the removal of 0.7 million cubic yards of rock and clay and the creation of a cutting over seventy feet deep. (Unlike Moseley Tunnel on the Camp Hill line this was not just a cosmetic structure created to appease awkward church authorities.) The plan was to gradually remove the huge tonnage above the tunnel, eventually exposing the brickwork from above prior to demolition. Large rectangular areas of brick, christened 'windows', were to be removed near the top of the tunnel arch, then explosive charges were to be placed. The train service continued as work proceeded, with a speed restriction of 30mph (up line) and 20mph (down), both reduced to 15mph as more rock was removed.

It was already known that the tunnel lay across a geological fault and as the work of widening the cutting on the southern approach progressed it was decided that a concrete reinforcing wall forty feet high and three hundred yards long was essential in

The demolition of Cofton Tunnel in progress, 1928, new concrete retaining wall to the right. The heavy engineering of the contractor's crane is in stark and alarming contrast to his lightly engineered track.

(Roger Carpenter collection)

order to minimise the risk of subsidence. This added to the cost in both time and money. The wall was begun in the spring of 1927, and the need for it became apparent with the onset of a series of violent thunderstorms in July, culminating in a downpour of over two inches in an hour on the evening of 11th (the rain gauges failed to cope with the amount, hence the estimate) causing local drain covers to pop from their frames like champagne corks. Parts of the cutting at Cofton which had not been concreted subsided and blocked the track. Four trains were held near Barnt Green and their passengers were eventually transported by road round the blockage. The line was partially reopened the following morning.

As preparation work continued and the top brickwork was exposed, the tunnel was divided into sections for ease of demolition, windows of brick were removed and demolition was scheduled to begin over the weekend of May 12th-13th 1928. The previous afternoon many men were working on the first section, some removing the last spoil from above and some within placing old sleepers between the running lines so as to diminish damage to the track from falling brickwork. Without warning, at 3.28pm, the section collapsed, killing four men and injuring four more. (The Inspector's report into the tragedy found that the windows had weakened the structure to the point of collapse.) The bodies and debris were removed and a crowd soon gathered to see what was going on. By 7pm trains were running again, restricted to 5mph and only one at a time allowed within the tunnel. Train movement was banned from midnight. The next morning a workman making holes for the explosive charges gave the brickwork just one blow with his pick and noticed that the whole section moved. Charges were gingerly but quickly placed as dust and debris fell all around and the section was demolished without further incident.

Further sections were removed as more brickwork was exposed over the next eight months. The last 140 yards were split into three sections and blown up late on the evening of January 26th 1929. It was a Saturday and a crowd of several hundred had come to watch. Afterwards two hundred men worked round the clock to shift three thousand tons of rubble in time for re-opening of the line at 6.45am on Monday morning.

There remained a layer of rock twelve feet thick, twenty-five feet wide and half a mile long alongside the existing track. This all had to be removed before the two new tracks could be laid and the work was only finally completed in May 1930. Sixty-one years later the rock at this location was to prove stubborn again when the foundations for the electrification masts were excavated.

Between the wars cartographers struggled to keep their maps up to date when housing developments mushroomed as never before. Changes on the railways were a low priority and even some post-1945 revisions show Cofton Tunnel. As war loomed the German High Command, using British maps, earmarked sites for bombing, including Longbridge car works. The Luftwaffe, flying from the south, were instructed to follow the railway line and bear left at the tunnel.

Meanwhile, in 1930 the LMS announced further improvements to the main line, to include quadrupling from south of Bromsgrove station to Stoke Prior, at the junction with the loop line to Worcester. Work began in May 1932. This left the intervening section from Barnt Green down the Lickey Incline as double track. Nobody, for obvious operational and financial reasons, suggested quadrupling it, but what a sight *that* would have been!

BARNT GREEN : A RAILWAY VILLAGE

Barnt Green is the oldest of today's Cross City stations, having been in continuous use, on more or less the same site, since September 17th 1840. Many people are aware of railway towns that grew from nothing; Crewe and Swindon are familiar examples. Railway villages are less obvious, but Barnt Green is one of these. There were no works here, the site was of no strategic importance, yet before the railway there was no village, just fields and lanes with a sprinkling of cottages and farmhouses. There was no centre and no parish church. The population at the 1851 census was still only 46, when the station was already ten years old. The first station master, a Mr.Hutt, stayed for forty years.

The building of a station at such an isolated spot was a speculative venture, encouraged by the local big landowning family, the Windsor-Clives of nearby Hewell Grange, who thought it would be of use to their tenant farmers in the district. The opening of the Redditch branch in 1859 had no more immediate effect than the coming of the main line and it was not until the 1880s that houses began to be built near the station and a discernable village centre was formed. Shops, pubs and a temperance hotel were built. By 1900 the first large houses were appearing on the slopes of the Lickey Hills, just to the west of the station. The station footbridge was, and remains, a useful right of way between the two parts of the village. More modest houses were erected east of the railway. For rich or poor Barnt Green was becoming established as a commuter village as many of its inhabitants travelled to work by rail, to the city centre, to Bournville or to Redditch.

The original station had staggered platforms. The down main line platform has always been in its present position, the up main line platform, which had been nearer Birmingham, was relocated opposite it in 1929. The branch platforms were extended around 1900 when the Midland Railway began running longer trains through Redditch.

Barnt Green acquired all the typical trappings of a busy country station. Oil lamps gave way to gas, enamel advertisement panels sprouted like weeds and by 1920 there was a telephone kiosk. A weekly cattle market was held on Wednesdays at the stockyard near the station and the animals were herded to it along the unpaved village street. The cattle were kept penned overnight at the cattle dock before travelling to slaughter, and the noise they created meant disturbed sleep for those living nearby.

This was not the only cause of broken nights, as freight trains approaching Barnt Green round the curve and up the 1:74 from Redditch were not disposed to do so quietly. If there had been rain, making for greasy rails, some such trains would wake the entire village before reaching the station, with furious wheelspin and agitated noises from the exhaust, despite generous sanding of the rails by the train crew. Some of this traffic was seasonal. Mrs.Winifred Brunton, who spent her childhood and adolescence at Barnt Green in the 1920s and 30s, recalled -

> "We were occasionally wakened during the night
> in late summer by freight trains struggling up this
> line loaded with plums from the Evesham area.
> These lovely yellow egg plums have now almost
> ceased to exist."

Fowler 0-6-0s, Stanier 2-8-0s and 'Black Fives' were most frequently used for the overnight fruit trains. Towards the end of steam, in the 1950s and early 60s, they were often hauled by B.R.Standard Class 9F 2-10-0s.

The cattle market, though not the cattle dock, had to move.

Mrs.Brunton again ...

"At that time (1926) a weekly livestock sale was held on railway land below the embankment, but this had to be found another site as the ground was used for tipping spoil from Cofton Tunnel...... there were also coal stacking plots, as most of the local coal merchants received coal by rail."

"During a very heavy snowfall about 1935 the first train to Birmingham struggled into Barnt Green at midday. There was a lovely coal fire in the waiting room to keep us warm. There were occasions when the trains provided the only way out of Barnt Green for car drivers who often got stuck in snowdrifts on the hills out of the village, and they were often the first to complain that the trains were late."

"During the Second World War Barnt Green used to be the stopping point for occasional loads of wounded servicemen on Sundays, where they were provided with refreshments by the W.V.S. before being taken on by road to local hospitals."

Racing pigeons were brought in by train. It was the duty of station staff to release them and note the time at which they did so. This was a common sight at many stations for decades, but one which has now entirely vanished. At Barnt Green the favoured release point was on the embankment just north of the junction.

The sidings near the cattle dock were considered secure enough for the overnight stabling of the Royal Train. One such occasion was in March 1938. The King was on board and all railway staff were barred from shouting instructions or using lamps so that he could have a good night's sleep. Presumably there were no cattle noisily waiting for their early morning train. The next day he travelled to Cofton for a visit to a new shadow factory making armaments. War was coming, the Austin factory, also producing armaments, would be a prime target so it was camouflaged and smaller, satellite factories - shadows - were built in the area, making it more difficult for enemy action to cripple output.

Early experiences can have a lifelong influence. In 1924 an eleven year old boy, Don Powell, moved with his parents to their new house near Barnt Green station. From his bedroom window Don could hear the bells in the signal box and see the movement of the arm of the nearest signal on the up main line. This fostered an interest in railways in general and signalling in particular which grew until, although never employed on the railway, he gained a wide knowledge of the subject. Mention a long demolished box almost anywhere in England and Don will have visited, photographed and catalogued it; ask about almost any type of signal and he will describe its workings and its purpose within moments. As his youthful interest developed he enjoyed visiting and working in signal boxes where possible. This was highly irregular, of course, but indulgent signalmen frequently risked discipline by letting enthusiastic amateurs take a turn at the levers.

A visit to a preserved railway or some of the remoter corners of the BR network can serve as a reminder of how railway signalling used to be only a generation ago. Everything was mechanical, of course, with wires for the signals and rods for the points, and all sorts of devices and hinges for transferring the energy of the signalman's pull around corners, under running lines and up signal posts. Signals with a red arm were either 'home' or 'starter', the latter to start the train running into the section controlled by the next box. Trains not allowed to

Barnt Green main line platforms, October 1921, the Midland signal, with tapered wooden post, set clear for a Birmingham bound train. *(W.L.Good : Don Powell collection)*

pass when these were set at danger. On entering a new section the first signal was a 'distant' or warning signal, coloured yellow with a fish-tail arm which, if in the danger position, warned of a likely stop at the next signal, a 'home'. Where two signal boxes were close together the starter signal of one shared a post with the distant signal of the next, as at Barnt Green.

There were two signal boxes here, known simply as "Barnt Green Main Line", which was on the up side opposite the cattle dock, and "Barnt Green Single Line", which stood where the two tracks of the Redditch branch merged into one. The main line box came with the quadrupling of the line and replaced an earlier one on the same site. It had a 70 lever frame and opened on September 15th 1929. The single line box dated from 1889.

Don Powell had considerable 'hands on' experience in these boxes, both of which eventually closed on 8th September 1969.

"In 1931 I got acquainted with two signalmen who worked the main line box, and I used to make regular visits at evenings and weekends. After some time I used to work the box completely with the levers and all instruments. One Saturday I got to the box about 2.30 and by 9.30 we had passed about 65 trains. About 9.30 the door of the box suddenly opened and in walked Inspector W., a tall lean man about 6'2" wearing a bowler hat covered with dust. He shouted at me, 'I heard you could work this box as well as the signalmen and I have seen you do it, now get out!'. He turned to the signalman and said, 'You know what this means L.?' However, my father had a large timber yard at Monument Lane Carriage Sidings, with a private

Despite earlier incidents, Don Powell eventually came back for more 'hands on' experience, and is seen here in Barnt Green Main Line Box, around 1960. Renewed by the LMS in 1929, the box was fitted with a 70 lever frame.

(W.H.A.Thompson : Don Powell collection)

siding, and we used to have a lot of traffic with the LMS. He went to see the Chief Operating Officer at Saltley and pleaded with him to be lenient with signalman L., who got a few days suspension, but not the sack! However, I never discovered how Inspector W. got to know about me working the box, but I naturally did not go there again."

This close encounter did not dampen enthusiasm, nor lessen the risks. The other box was just as interesting and nearer the fish shop.

"In 1932 I got to know one of the signalmen at the single line box and used to go and work it most evenings, Saturdays and Sundays. It had a 12 lever 6" M.R. Tumbler Frame with three spare levers and a Tablet Instrument (Tyers No.6 type) for the single line section to Redditch North. On Saturdays I used to get kippers from Macfisheries fish shop in Barnt Green and cook them on the square coal stove in the box for us both. The signalman lived in Alvechurch and had a large family. As his wages were only 57/6 (£2.87) per week, the cost of living and feeding them was rather difficult. On Sunday mornings he used to put down rabbit snares by the track as he walked to the box from Alvechurch. I used to put on his railway issue coat plus cap and work the box, taking and giving tablets. There were quite a number of fishermen's trains on Sundays to Evesham etc. Signalman F. used to go back down the track to see if he had bagged any rabbits and

came back later on to see if all was well! However, there was a farmer's overbridge down the line and on one evening we were talking in the box when suddenly we saw the top of a bowler hat bobbing about just above the parapet. Signalman F. said, 'It looks like Inspector W.', and after the episode at the main line box I made tracks for home. Once was enough!"

Today all is apparently uniform. The colour light signals on the Cross City Line are virtually indistinguishable from those anywhere else, the subtleties of three aspect and four aspect lights notwithstanding. This makes for an efficient and safe railway, with a straightforward signalling system understood by railwaymen everywhere. Previously signals, boxes and associated equipment came in all shapes and sizes, normally identifiable with the local railway company, which had acquired a recognisable house-style long before the end of the nineteenth century. Barnt Green was no exception.

The 1921 view of the staggered main line platforms shows a splendid example of a tall tapered wooden signal post, which was pure Midland Railway. The two photographs of the Single Line Box date from around 1960 and feature a platform for the signalman when exchanging the token and an oil lamp for that duty after dark. By this date the Midland signal post had been replaced by an LMS one. Unusually the lower arm is the outer distant for the main line box, rarely used and a strain to operate, connected to its lever via half a mile of wire round a sharp curve. Despite the indicator blind the train is headed for Birmingham.

Another unusual signal at Barnt Green was a split gantry, with two signal posts (dolls) and three signal arms. It was also

Signalman Harry Wood exchanging the token at Barnt Green Single Line box. The train is the 20.45 from Redditch, June 1960 *(Don Powell collection)*

Barnt Green Single Line box, with platform and oil lamp for token exchange. The lower signal is the outer distant for the main line box. June 1960. *(Don Powell collection)*

situated on the branch approach to the main line, just south of the station. The top arm doubled as the Single Line starter signal and the Main Line outer home. In this way the Main Line signalman could hold a train a quarter of a mile from the junction. This gave him freedom of acceptance but it also blocked the single line. This signal had to be operated from both boxes before it could clearfrom the danger position, but could be put back to danger by either box. The other two arms were split inner distant signals for the fast and slow main lines, which were operated from the Main Line box alone, but only after the upper arm had been cleared first. The array of balance levers at the base of this particular signal post, to ensure safe working, was impressive.

The snowy picture, probably dating from the unforgettable winter of 1947, features the gantry at the north end of the up main line platform, with unusual co-acting signal arms lower down. This was a kind of insurance policy in case the station footbridge had obscured the train crew's view of the upper arms.

In 1945 about 50 000 passenger journeys were being made every week on the Birmingham-Redditch line. When Midland Red announced its intention of running a bus service (route 142) via Barnt Green in the early 1950s British Railways opposed them in court, unsuccessfully, on the grounds that a regular train service already existed. This was not to last.

By 1970 everything had gone; freight facilities, sidings, signal boxes, staff and buildings. What remained was a semi-derelict halt, unkempt, unloved and almost without trains. 1968 was typical of the long lean years, with departures for Birmingham at 07.36, 08.04, 08.14, 08.34(SX), 12.44(SO), 13.45(SO), 16.56 and

17.34, with a similar flow in the other direction.

Cross City trains began running in May 1978 but the service south of Longbridge was as sparse as ever at first, slowly improving in stages until 1989, when the present pattern of an all day service seven days a week was established. The station remains unstaffed.

In May 1989 a shuttle service was introduced between Barnt Green and Worcester, operated by a Class 120 single car dmu. This was mainly an attempt, within severe financial constraints, to improve the dire level of service at Bromsgrove. Barnt Green became the interchange point for Bromsgrove passengers transferring to/from Cross City trains. In addition it became possible once again for passengers from Barnt Green and Redditch to travel direct to Worcester and be able to come back on the same day! This shuttle service was severely cut back in 1992. Few people were using it, especially after Bromsgrove was provided with a two-hourly fast link with Birmingham. If *these* trains were to call at Barnt Green, passengers from the village and the Redditch branch would have convenient rail access to the south without having to go via New Street first. New custom would be generated.

In the 1993 summer time-table the train which left New Street at 09.15 and Barnt Green at 09.29 was formed by a Class 166 Turbo dmu and provided a through service, via Worcester, from New Street to Paddington, the village's first ever direct link with the capital. The return working, leaving Paddington at 12.48, ran non-stop between Bromsgrove and New Street.

Double insurance policy. Co-acting signals, Barnt Green main line, looking north, 1947.   *(Don Powell collection)*

Stanier 'Black Five' No.44810 heads north through Barnt Green's main line platforms with an express, 31st July 1954. Everything in this picture - the field behind the station where houses now stand, the neat little bookstall, the gas lamps, platform trolley, even the baggy trousers and the hint of Brylcreem - belongs to a vanished era.

(P.J.Shoesmith)

A COLOUR TRIBUTE

The majority of these photographs show the Cross City line in the final days of diesel operation before the erection of electrification masts had begun. They are offered as a pictorial tribute to the dmus near the end of their long lives, to the crews who operated them on good days and bad, and especially the men of Tyseley depot, who often fought against the odds to keep their ancient charges in running order. *All photographs by John Boynton.*

The graves of the two railwaymen killed in the explosion at Bromsgrove, November 10th 1840, complete with artists impressions of the American Norris locomotives which often worked trains through to Curzon Street, over part of todays Cross City Line. Norris pirated the designs from British built locos (designed by Edward Bury) exported to America in the 1830s. His locos came in three classes; B, A and A Extra, weighing 8, 10 and 12.5 tons respectively. They were very similar to each other in appearance. The Birmingham & Gloucester Railway wanted just three A Extras for the Lickey, but Norris's high pressure salesmanship resulted in their buying three As and seven Bs as well.

The first southbound Cross City train, the nine-car 06.19 from Lichfield City, departs empty stock from Longbridge as the 07.32 to Four Oaks makes ready to leave from the other platform, May 8th 1978. The white livery did not remain smart for long.

Five Ways, looking towards the city centre, November 20th 1990. The West Suburban line and the Worcester & Birmingham Canal are separated by the trackbed of the old line to the Central Goods depot.

Another view of Five Ways taken on the same day, this time looking south. The confined site is obvious, making this busy station virtually out of bounds for disabled passengers. Happily, funds have now been found (1993) for the installation of much needed lifts between street level and the platforms. The university clock tower can just be detected on the horizon.

Seen from the canal towpath a train to Redditch passes the site of Somerset Road station as train services returned to normal following heavy snow, February 14th 1991

Selly Oak, with a train for Lichfield Trent Valley about to depart, December 3rd 1990. The nineteenth century terraced cottages in the foreground have seen the full range of rail facilities in Selly Oak, from the single track Birmingham West Suburban Railway to the electrified Cross City Line. In the background is Birmingham University. The clock tower is modelled on that at Siena, while the great hall is meant to suggest Constantinople.

Workmen renovate the canal bank as a train to Longbridge slows for the stop at Bournville, November 20th 1990. The bridge in the background once carried Cadbury's 'siding' over the main line, providing a rail connection between the factory and their wharf.

End of the line at a green and busy mid-morning Redditch. The train will form the 11.53 to Lichfield, May 22nd 1990. The new station building now stands where the cars are parked and the buffers are alongside where the shelter stood.

Butlers Lane, with pupils from the Arthur Terry High School anxious to get home as the Redditch train approaches, October 4th 1990. This school was in the forefront of the campaign of safety awareness during electrification.

A train for Lichfield City is about to leave Four Oaks, October 4th 1990. The down platform buildings and original footbridge were replaced some time ago, but the original buildings on the island platform survive and flourish. What is the collective noun for buffer stops?

Wylde Green, looking north, two trains in view, November 5th 1990. The platform canopies had just been installed.

Vauxhall or Duddeston, depending on which sign is correct, with a train for Lichfield City. The island platform beyond is redundant, although happily the original Grand Junction engine shed of 1840 is not, neither is the early 1950s tower block, which almost looks ripe for a preservation order.

A train for Redditch leaves Bournville, December 3rd 1990. A low winter sun highlights the new dip in the track under the Mary Vale Road bridge, excavated to provide sufficient clearance for the overhead wiring.

Wirescape at Lichfield Trent Valley, the main line looking towards Euston, complete with ex-LNWR signal box, which sways with the passage of InterCity trains. The spur linking Trent Valley and Cross City lines curves away to the left. This useful link was not to be electrified as part of the Cross City scheme. A six-car Cross City train has just arrived at the high level platform. November 5th 1990.

The electric service begins north of Birmingham. Monday 30th November 1992 was wet and gloomy and more than half the trains were still diesel operated. The sombre mood is reflected in this dank scene at Lichfield City, as emu 310 106 arrives on its way to New Street.

Three Centro-liveried Class 323 emus seen in close proximity, in secure store at Kineton Military Railway prior to delivery to BR. Units are 323 304 (left) and 323 305, with 323 306 at the rear, April 15th 1993. *(courtesy of Kineton MR)*

DECLINE AT REDDITCH

Today's railway at Redditch is successful and efficient. Services are faster, more frequent and busier than at any time in the line's history.

Nevertheless, for all this recent revival there can be no doubt that the railway is less important to the town in overall terms than it once was. This is true for most British towns still served by the rail network. There are fewer opportunities for work on the railway. Most people now have access to a car so even if they are daily rail commuters they no longer rely on train or bus for all their travel needs. Most noticeable of all, in Redditch as elsewhere, the considerable volume of rail freight traffic that serviced the town's industries and shops barely a generation ago has entirely vanished.

Harry Jay, a retired driver who was based at Redditch between 1941 and 1963 estimates that during the 1950s the railway provided employment for almost a hundred people. If this sounds excessive to modern ears, consider:- the four locomotives at the engine shed each needed two crews of two, plus staff for the shed itself, the goods office employed thirteen clerical staff, the yard needed shunters etc., the fleet of eight 3-wheeled Scammell mechanical horses for door-to-door deliveries all required drivers, the four cranes in the goods shed needed drivers, both signal boxes were manned round the clock, not to mention ticket clerks, porters and a station master.

One small duty was unique to Redditch. The water column at the station was fed from a spring which also seeped into the tunnel; this constant source meant that the column never went dry - except when the duty railman forgot to switch on the pump. During the severe winter of 1963 the icicles in the tunnel hung down to track level, as Harry Jay discovered one morning when he and a colleague went in to see it if was safe for trains to pass through.

The small engine shed at Redditch was situated about half a mile north of the station, was built at a cost of £3,800 and opened in 1872. It was not a roundhouse but a simple structure 118' long, served by a single track. In the early years there was a turntable just outside the entrance. At just 40' long this was even shorter than Bournville's. It was removed as useless around the turn of the century and never replaced. At first the shed normally housed half a dozen of the small 2-4-0 locos that worked the passenger service. These were supplied by Saltley, even after Redditch officially became a sub-shed of Bournville. The Deeley 0-6-4 'Flatiron' tanks took over the passenger service when they were new and they were joined by a solitary 3F 0-6-0 for freight traffic.

Late in the day, in 1957, improvements were made. The track was renewed and a new concrete ash pit installed. By then Redditch housed four locomotives which helped operate what was still an all-steam passenger and freight railway from New Street, through Redditch, to Evesham and Ashchurch. As at Bournville there were few concessions to progress, and the manual coaling stage, which survived until the early 1960s, was a case in point. This was a simple wooden platform, with a primitive shelter, alongside a siding. Coal was off-loaded manually from the wagons and stored on the platform until required by the locomotives. Not for the likes of Redditch the huge automatic coaling bunkers of the larger sheds; this was still very much the sort of operation George Stephenson would have been familiar with.

Redditch was transferred to the Western Region in February of 1958 and became a sub-shed of Bromsgrove. Soon alien life forms were to be seen in the shape of ex-Great Western 0-6-0 pannier tanks. The novelty did not last long, because the need for the shed itself was rapidly diminishing. Diesel multiple units took

over the Birmingham - Redditch passenger service on 25th April 1960, but through trains between Birmingham, Evesham and Ashchurch remained steam- hauled until the end, so the shed continued in being to house two locomotives for passenger and parcels duty and a tank engine (usually the ex-GW) to act as yard pilot. The end of services south of Redditch made closure of the shed inevitable. It came on 1st June 1964. The goods yard followed five years later; meanwhile a Class 08 diesel shunter became yard pilot.

Redditch had carriage sidings, goods sidings, timber sidings and a branch to the gas works, which relied entirely on coal gas in the days before the bed of the North Sea had been explored. 'Gas coal' came from the Yorkshire, Nottinghamshire and Warwickshire coalfields. On arrival the wagons were kept in the sidings at Clive Road and taken as required, ten at a time, onto the gasworks branch, where they were turned upside down and unloaded automatically.

The yard shunting engine was usually a Fowler 'Jinty' 0-6-0 tank. Shunting went on for most of the day, such was the volume of traffic. The sheer variety of goods serves to emphasise the importance of rail borne traffic in the economy of any medium sized town before the mistaken idea that rail could only handle bulk trainload traffic became accepted political dogma in the 1960s.

Samples of freight handled at Redditch during the 1950s

INCOMING

*   domestic coal from the Staffordshire and Shropshire coalfields, distributed by local coal merchants.
*   timber to John Wright, usually 200 ton consignments.
*   aluminium ingots from Canada by rail from Ellesmere Port to Reynolds Tubes and High Duty Alloys.
*   bulk seasonal deliveries of fertilisers from Shell, ICI and Fisons, also deliveries of Silcox's cattle food.
    (All the above had warehousing at the goods yard.)

*   general freight for retailers eg; Woolworths.
*   consignments of Sheffield steel for use by the numerous small factories.
*   small containers (pre-Freightliner) from the Dunlopillo factory at Llanelli to be forwarded to Dunlop's depot at Hunt End.

OUTGOING

*   guns from B.S.A.
*   motor cycles and diesel engines from Royal Enfield
*   50 - 60 tons of tyres per week from Dunlop
*   small individual consignments of leather goods, fishing tackle and needles.
*   daily wagonload traffic to London, Birmingham and Liverpool; twice weekly to Glasgow, Bristol, Manchester, Leeds, Southampton and Hull.

The goods shed had nine loading bays and space for eighteen wagons. Loading and unloading was done with the aid of three gantry cranes and one 10 ton crane. A 10 ton freight lifter was sent from Birmingham whenever a consignment of aluminium ingots arrived. Such activity required clerical support and Mrs.Marjorie Tyson remembered the goods office when she joined the staff in 1948.

"There was no prejudice against ladies as such, although there was a different pay structure until the equal pay legislation of the 1960s. There were thirteen people in the office, two of whom were ladies. There was a "National" accounting machine, an adding machine and a single typewriter. All accounts and invoices were worked by hand. The goods office was the proud possessor of three Dickensian accounting desks, complete with high working surfaces and brass rail surrounds. These remained there until closure."

Sheep were also handled in the goods yard and the first passenger train of the day from New Street, which for many years left at around 6.30am, carried boxes of fish which were on sale in Redditch by 9am.

There was a wide variety of locomotives to be seen at Redditch, ranging from Johnson six-wheeled tender engines and 'Jinties' on shunting duties, through 'Crabs', so-called because of the motion of their connecting rods, to mixed- traffic Stanier 'Black Fives' and Stanier 2-8-0 freight engines. There were occasional more rare visitors, especially on the fruit trains from Evesham, including members of the final B.R.Standard class, 9F 2-10-0s.

During the summer of 1962 substantial engineering work took place on the Lickey route, which meant diversions through Redditch between Barnt Green and Ashchurch. Mike Goddard, who was a lad at the time, recalled -

"To the local enthusiasts this indeed was an event unprecedented in our time. The Redditch shunter was in steam on Sundays, banking heavy trains to Barnt Green, and trains passing in all the loops at Redditch, Alcester, Broom and Evesham. It brought exotic beings like Royal Scots, Patriots, Jubilees and Standard 2-10-0s, some even double-headed! We couldn't believe it, this was seventh heaven, and we hadn't time for such mundane things as Sunday lunch!"

This was the final spectacular act in the history of the Redditch line as a through route, because the section between Alcester and Evesham was closed on October 1st 1962 when the track was found to be unsafe. Could this have been anything to do with the pounding it had received that summer? Within two years there was complete closure and lifting south of Redditch.

The remaining service at Redditch - such as it was - came under threat of closure in 1964, but before looking at that episode it is worth remembering that goods traffic lingered on until 1981, twelve years after closure of the goods yard. By then it consisted solely of a daily roadstone train from Amey's quarry at Tytherington, Avon, to cater for the construction of the town's elaborate road network, with its numerous dual carriageways, flyovers and complex junctions. Once the road building was complete this traffic ceased.

Before the roadstone traffic finished the line was still signalled manually. The sole remaining box, at Redditch North, had fifteen operational levers, controlling signals and sidings, and was still lit by gas. The next box was Saltley. The distant signal on the approach to the terminus was permanently fixed, but the outer home, 819 yards from the box, had a small electric motor fitted to ease the strain on the signalman's gut when tugging on that length of wire - a sort of railway equivalent to power assisted steering in a heavy goods lorry. The fact that there was still a box on the Redditch line meant that more than one train could be on the branch at once, one moving between Redditch and Barnt Green and one in the station or sidings. It was then possible to run train departures from Redditch at less than 30 minute intervals. This was exploited in the morning peak hour throughout the lean years of the basic passenger service, when

Redditch North signal box, dreaming in the undergrowth during the hot summer of 1976 (Sunday 6th June) after closure of the goods yard to all but roadstone traffic and withdrawal of all but peak hour passenger trains. *(M.A.King)*

two trains to Birmingham left within twenty minutes of each other.

The signal box was absurdly uneconomic to operate. By 1981 there were no evening movements of any sort between the departure of the freight, with roadstone empties at around 19.30, until the arrival of the last passenger train of the evening - the only passenger train of the evening - at 23.30. The branch, and hence the box, had to remain open for this county council-supported service, which sometimes carried no passengers. The box was operated by two signalmen, one per shift, and was normally manned from 6am until the arrival of the last train.

The signal box closed and was demolished, all sidings were removed and the Redditch line was worked by remote block control from Saltley, with only one train at a time being permitted beyond Barnt Green. The branch was worked as a siding. In the final days of diesel operation it was very intensively worked, with a train somewhere along the branch for fifty-eight minutes out of every hour. Trains passed in Barnt Green station and, if both were running to time, there was a two minute interval after the Birmingham bound unit left the single line before the Redditch bound train entered it. But what of the passenger service before the days of the Cross City Line?

In the immediate post-war years the Redditch line, like so many other secondary routes, seemed relatively busy and untroubled. The fifty thousand passenger journeys per week were in wooden carriages, many non-corridor, hauled mainly by Midland 4-4-0 'Compound' type locomotives, or the newer LMS Ivatt 2-6-0s, incredibly ugly with their very high running plates and exposed guts oozing steam below. Bus competition was trifling, that from cars even less so, with petrol rationing in force until 1953. Post war austerity, a lack of investment and a certain amount of complacency ensured that the service stagnated. It was slow, shabby and dirty, operating at anything but regular intervals and - in common with the rest of the network - the continued use of the term 'third class' and an illogical fare structure seemed to symbolise a transport system that lacked direction. In 1949, for example, a 3rd class single from Redditch to Birmingham cost 3/3d (16p), but the day return was only 2/1d (just over 10p). The prices may have changed but the silly fare structure persists, and has been endemic throughout the system for longer than most of us can remember.

Diesel multiple units began operating the Redditch-Birmingham service in 1960. They were welcomed by the men, including Frank Beardmore:-

"The diesel multiple units soon began to replace the steam engines, and we were trained on the line by an instructor from Saltley and also spent three days at Didcot at the training school. ....The diesels were very easy and pleasant to drive ... you just pressed a button and away you went.

The Beeching Report was published in 1963. In relation to this document it is worth remembering Dr.Beeching's approach to a problem. This chemist from ICI, whose knowledge of railways was small, once told a colleague, "If you have a sticky problem, work out an answer, create chaos and then offer up a solution." (Nicholas Faith, 'Heroes & Villains', Independent Magazine, 29/12/90). Lines all over the country were feeling the effect of this warped way of thinking, including what was left of the service to Redditch.

The notice of closure was published in 'The Times' on 12th August 1964 and in the 'Birmingham Post' on 25th September. It included all stations from Selly Oak to Redditch, plus Bromsgrove, the latter as part of a plan to route all Birmingham-Worcester local trains via Kidderminster. Objections had to be lodged by November 13th, by which time 948 had been received, 638 from individuals pleading hardship, 197 from Barnt Green alone. The remainder were from local authorities, factories, schools, other official organisations and people submitting 'block' objections.

The ostensible reason for closure was that the line operated at a loss, which amounted to £45,940 in 1963. Following dieselisation in 1960 no further improvements were attempted and then - as now - no account was taken when proposing closure of any rail line of the adverse effects and costs this would have on the overall local environment in the form of increased road traffic, accidents, unemployment of people whose travel patterns were severed, etc.

Six businessmen, led by P.J.Cooke, formed the Redditch Passenger Action Committee within days of the announcement, leafleting stations and galvanising public opinion. The local press, Redditch Trades Council, Redditch Chamber of Trade and the Transport Users Consultitative Committee, among others, all saw the folly of axing the rail service just as Redditch was about to be developed as a government designated New Town. The Chamber of Trade objection highlighted the fact that some important bus stops were situated at the top of Unicorn Hill, a stiff climb up from the station. Its suggested re-routing of buses foreshadowed the easy interchange which now exists. Numerous individuals objected on the grounds that the Birmingham bus route was further from their homes than the station and that the increased journey time, especially on congested roads, was as much as half an hour. The written objection of Anne Thomas, of Birchfield Road, was typical:-

"My nearest alternative bus service is a ten minute walk away and the journey into Birmingham takes 30 minutes longer. The trains are more comfortable and especially in winter the train is quicker and far more reliable."

The British Railways Board had completed a passenger census (see page 60) before publication of the closure notice, on Monday-Saturday 13th-18th July 1964. In the roundest of terms these figures show that 2,400 passenger journeys were made on the line daily. This was 720,000 journeys per annum (assuming 300 working days per year and the absence of a Sunday service), so the annual support of almost £46,000 amounted to just over 6p per journey. The service was not promoted, there were no off-peak travel inducements and peak hour fares had recently been increased, leading to fewer passengers. A second survey, during the last week of May 1964, showed a sharp drop in the average number of daily journeys on the line to 1,538, rising to 1,788 during a third survey from February 22nd to 27th 1965.

The buses of the Midland Red, meanwhile, would not be capable of handling these extra people should the line close; the company's attempts to even maintain existing services were descending to the level of farce, as the 'Birmingham Post' pointed out on October 14th 1964:-

"Because the shortage of bus crews has become so acute, Midland Red is training its clerks and other office workers to drive buses in the evenings after finishing their normal duties. Typists are helping as conductors. A spokesman for the company said last night, 'We are now more than 1,400 drivers and conductors short. The situation is very bad, but it could be a lot worse if we did not have volunteers from our office staff willing to work for a few hours in the evening'."

The public hearing into the closure was held at the Grand Hotel, Birmingham, on Tuesday 16th March 1965, not suitable for any objectors unable to have time off work. After the hearing nothing was heard from the Transport Minister, Tom Fraser, save for an exchange in the Commons with Ioan Evans M.P., when he resisted the temptation to rush:-

"It seems to me important that I should take the right decision rather than a quick decision"

and he also refused to contact the Chairman of British Railways about the closure on the limpid grounds that:-

"I think it would be better .... if I were fully to accept my responsibilities which lie upon me to take the decision at the end of the day."

(Hansard Vol.711 No.103, 28/4/1965)

That decision was eventually announced on 9th August. Closure consent was refused (except for Blackwell and Stoke Works on the Bromsgrove line) but only a threadbare peak hour service remained, the Minister even 'asking' that:-

"the Board make all possible economies consistent with the maintenance of a minimum peak hour service for commuters from these stations to Birmingham."

For Redditch this meant three morning trains to Birmingham, with three returns in the evening; for Bromsgrove there was to be but a single train each way. In the climate of the time it was perhaps inevitable when this almost total defeat was hailed as a victory - "Passengers Win the Battle of the Railway Line", trumpeted the 'Birmingham Post'. The secretary of Redditch Chamber of Commerce, Pauline Meller, was a little more perceptive when she was quoted as saying:-

"With things as they are at the moment, one can only think that the decision is a satisfactory one, because the line stays open and therefore leaves the door open for a possible increase in the service later on when the New Town develops at Redditch."

The Minister had reserved his position on Selly Oak and Bournville stations and two more years were to elapse before his successor, Barbara Castle, was to lift the threat and refuse consent to their closure on 25th October 1967.

Redditch line – average number of weekday passengers, July 1964.

Passengers joining trains to Birmingham at:-

Redditch	278
Alvechurch	87
Barnt Green	199
Northfield	334
King's Norton	116
Bournville	125
Selly Oak	73
Total	1,212

Passengers alighting from trains to Redditch at:-

Selly Oak	58
Bournville	67
King's Norton	167
Northfield	278
Barnt Green	196
Alvechurch	169
Redditch	318
Total	1,253

A superb photograph of a vintage railway sorely in need of modernisation and investment. This is Northfield on April 7th 1963, with the goods yard crane, station buildings and semaphore signalling reminiscent of a bygone era. The Bristol-Newcastle express might be powered by Peak (class 45) No.D63, but the ex-LNER Gresley carriages look almost as antiquated as the grounded pre-Grouping van body on the platform.   (P.J.Shoesmith)

In July of that year a few extra trains were run on the edge of the peak hours and on Saturdays. They were not a success and were taken off the following May. P.J.Cooke, of the disbanded action group, could only lament accurately:-

> "Since services were slashed 18 months ago the public has ceased to be train conscious. While only a commuter service was operating people got out of the habit of using trains. It will take a lot to win them back."

Stations were reduced to unstaffed halts in May 1967, but on the first day the guard of the 8.05 from Redditch had not been trained to use a ticket machine, neither had he been told to collect tickets, so everyone enjoyed a free ride, at least as far as the excess fare booth at New Street!

The twilight minimal peak hour service continued to grope along as best as it could from one year's end to the next. Stations decayed gently, or suffered ruder outbursts of vandalism, as at Northfield and Alvechurch. Northfield and King's Norton enjoyed an extra morning peak hour train in the form of the first train of the day from Bristol, which started from Gloucester in later years. This added luxury was not always successful, particularly at the start of a new time-table, as some Bristol drivers failed to stop there. Geoff Hilton, one of the rare breed of Northfield commuters at the time, recalled:-

> "There was a good deal of umbrella waving if the train came thundering over the bank and shot past us. On more than one occasion it stopped beyond the station and edged its way gingerly back to us."

Nothing was done to encourage use of this important artery for over ten years. Even though the neglect was finally swept away with the start of the Cross City service in May 1978 it would be eleven more years before the Redditch branch felt the full benefit.

Redditch looks bright and cheerful in midsummer sunshine, as 4-6-0 No.46443 arrives on a train from Birmingham, 1st June 1963. The handsome station was then ninety-five years old and appeared in good shape. Nevertheless, everything that seemed so permanent was swept away nine years later and the town bus station now occupies this site. What seemed more temporary lives on, as the locomotive now has a new home on the Severn Valley Railway.

P.J.Shoesmith)

CROSS CITY NORTH, between Birmingham and Lichfield

(A Grand Junction : The Sutton Coldfield Railway : The first train to Lichfield will be somewhat delayed : The Sutton Coldfield Disaster, 1955 : Push-Pulls, Diesels, Small Boys and Motorists : Decline)

A GRAND JUNCTION

Between Duddeston and Aston the Cross City Line follows the route of the Grand Junction, an early main line and the first railway to arrive in Birmingham. Even at the dawn of the railway age Birmingham was seen by industrialists with an eye to their profits and by railway engineers with vision as the potential hub of a national network.

The Liverpool & Manchester Railway was an overnight success when it opened in 1830, making it certain that more railways linking other large centres of population and industry would soon follow. Where could be more populous or industrial than London and Birmingham? Why not join them with each other by the London & Birmingham Railway and then with the Liverpool & Manchester by means of a "grand junction", the first trunk line in the world?

It was no coincidence that Acts of Parliament authorising construction of the London & Birmingham and Grand Junction Railways were both passed on May 6th 1833. Joseph Locke engineered the Grand Junction, which had been surveyed by George Stephenson, whose son, Robert, engineered the London & Birmingham line. At seventy-eight miles long, the Grand Junction was intended as the first vital link in a chain of lines linking London with the industrial Midlands and North, which would also offer a through route to Scotland and another to Holyhead for Ireland. The London & Birmingham and Grand

Junction were both under construction at the same time, each employing thousands of men, many of whose fathers and grandfathers had earlier built canals.

The Grand Junction passed through generally easier country and was shorter than the London & Birmingham, without difficult works on the scale of Tring Cutting or Kilsby Tunnel, so it reached Birmingham first, with a temporary station at Vauxhall opening on July 4th 1837. The first train, departing at 7.00am, was made up of eight 1st class carriages pulled by a 2-2-2 locomotive "Wildfire", built by Robert Stephenson, with 5' driving wheels and a weight of just under ten tonnes. What this engine lacked in size it made up for by efficient hard work, running over twelve thousand trouble free miles in its first three months. This represents a round average of 130 miles per day, seven days a week, outstanding for the time. Others of its class proved equally reliable and ensured a good commercial start for the Grand Junction.

Thousands of cheering and waving people lined the route, but there was no official opening ceremony, partly because the country was still in mourning for William IV, who had died on June 20th. When the Liverpool & Manchester opened with festivities in 1830 the day was marred by an accident in which the "Rocket" ran down and killed the Liverpool MP William Huskisson. Joseph Locke, the Grand Junction engineer, had been driving the "Rocket" on that occasion and the effect on him was profound. The Chairman of the GJ and his deputy had witnessed the accident and all three men requested that there should be no opening ceremony. Commemorative medals were struck, which were inscribed with the company's title, opening date, engineer and cost of construction - £1,500 000.

The lack of ceremony did not dampen the enthusiasm of the crowds gathered from miles around, many since dawn, to catch a glimpse of their first train. The southbound trains suffered delays as the day wore on, because they were mobbed at stations and the track was invaded, especially near Birmingham. The 2pm arrival at Vauxhall could not get in until 4pm for this reason.

Facilities were not ready for goods traffic until February 1838, but a healthy revenue was generated by the 232,202 passengers who travelled in the first six months, all without incident.

As on other early railways luggage was carried on the roof and passengers could opt to ride there too. With increased speeds and smuts from the engine few of them did and the practice soon ceased. Those with their own horse and carriage could transport them on flat trucks. No smoking was allowed on GJ trains, "even with the consent of other passengers". One compartment of the mail carriage could be converted into a 'bed carriage' even though there were no overnight trains. There were six trains each way per day, two on Sundays, taking about four and a half hours at an average speed of 22 mph. There was as yet no provision for third class passengers.

Vauxhall station, sited at Erskine Street bridge just south of the present Duddeston station, was necessary until the 28 arch viaduct leading to the terminus at Curzon Street was completed. Passenger amenities at Vauxhall were basic, consisting of a booking office, waiting room, two platforms and overall wooden roof. The roof rested on iron pillars only, there were no side walls and hence no real protection from rain and wind. It was a mile and a half to the town centre. Those who did not walk could take a cab - perhaps even a new Hansom cab (patented 1834) to the Town Hall (also by Joseph Aloysius Hansom, also 1834) - though they would have been outraged at the exhorbitant fare of 1/- (5p).

There was one special moment in the brief life of this station. A railway horsebox was converted into a Post Office sorting carriage, the first in the world, and it began operating between Vauxhall and Liverpool on January 6th 1838. The concept of speeding up communications by sorting the mail on the move was simple but effective; the 'West Coast Postal' and all such mail trains worldwide owe their origins to this ex-horsebox. It was so successful that by September of the same year it was replaced by a purpose-built vehicle equipped with newly devised 'mailbag exchange apparatus' that could discharge and collect mailbags at speed.

The GJ terminus at Curzon St., alongside the L.& B. station of the same name, opened in January 1839, although the GJ time-table had been recast three months earlier in anticipation, to allow through running and good connections between the two. Both stations were built by the same contractor, Grissell & Peto. The GJ station could not boast of a grand arch like its L.& B. neighbour but had instead a long pleasant classical facade, with four large entrance doors and nine empty niches which looked as though they should have contained statues.

Vauxhall was now surplus to requirements and closed some time in 1839-40, although company records make no reference to this. It is only certain that it was gone by 1841 and a new station, variously named "Vauxhall", "Duddeston" or "Vauxhall & Duddeston" throughout its life, was opened on the present site in 1869.

The GJ terminus at Curzon Street became a goods station when New Street opened. In more recent times it looked very neglected, was never the subject of a preservation order and was demolished in 1971. One building in Birmingham from Grand Junction days survives intact, the engine shed alongside Duddeston station. It was extended around 1841 - records are again vague - and is now used as a repair depot for British Rail's civil engineering fleet. Ordinary and unknown, it is important as one of the oldest engine sheds in the world. Long may it continue as a living workplace.

On New Year's Day 1846 the Grand Junction and London & Birmingham became two of the key components of the new London & North Western Railway, the self-styled 'Premier Line'. Most of the Grand Junction still serves as part of the West Coast Main Line, though not this section, which continues north of Aston and through Bescot before regaining the WCML at Bushbury Junction, Wolverhampton. Nevertheless, it remains obvious as the train runs between Duddeston and Aston that this is a well engineered main line designed for smooth fast running, a worthy first fragment of today's Cross City Line.

THE SUTTON COLDFIELD RAILWAY

It took a quarter of a century for the idea of a railway at Sutton to become reality. When the Grand Junction opened in 1837 it was already making plans for a branch from Birmingham to Derby via Sutton and Lichfield, but nothing came of them.

During the Railway Mania of 1845 all sorts of lines were proposed all over the country, some practical, many fanciful, most were destined never to be built. To the inexperienced small investor it seemed possible to make a fortune with ease, but reality was different. Some companies sprang up and then vanished like the morning mist whenever good intentions were not matched by hard cash; others were rapidly absorbed by competitors so as to be strangled at birth.

The unreal atmosphere of that summer and autumn reached the Hen & Chickens Hotel in Birmingham on September 16th when a gathering of interested parties met to form the Birmingham & Lichfield Railway Co. In Lichfield, just two days later, the board of this company met the promoters of a Lichfield & Manchester Railway, promptly amalgamating with them to form the Birmingham, Lichfield & Manchester Railway Co. Their surveyor, John McLean, reported a month later on the possibilty of two routes, one through Sutton, the other by-passing the town and crossing the park near Banners Gate. He recommended the latter because:-

"(Sutton Coldfield) has little trade, and principally composed of an agricultural population, to whom rapid conveyance is not essential, I would advise you to adopt the line through Sutton Park."

A noisy protest meeting was held in the Moot Hall lamenting this attitude. As the BL&M Railway wanted a smooth passage of their bill through Parliament they relented a little, promising to construct a branch to the town centre. Provision was made in the bill, which became an Act on July 27th 1846.

Politics continued to move swiftly along, while the actual construction of any railway happened not at all. In September the BL&M was taken over by the newly formed London & North Western Railway, whose internationally famous joint engineers, Joseph Locke (ex-GJ) and Robert Stephenson, each enjoyed salaries of £2,000 per annum as well as a lump sum of one thousand guineas (£1,050) they had received when the company

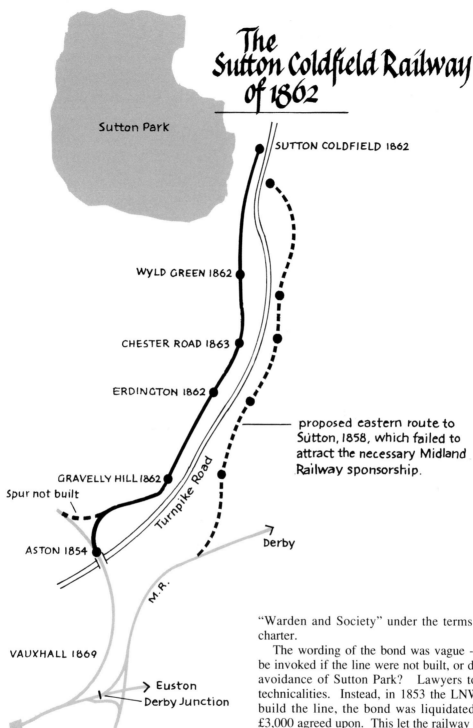

The Sutton Coldfield Railway of 1862

Sutton Park

SUTTON COLDFIELD 1862

WYLD GREEN 1862

CHESTER ROAD 1863

ERDINGTON 1862

proposed eastern route to Sutton, 1858, which failed to attract the necessary Midland Railway sponsorship.

GRAVELLY HILL 1862

Spur not built

Turnpike Road

Derby

ASTON 1854

M.R.

VAUXHALL 1869

Euston
Derby Junction

NEW STREET

had been formed. Locke was approached by some of Sutton's more prominent citizens anxious for a railway, as a result of which he surveyed a route to the east of the turnpike road, the ancestor of today's A5127.

An Act was passed in July 1847 enabling the LNWR to build this line but, like many of the lines proposed in the depression which followed the mania, it never left the drawing board. Nevertheless, the town did benefit. The LNWR had agreed to build the railway within five years and avoid Sutton Park, otherwise there would be a penalty of £20,000 to pay. The agreement was not an integral part of the 1847 Act, but was originally made at the time of the 1846 Act. It took the form of a bond between the Birmingham, Lichfield & Manchester Railway and Sutton's Mayor and Corporation, who were quaintly styled

"Warden and Society" under the terms of Henry VIII's 1528 charter.

The wording of the bond was vague - could the penalty only be invoked if the line were not built, or did it refer mainly to the avoidance of Sutton Park? Lawyers today wax rich on such technicalities. Instead, in 1853 the LNWR abandoned plans to build the line, the bond was liquidated and compensation of £3,000 agreed upon. This let the railway off lightly and provided enough money for a spanking new Town Hall in Mill Street, which later became a masonic hall.

Nine more years went by before the railway reached Sutton. During that time there were constant differences between those who favoured an eastern or western route. These were compounded by a vocal minority who did not want a railway at all. A petition against the 1847 Act said "any railway would make Sutton a smoky and degraded suburb of Birmingham" and an 1860 history of the town by a certain Miss Bracken was no less forthright;

> "Long may it (the Sutton Coldfield air) be worth the seeking - long may the gallant old Beacon hold his ramparts against the sappers and miners of the West ...Sutton may readily be spoiled.... At the present time there is not a steam engine in the parish."

A Class 101 dmu on a New Street-Four Oaks working at Chester Road, 13th December 1967. The scene is framed by the tall distant signals of Erdington (left) and Wylde Green. The tower blocks of Erdington dominate the horizon, but nearby some of the 'better class of villa residence' which the promoters of the line hoped to attract, are much in evidence.

(P.J.Shoesmith)

During 1857 efforts to get a line built were resumed, thanks largely to Mr.Baron Webster, who was Warden of Sutton that year. His approach to the Board of the LNWR met with a cold reply. It said, in effect, "you provide the capital, contruct the line to our approval, guarantee that there will be no operating losses and we will be happy to run your railway for you". Neither Webster nor others were discouraged for long. The following year three routes were surveyed, two east of the turnpike road and one to the west. All were intended as single track branch lines.

By the autumn of 1858 support among Sutton's prominent citizens had crystallized. Some, led by Webster, favoured an eastern route to Sutton from a junction with the Midland Railway's Derby line. They issued a share prospectus for a "Birmingham, Erdington & Sutton Coldfield Railway Co." with capital of £60,000. Others were led by Thomas Attwood, who lived in Erdington and was the son of Birmingham's first MP. They supported a western route from a junction at Aston; they also issued a prospectus for a railway of the same name, also with capital of £60,000. A few of these landowners, well before the term 'Nimby' had been invented, backed whichever was the further route from their own property.

Extracts from both prospectuses show that the promoters understood that Erdington and Sutton could soon be dormitories for Birmingham and that, in any event, the inhabitants wanted the cheap coal that only a railway could supply. From the eastern prospectus:-

> "The district of country from Gravelly Hill and Erdington to Sutton possesses advantages beyond any other in the neighbourhood of Birmingham and so much has this been felt, that, although without Railway accomodation, buildings of the first class have rapidly sprung into existence, and the whole country for some distance on each side of the proposed line is now being sold as building land.

And from the western:-

> "...It is found that a line of Railway commencing at the Aston Station ....is the best, being the shortest and cheapest route from Birmingham to Sutton.....

It is obvious that any Railway, to really benefit the population, should be in connection and alliance with the London and North Western Railway Company, in order to secure the important privilege of using the New Street Station, at Birmingham, and a direct communication with the populous and mineral district of South Staffordshire, which will afford a good and cheap supply of Coal, Lime, etc., to the District through which the Line passes."

Webster and Attwood worked hard to bring supporters of the two routes together. Both men were perceptive enough to see that the need for a railway was greater than petty rivalries about a route. They quickly realised that either route would need financial backing from the supporters of both if it were to be viable. Many of their board members were not so wise. In January 1859 the promoters of the western line suggested that they sink their differences, withdraw the separate bills they had placed before Parliament, and draw up a mutually acceptable bill in time for the 1860 session. The eastern line promoters refused to withdraw, neither did they accept proposals from the LNWR in June 1859. At this the LNWR broke the impasse by adopting the western route as its own and absorbing the western company.

A Parliamentary Select Committee met for four days in July to consider the two routes. The Midland had had no time to adopt or absorb the eastern route, whose promoters were, in effect, 'sent naked into the conference chamber'. Their trains would have channelled more traffic into New St. via the Midland junction at Lawley Street, already recognised as potentially dangerous because of speeding trains and cluttered signalling. (This junction was later the scene of a fatal collision between MR and LNWR expresses in 1892.) In contrast to its attitude three years earlier when responding to Webster, the LNWR gave evidence that it was now prepared to finance and construct a double tracked western line. The result was inevitable and the Act enabling this line to be built was passed on 8th August.

It took a year to the day before the contract to construct the line was signed and work could begin. It cost £85 000 and opened for passengers and goods on 2nd June 1862, just within the three years stipulated by the Act.

At first there were seven trains each way (three on Sundays) taking 25 minutes for the seven and a half miles to New Street. By the turn of the decade there were fifteen weekday trains each way. Six of these - the Sutton departures at 08.00, 08.30 and 08.35, plus the New St. departures at 17.15, 18.15 and 18.35 - were aimed at those with business in Birmingham. Four of the six omitted stops, were two or three minutes faster, and could perhaps be classed as semi-fast. The Sutton commuter had arrived! (The population of Sutton increased from 4,662 at the 1861 census to 7,737 by the 1881 census.)

Traffic flow was not all in one direction though, because excursion and weekend relief trains were run to Sutton to build on custom that was already there. Before the arrival of the railway the value of Sutton Park as a place of relaxation was appreciated by the hundreds who travelled from Birmingham by horse bus every weekend, especially but not exclusively in the summer, as skating on the frozen pools drew many to the park in the depths of winter. Now the journey was more comfortable, travelling time was reduced to twenty-five minutes and the third class single fare of sixpence ha'penny (2.75p) was half the bus fare. There were no third class return fares when the railway opened but even first class passengers paid only 1/6d (7.5p) return, just 5d more than two third class singles. The only drawback was that New Street then - as now - found it difficult to cope with the volume of traffic at the busiest times. When this was the case, on summer Saturdays and particularly on Bank Holiday Mondays, Sutton excursions started from the far less convenient Curzon St., which saw its very last passenger train, a Sutton excursion, on Whit Monday 1893. After this date, for several years, Sutton excursions ran to/from the even less convenient stations at Vauxhall and Saltley (for the Midland Railway's Sutton Park line.)

The 1862 station at Sutton was fitted with a canopied departure platform, an island arrival platform, turntable, sidings, crane, cattle dock, goods shed, refreshment rooms, coal offices, signal box etc. There was even a short transverse siding and dock - reached via a wagon turntable - where road carriages were mounted onto flat trucks before attachment to the main train; this a century before cars boarded the Motorail trains at exactly the same spot. All has now entirely disappeared, apart from a short length of the main platform and a remnant of its buildings.

THE FIRST TRAIN TO LICHFIELD WILL BE SOMEWHAT DELAYED

In fact, Lichfield's first railway had nothing directly to do with what is now the Cross City Line, neither was it delayed, but it is worth a brief description, as it was intended as a solution to problems in Birmingham.

It was apparent very early in the railway age that the original main lines linking London with the industrial Midlands and North-West England - the London & Birmingham and the Grand Junction - would soon be inconvenient and inadequate. The volume of traffic between London and the North-West was sufficient to justify a fast direct link, in effect a Birmingham by-pass, routed along the valley of the River Trent. The Trent Valley Railway Act, for the line as built between Rugby and Stafford via Lichfield, was passed in the summer of the Railway Mania on July 21st 1845. The line was bought by the newly formed LNWR in April 1846 and it opened to a limited passenger service of two stopping trains each way daily on September 15th 1847. The station at Lichfield was at the hamlet of Streethay, a mile north of the city. The original buildings, demolished in 1971, were similar in appearance to those at Atherstone, which were sensitively restored during the 1980s. There was a useful by-product to the opening of the Trent Valley Line. Until then all towns of any size kept their own time relative to Greenwich. Birmingham, for example, was seven minutes behind, so any early Victorian passengers on the L.& B. who were lucky enough to own accurate watches had to adjust them, just like long distance air travellers today. The Trent Valley Railway offered a second route between the capital and Manchester, which meant double the potential difficulties for proper time-keeping. Common sense prevailed and the full opening of the Trent Valley, on December 1st 1841, was the day when the LNWR adopted 'London Time' throughout its system. The further spread of railways hastened the extinction of local times.

The line linking Lichfield's Trent Valley and City stations, the northernmost tip of today's Cross City Line, started life as part of the South Staffordshire Railway, which ran from Dudley via Walsall, Brownhills and Lichfield to a junction with the Midland main line at Wichnor, south of Burton-on-Trent. It was a cross-country alternative to the Midland Railway's Birmingham-Derby main line. Unusually for the time, there was virtually no opposition to the building of the line, but there was plenty of chaotic in-fighting amongst the directors. Nominally an independent company, the South Staffordshire's board was split three ways among those with Midland interests, those influenced by the LNWR and those who managed to think for themselves.

The line opened from Walsall to Wichnor Junction on 9th April 1849, with stations at Rushall, Pelsall, Brownhills, Hammerwich and Lichfield (City), and running powers through to Burton-on-Trent. There was a civic dinner in Lichfield and a ball at the Guildhall, although no trains appeared in any time-table before June and the South Staffs station at Trent Valley did not open before August. Compared with the Grand Junction, which managed to run an efficient, regular and fast service from Birmingham Vauxhall from the very beginning, the South Staffs started life as a ramshackle outfit. The first time extra traffic was expected, for the Whit Monday Fair at Lichfield, there were

The Lichfield Extension
and associated lines

Notes on stations

LICHFIELD TRENT VALLEY
Trent Valley platforms opened 1847 – moved to present site 1871
High Level (South Staffs) platforms opened 1849 – moved to present site 1871 –
closed to passengers 1965 – 88.

LICHFIELD CITY
Opened 1849. New station built slightly to west, 1884.

BUTLERS LANE
Demolished October 1991. New station on same site opened March 1992.
Served by buses from Blake Street during this time.

SUTTON COLDFIELD
Original 1862 terminal buildings and platform continued in railway use
long after the opening of the through platforms in 1884.

insufficient carriages. It is not as though the railway had had no warning, because the Lichfield Bower was - and remains - an annual event dating from the Middle Ages. Open trucks with hastily and badly installed planks for seating were used - not a good introduction to rail travel for the miners and cottagers of Pelsall, Brownhills and Hammerwich. Later stock shortages were relieved by cattle trucks, and if Neele's "Railway Reminiscences" are to be believed, the urchins of Lichfield delighted in gathering near the station to mock and moo at the passengers.

During the nineteenth century the city's most important industry was brewing. The arrival of both railways at Trent Valley stimulated growth in the area, including the Railway Tavern (1854) the Trent Valley Brewery Co. and cottages for its workers, the Brewery Row of 1881. The area around Trent Valley station is now a trading estate, which is thriving because of convenient access to the A38 trunk road.

There were excursion trains to Lichfield, stock shortages notwithstanding, and people came to view the cathedral and picnic on Borrowcop Hill, near the present site of King Edward VI School. Despite these early tourists Nathaniel Hawthorne, in his "English Notebooks" of 1855 said:-

"The people have an old-fashioned way with them
and stare at a stranger as if the railway had not yet
quite accustomed them to visitors and novelty."

By 1856 there were five trains each way, two on Sundays,

A steam shovel pauses for the camera during the building of the Lichfield extension. The location and date are both uncertain, but are believed to be just north of Four Oaks, during 1882, on the occasion of the first outing of the newly-formed Birmingham Photographic Society. *(courtesy of Birmingham Central Library)*

between Walsall and Burton via Lichfield. This was now developing as a secondary route, as the promoters had intended. Not that all was plain sailing. Differences among the three factions on the board had been papered over in 1850 when the company's engineer, John Robinson McClean, had personally leased the line for 21 years. He gave up the lease in 1861 and it was transferred to the LNWR, which relished the prospect of running its trains to Burton, deep in Midland territory.

There were extraordinary scenes at Wichnor Junction as the first LNWR train approached. It was confronted by a large gang of Midland men and three locomotives, one of which had been made ready to uproot part of the track should the LNWR train be foolish enough to attempt to continue. The train was halted and there followed an uneasy stand-off. The Midland failed to follow up this threatening behaviour and conceded defeat on the same day. The first LNWR train to enter Burton did so with all guns blazing, or at least with constant shrieks from the whistle. Having inherited running rights to Burton from the South Staffs on paper the LNWR certainly earned them in practice.

Six months later, on June 2nd 1862, the LNWR branch from Aston to Sutton Coldfield opened, ending, most definitely, in a terminus. The line from Birmingham to Sutton had been seen as part of a route through Lichfield to the north from the beginning, even in the earliest GJ scheme of 1837.

During the years that Sutton remained a terminus there were

two Acts of Parliament enabling an extension to Lichfield to be built; in 1863 for the Birmingham & Sutton Extension Railway and in 1872 for the Birmingham & Lichfield Junction Railway. An Act of 1873 allowed for a spur at Sutton, connecting the Lichfield extension to the Sutton Park line. All these powers lapsed. Eventually the LNWR promoted its own plans for a Lichfield line and the enabling Act received the royal assent on June 29th 1880. The service began on December 15th 1884 - *this* was the train that had been somewhat delayed! The "Lichfield Mercury" reported:-

Lichfield & Sutton Coldfield Railway

"This new branch of the London & North Western Railway was opened for passenger traffic on Monday last. Considerable interest was taken in the event not only amongst the inhabitants of Lichfield but also of Shenstone and Sutton Coldfield and the inhabitants of the hamlets of Blake Street and Four Oaks, the latter two with Shenstone intervening between the termini of the line. We regret to state that the occasion was marked by an incident of a most melancholy nature. While the bells of Shenstone church were ringing a joyous peal, and fog signals were being exploded as the first two trains passed up and down the line respectively, a man named Fields, engaged in some work at the

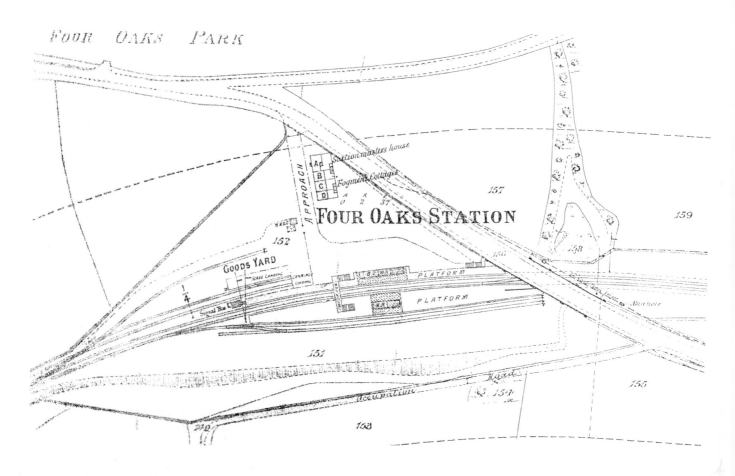

LNWR plans of Four Oaks station, 1882, on a green fields site. The land all around was owned by William Hartopp. Over the next two decades it was sold for development and some fine houses built. Beyond the station drive, on the far side of the main road, Four Oaks Park was developed at the turn of the century. The houses built then, especially those along Hartopp Road, remain some of the most opulent in the Midlands. The station cottages and goods yard have gone, replaced by a 252 space car park which may now in its turn be superseded by a multi-storey car park. The grey areas on the map mark the dust of ages as it lay in the archives, rolled up and undisturbed for decades.   *(courtesy of Lichfield Record Office)*

Shenstone siding, was run over by a truck and so shockingly mutilated that he died in the course of an hour or two .....

At a considerable period before the new booking office was opened at either end of the new line, a good number of passengers assembled, and the first trains were well loaded, but not to any extraordinary extent, or even to the extent that was anticipated. The engines drawing the trains throughout the day were gaily decked with flags, holly, etc. The trains ran smoothly and evenly, and but for the evidence of recent construction all along the route and the partially finished stations none would have imagined that this was the first day the line had been opened for passenger traffic.

...(This is the) ultimately successful attempt to open up direct communication through a long isolated district with the ancient city of Lichfield and the important town of Birmingham. The new line has reduced the railway distance between Birmingham and Lichfield by four and a half miles" (the former route was via Walsall) "but it is noticeable that the fares have not been reduced in due proportion. The fare is now 2/9d (14p) return for a journey of 31 miles." (sic. for 31 read 18) "The new line will afford a shortened direct route from Birmingham to Lichfield, Burton and Derby,

placing the LNWR, in respect of distance, on more than equal terms with the Midland Railway."
(and this inter-company rivalry, symbolised by the rumpus at Wichnor Junction, was the real reason for the building of the line)

"The constituting of this branch main line also relieves traffic on the old Grand Junction line to Bescot and Walsall, and so enables the services of trains to be quickened and facilitated on both routes....

The beauty of the country and the advantages of ready communication with Birmingham will lead to an extension considerably beyond Sutton of that system of villa residence which has sprung up all along the line as far as its present terminus. An addition to the excursion traffic may also be anticipated".

It is a mistake to view the subject of any book in total isolation. A brief glance at other items in the same edition of the "Lichfield Mercury" gives some slight impression of the world that the new railway emerged into. Sewing machines were offered for sale at twenty shillings (£1); Lichfield Workhouse was being extended; teachers at Cannock were keeping children in after the end of official school hours "perhaps in the hope of extra grant" but the children were overworked; Aston Villa, who were to win the FA Cup for the first time two seasons later, beat Cambridge University 3-1 at Perry Barr in Cambridge's first defeat of the season, "Villa displayed their very best form", and:-

"Miss Outhwaite intends to open a MORNING CLASS, in a central position in Lichfield, after Christmas, for the Daughters of Gentlemen. Terms & particulars on application."

Lichfield City was the only station completed in time for the opening day, although all the others were open for business. The original stations have survived in some measure, apart from Blake Street, which was rebuilt in the 1960s. The new station here is a delight, an improvement on the original. The two storey entrance hall and the island platform buildings at Lichfield City retain their integrity, but a horse and carriage landing for meeting trains, several sidings including a loop on the up side "for Walsall trains to stand on" and through goods loops have all vanished.

Plans of Blake Street and Four Oaks stations, drawn up when the line was under construction in 1882, show that they were both surrounded by fields. The inclusion of a bay platform at Four Oaks shows that this was to be the new terminus of Sutton local trains from Birmingham. If this attractive area near the park, ripe for the better sort of 'villa residence', was to fulfill its potential it would need a reasonable train service, irrespective of what was happening further north.

The Lichfield extension soon settled into a steady rural rhythm. The three new stations all had sidings served by pick-up goods trains. Four Oaks became a highly desirable commuter area with handy peak hour services to and from Birmingham, although the off-peak trains along the whole line were infrequent and irregular until just before the arrival of the diesels in 1956. Lichfield trains were often semi-fast south of Sutton and some went through to Derby.

Blake Street, a typical LNWR wayside station. Note the fence mounted oil lamps and the almost obligatory enamelled advertisement for Virol. *(Lens of Sutton)*

The enlarged 1884 station at Sutton Coldfield had a standard LNWR footbridge at the south end, in addition to the covered way linking both platforms to the booking office and each other. This photograph, taken from on top of the water tower, shows it being dismantled during the summer of 1931. Crane No.8 is on duty. The passenger stock in view is a rake of Lancashire & Yorkshire Railway 54' arc-roofed non-corridor coaches. Numbered amongst the freight vehicles are three LMS and three LNER wagons, together with some which are private owner. One belongs to J.Mills & Son, Birmingham, and illustrations of that company's wagons are extremely rare. *(A.Holme-Barnett)*

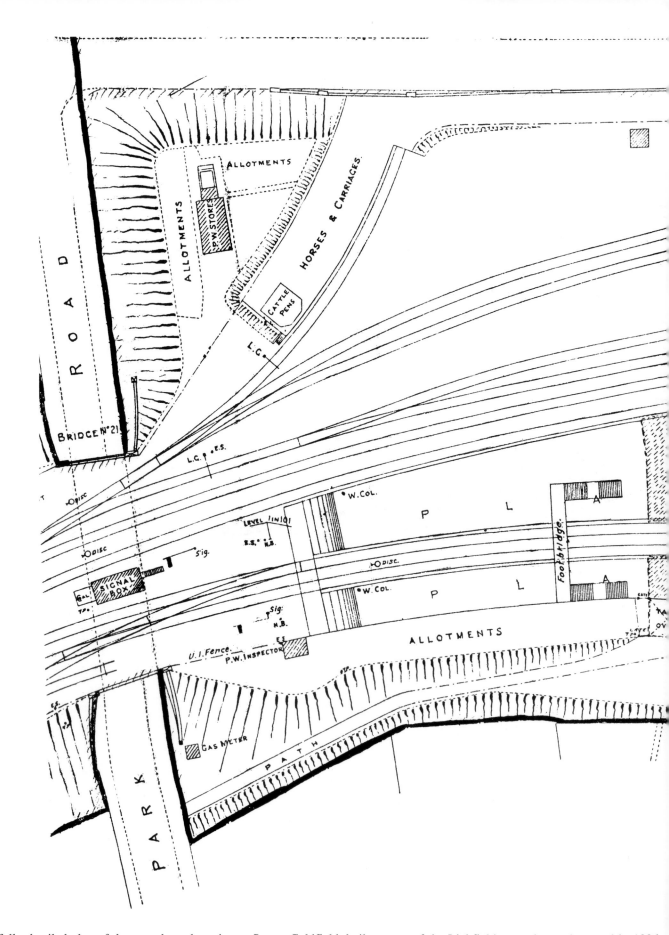

A beautifully detailed plan of the new through station at Sutton Coldfield, built as part of the Lichfield extension and opened in 1886. The hatched areas mark the platform canopies. Note also the canopy over the approach road for those arriving by carriage or cab, with the cabmen's shelter opposite. Milepost 5 on the down platform indicates the distance from Aston. The double line linking the booking office with this platform is the slope known as the 'wooden hill'. *(courtesy Birmingham Central Library)*

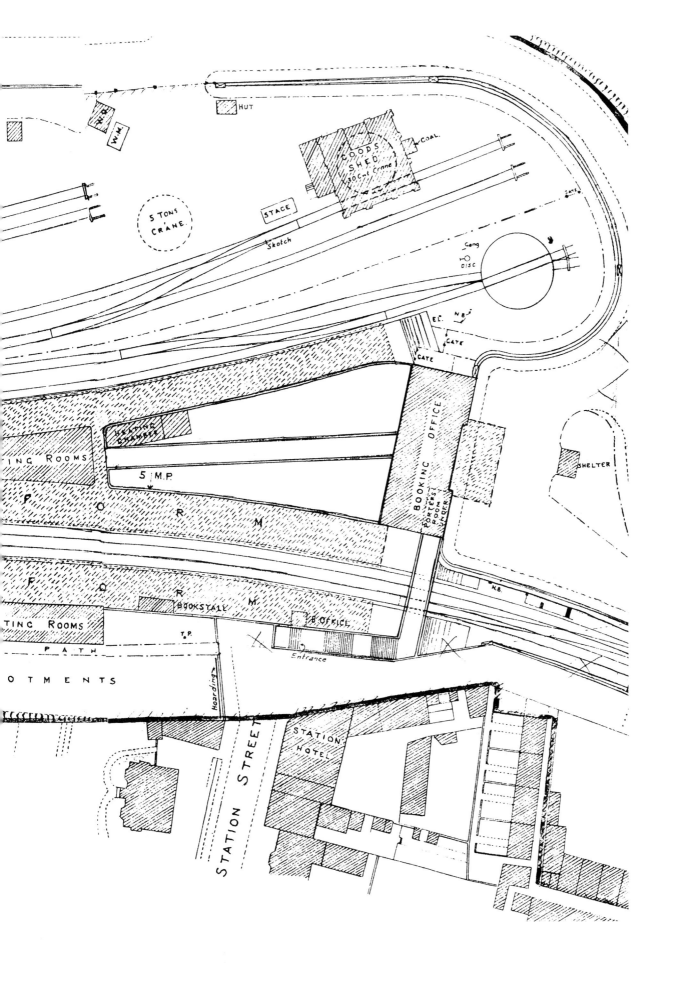

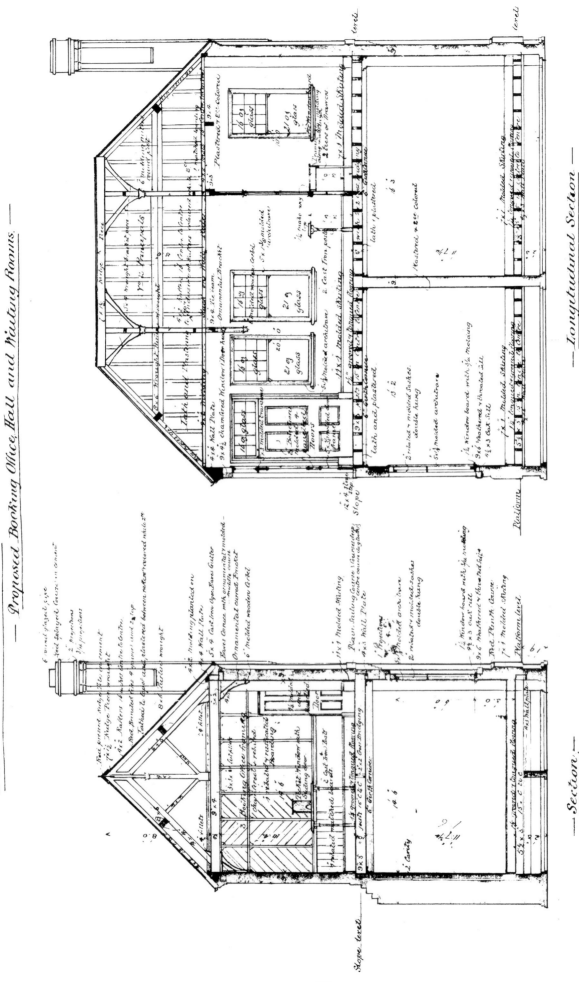

— L. N. W. R. – GRAVELLY HILL. —

— Proposed Booking Office, Hall and Waiting Rooms. —

— Section —

— Longitudinal Section —

The up platform buildings at Gravelly Hill date not from the opening of the line, but from the extension to Lichfield, when the station was improved. These LNWR plans were tendered by Joseph Evans on July 29th 1884. The two storey structure is on a difficult site in a cutting. The well proportioned booking hall, with wooden herring bone panelling and wainscot below, is on the upper floor. The waiting rooms, general and ladies, are eleven feet below at platform level. This building remains largely unaltered today.

(by permission of British Rail)

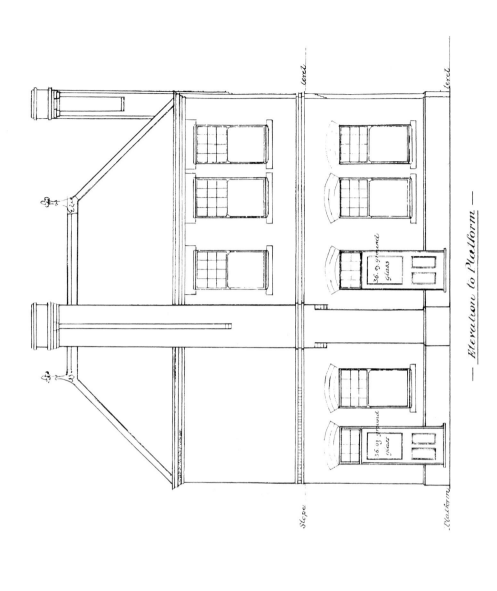

— Elevation to Platform —

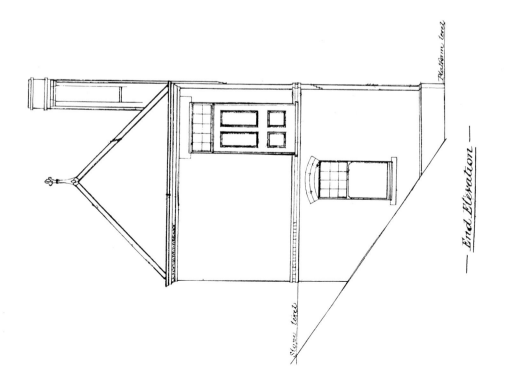

— End Elevation —

73

THE SUTTON COLDFIELD DISASTER, 1955

Sutton Coldfield was the scene of a spectacular tragedy early in 1955. There were no local Sunday services at that time but the line was regularly used as a diversionary route. On Sunday January 23rd the York-Bristol express, travelling at roughly double the permitted speed of 30mph, failed to take the curve at the station, mounted the down platform and demolished some of the platform buildings. All but one of the passenger carriages were steel-bodied standard LMS Stanier vehicles, mercifully, otherwise the death toll from such an impact on a whole rake of wooden stock (eg; Harrow 1952) would have been much higher. Seventeen people died at Sutton, including the fireman and pilot driver. The regular driver did not know the road, so he had taken a pilot on board at Burton-on-Trent, as the rule book demanded. He then rode in the train rather than the loco cab, contrary to the rules, and for this he was criticised at the subsequent enquiry.

The locomotive, a Stanier Black 5 4-6-0 No.45274, ended up on its side on the down platform, the less heavy tender was wrenched adrift and flung further afield. Of the ten carriages the first four were wrecked and the next five derailed. They remained upright, some in the tunnel. Only the final carriage, the other side of the tunnel, remained on the track.

The events were summarised in the March 1955 edition of "Railway Magazine", which stated that prior to the accident there was nothing wrong with the locomotive, coaches or track. At the time of the accident, 4.11pm, it was still full daylight, the weather was fine and clear and the rails were dry.

There were about three hundred passengers on board, twelve of whom were killed outright, with two more fatally injured. The dead included two children, aged five and eight, returning with their parents from a family wedding in Leeds, and five car delivery drivers from Coventry, travelling home together after taking cars for export to Newcastle docks. Both men on the footplate were killed and a driver travelling to work in the train died later. Forty passengers were taken to hospital, twenty-three of whom were detained.

The response of the emergency services was swift because the noise of the crash was heard by officers on duty at the police station, just fifty yards away. They ran to the scene, which confirmed their worst fears, then the superintendent returned immediately to raise the alarm. The first fire engine arrived within eight minutes, followed two minutes later by the first three ambulances, then the first doctor. By 5.00pm seventeen fire service vehicles, sixteen doctors, a blood transfusion unit and a mobile surgical unit were at the scene. Twenty-one ambulances were busy ferrying casualties to hospital, twelve more were standing by and up to seventy police were on duty. The last of the injured were out of the train by 7.00pm and the last body was recovered at 11.30pm the following day. Normal train services were resumed on Wednesday morning.

As is usual in such large scale tragedies, lying behind the bare facts were acts of bravery and courage by ordinary people suddenly catapulted into the middle of a crisis. Master Pilot

The scene on the morning after the crash, Monday 24th January, with clearing up operations under way. No.45274 lies on its side next to the first of ten carriages, the only wooden-bodied vehicle in the train. The forces which acted upon the train at the moment of derailment resulted in the tender being wrenched apart from the locomotive and flung ahead of it. It lies out of camera range, to the left.

(courtesy B'ham Post & Mail : A.Holme-Barnett collection)

A.Kepczynski, a Polish veteran of the Battle of Britain, had been travelling near the front of the train. After rescuing two terrified children he organised his RAF colleagues into a rescue team, then worked with great determination and energy until he collapsed.

Both the official Accident Reports, by the Warwickshire Police Force and the Ministry of Transport and Civil Aviation, mention Arthur Attenborough. He was a ticket collector, travelling to work at New Street in the last carriage with the guard. After the impact the last thing Arthur thought of was himself; the first thing he realised was that a northbound diverted express was due and that Sutton signal box would not be manned, it was 'switched out' with its signals at clear during Sunday working. He ran through the tunnel and along the platform, somehow forcing his mind to ignore the carnage, and arrived at the signal box. There he found another railwayman who had been on his way to work, fireman Derek Smith, dazed and badly shocked, attempting to do something but unable to speak. Arthur told him which levers to push back, and in what order, to set the signals to danger. At the same time he rang the general alarm bell code to alert all neighbouring boxes. By this time Derek had recovered sufficiently to place detonators on the track. Two years earlier he had found himself in a similar situation in Derbyshire, when he alerted a signalman who was able to stop a train before it reached the site of a collapsed culvert under the track. For that he was rewarded with one guinea (£1.05).

Mrs.Marjorie Fairey, a Red Cross nurse, was painting her house overlooking the line when she heard the noise of the crash in the distance. Her son saw the northbound train and yelled to his mother, who jumped onto the track waving frantically.

It was a close call. The driver of the northbound express noticed that Sutton distant signal was clear when he first looked for it. This was only to be expected as he knew that Sutton box was switched out. Had he then been distracted for any reason his train would have gone on to increase the wreckage and add to the death toll. Glancing at the signal again he saw that it had reverted to danger, so a full brake application was made. The Ministry report said that this train stopped 470 yards short of the accident, or, as the "Daily Mirror" put it:-

> "The woman in jeans ran down the track wildly waving her arms to the oncoming train. The driver saw her and crashed on his brakes. His train screamed to a standstill only 200yards from the wrecked express."

These then are some of the sad facts about the Sutton accident. When researching this event what interested me as much as the crash, with its mixture of tragedy and bravery, was the primitive working practices still in force. Here was an irregular sharp curve through a station of some importance, subject to a permanent speed limit of 30mph, with a general radius of 15 chains (330yds) and a short knuckle whose radius was only 8.25 chains (181.5yds) and there were no warning signs to aid drivers' route memory!

One of the two steam cranes on duty grapples with the mutilated remains of the wooden bodied carriage over the top of the wrecked locomotive.

(Colin Smalley collection)

This was nothing unusual. Over the previous hundred years the technology of rail safety had developed, particularly the signalling; from the first basic signals, through fully interlocking manual systems to colour light signals. Apart from signalling, other aids to safety were often primitive or non-existent. It was not considered necessary, for example, for railmen working on the track to wear something bright so as to be more easily seen by train crews, not that many of them could see too clearly in any event. Apart from the smoke, steam locomotives were not always designed with clear forward vision as a priority. Even if you leaned out, much of the road ahead would be hidden by up to a hundred tons of steel. At night, especially if it were cloudy, moonless or away from any town, the darkness was total. Judging speed was, even to the most experienced and skilled railwayman, nothing more than an inspired guess, as most steam locomotives were not fitted with a speedometer until well after the Second World War. The fact that every day thousands of railwaymen worked perfectly safely in such circumstances is the greatest possible tribute to their expertise, commitment and dedication.

Before the Second World War the LNER had seen fit to erect permanent speed restriction signs at some locations, initially on busier lines where the restriction was markedly slower than the general line speed. The signs were of the now familiar type, with metal cut-out figures. They were still confined to the former LNER system at the time of the Sutton crash, and in any case if you did not reduce speed until you saw the sign you were too late. "Knowing the road" in railway terms meant just that; every quirk, every speed restriction, every farmers crossing, every potential hazard of any kind, come rain, come shine, come inky black night. Those whose memory lapsed, even for a moment, risked paying the ultimate price, as did the Sutton driver.

Two years after Sutton, in April 1957, the "Railway Magazine" reported that:-

> "British Railways is to adopt as standard the former LNER type of lineside sign, with metal cut-out figures, as an aid to drivers to indicate the commencing point of permanent speed restrictions. Some 11 250 signs will be needed and their general introduction is expected to prove of considerable value in view of higher speeds which will develop under the Modernisation Plan."

An overview of the wreckage, as clearing up continues. The improvised beams and planks, which aided the removal of stretcher-borne casualties, are still in position. The way in which the carriage on the left has been almost buried by others underlines the horror of the scene. Beyond, the wooden bodied carriage has gone, but the loco is still there.
(Colin Smalley collection)

This was a start, and in accordance with the recommendations of the official Ministry of Transport & Civil Aviation Report into the Sutton crash, chaired by Lieutenant Colonel G.R.S.Wilson. It would be many years, after another crash due to excessive speed, which this time cost six lives and also took place on a curve through a station (Morpeth, May 7th 1969), before the next

logical step was taken. That Accident Report, by Colonel J.R.H.Robertson (HMSO, January 1973) recommended a positive advance warning of speed restrictions, illuminated at night and reinforced with an audible warning in the locomotive cab. Over five hundred such boards came into use on BR, a permanent legacy of the tragedies at Morpeth and, indirectly, at Sutton.

PUSH-PULLS, DIESELS, SMALL BOYS AND MOTORISTS

When British Railways came into existence, on 1st January 1948, the Birmingham-Lichfield line of the former LMS was, like so many others, in a rundown condition. Most suburban lines outside the London area had become working museum pieces, a situation brought about over more than two decades by lack of investment, increased road competition, the war, and post-war austerity.

The sort of train that operated between Birmingham and Lichfield at nationalisation had been a more or less familiar sight for decades. Those who can remember such things may do so with a degree of fondness induced by the passage of years and the onset of nostalgia, but the reality was quite different. The carriages were wooden bodied pre-war LMS stock, without benefit of corridors or toilets. The lack of toilets presented few problems on short journeys, and the lack of corridors made for fewer social problems than would be the case today; these compartments were ideal for graffiti artists or attacks on lone passengers, but instances of such behaviour were rare.

The carriages were a grimy crimson lake. Occasionally one would be re-painted, when it could briefly be seen at its best. The red was then quite smart and there was an unbroken length of black and yellow lining at door handle height, and a single yellow line above the windows. The roof almost managed to be silver and everything below platform level was an unassuming matt black. This smart appearance never lasted long and each carriage soon managed once again to blend with its scruffy fellows. Incredibly, such stock, the design modernised only in detail, was built until 1960.

Internally this stock boasted few amenities. The heavy slam doors closed with a force that could cripple unwary fingers. Each door window opened by a sharp tug on a leather strap which wrested the window frame off its ledge so that it could be lowered into a cavity in the door panel. There were holes in the strap and the amount of ventilation was adjusted by placing the brass knob fixed on the door frame through the desired hole. Normally there were two air vents in the roof and three naked light bulbs. Each compartment had longitudinal seating stuffed with horsehair. The material was a dark red and one common design involved interlocking chevrons in various shades. It was quite comfortable, but with two major faults; it gave no support to the small of the back and it was almost invariably dirty even when it appeared clean, because of the all-pervasive grime from the steam locomotives. Travelling by train in good clothes could be difficult. Ladies wearing gloves were at particular risk.

Below the seats were the heating pipes, supplying steam direct from the engine and controlled from within the carriage. These made the compartments very cosy in winter, although the frequent seepage of steam as the stock grew older and less cared for meant that trains left stations shrouded in white, sometimes inside as well as out.

In the panel above the seats were sepia photographs which were at least thirty years old, and a mirror. Finally, near the roof, four brackets on each side supported a sagging string luggage rack. Each window could be covered by a spring loaded roller blind at night, in reality they were more likely to be used at any time of day when the compartment was occupied by a courting couple.

One carriage in a typical train formation would be a composite, with the middle three compartments designated first class. They were wider than third class, permitting greater leg room, occupancy was restricted to six, the seats had arm rests and headwings and were covered in attractive blue chintz material, trimmed with braid. Few people travelled in them, even fewer with valid tickets.

The guard's van would be familiar to those who know the layout of one on a first generation diesel multiple unit; they were very similar. The main difference was the greater volume and variety of things carried in steam days, often including large wicker baskets of pigeons, assorted parcels and at least one bicycle. Much of this traffic was regular and destined for local shops. For example, the first train of the day from Birmingham generally carried fresh cream etc. for bakeries and cafes and at least one box of Grimsby fish for the fishmongers at Mere Green - hopefully these two consignments were kept well apart - to be despatched by one of the three delivery vehicles that worked out of Four Oaks.

The locomotive for such a train, between Birmingham and Lichfield, was almost always a Class 2 Ivatt 2-6-2 tank engine. Built in the immediate post war years, from 1946, these sturdy little machines did duty on many LMS suburban and branch line services. The locos were worked by men from Aston and Monument Lane sheds. On the rare occasions when an Ivatt tank was not available a substitute was obtained from Walsall's Ryecroft shed. They naturally sent a loco they did not want themselves, sometimes an ancient 0-4-4 parallel boiler Webb tank which was returned from whence it came as soon as possible. Burton crews handled the line's through services to Derby, which were usually pulled by ex-Midland 4-4-0 Compounds.

The service north of Sutton Coldfield was erratic and sparse. The highlight of the commuting day in the early 1950s was the 8am 'express' from Lichfield (08.18 from Four Oaks), which served all stations to Wylde Green, then ran non-stop to New Street (except for ticket collection at Duddeston). An all-stations train left Lichfield for Birmingham ten minutes behind the express, but after this flush of excitement there was nothing for Birmingham until mid-morning.

Trains were more frequent south of Sutton, but there was no such thing as a regular interval service. This was true for all the local lines in the Midlands and, with the exception of the electrified parts of the former Southern Railway, for almost every line throughout the country. Most local railway services were becoming little-used relics of a former age, and their inability to move with the times resulted in many unnecessary victims for Beeching's bonfire.

By 1954 the quality of service on the Lichfield line could no longer satisfy the rising expectations of the increasing numbers of commuters. At the 1951 census the population of Sutton stood at 47,000, more than double the 1931 figure. Many professional people had moved to the expanding northern suburbs of Sutton. The most efficient link between home and office, a decent train service, was sadly lacking. Local British Railways management were aware of the need to improve what was even then the busiest commuter line into Birmingham. An hourly regular interval steam hauled service was introduced between Birmingham and Sutton Coldfield in 1954. This was extended to Four Oaks in a matter of weeks, following complaints from would-be passengers, and the trains terminated in the bay platform there. The standard push-pull formation was used, the rolling stock continued to be scruffy, but overnight the service became frequent and reliable. "Push-pull" trains were distinguished by the end windows in the guard's compartment at the rear, which became the front when the loco pushed from behind. The locomotive did all the work, of course, but when pushing its movements were controlled from this compartment. This removed the need for the engine to detach and run round the train at termini, saving valuable minutes and making it easier to run a regular interval service. There are now many diesel and

Lightly loaded, short distance local trains were often operated on the push-pull system. More correctly known as 'motor trains', these usually consisted of two coaches and a small tank engine. One of the coaches was adapted to provide accomodation for the driver, from where he could see the road and drive the locomotive through a system of mechanical linkages. Such a train, with LMS period III motor driving brake third leading, arrives at Chester Road on a service to Four Oaks in the summer of 1955. *(A.R.Spencer)*

The fireman, of course, remained on the locomotive to maintain the fire and generally keep an eye on things. He is seen here casually leaning from the cab as Ivatt 2-6-2T No. 41320 gets the train under way again. *(A.R.Spencer)*

The first diesel in public service to arrive at Lichfield City was the 06.30 from Birmingham on 5th March 1956. Seen shortly after arrival at 07.15 the train is comprised of three two-car sets of Derby suburban (class 127) dmus, with driving trailer composite M79653 leading. The lack of ceremony is in marked contrast to events surrounding electrification 36 years later. *(A.R.Spencer)*

electric high speed successors to the steam push-pull trains, and the driving trailer vehicles (DVTs) on the East and West Coast Main Lines look remarkably like locomotives.

Steam push-pulls at Sutton meant that it was as easy to remember the times of the trains as of the competing "Midland Red" buses, which had run at regular intervals for years. Not surprisingly, usage increased. In 1955 there were about 750,000 passengers, which averages out at approximately 2,390 per day (there were no Sunday trains). This made it the most healthy suburban service operating out of New Street, the best of a sickly bunch. It was the prime candidate for the new diesel multiple units that were just being built. The service was completely dieselised, without ceremony, as from Monday March 5th 1956. As the "Railway Magazine" for April put it:-

> "Two-car diesel sets replaced steam trains on the Birmingham - Sutton Coldfield - Lichfield services on the LMR on March 5th. They each seat 9 first class and 105 third class passengers and are equipped with toilets; heating is by oil burning combustion heater. There are ten more services daily than hitherto from Lichfield to Birmingham and eleven more in the opposite direction, while the Sutton Coldfield - Birmingham services have been increased by eight each way. The journey time has been accelerated by 2 - 6 minutes."

There were now 35 down and 36 up trains linking Four Oaks with Birmingham each weekday. This was among the first dieselised lines in the country. There had been a temporary diesel service linking New Street with Castle Bromwich for visitors to the British Industries Fair in 1954, and some rural branch lines in Cumberland saw their first dmus that winter. The first urban diesel service began between Leeds and Bradford in June 1954, which resulted in 80,000 extra passengers in the first four months, bringing in an extra £4,500 revenue (average fare, 18p!).

There was a half-hourly service from Birmingham to Four Oaks, hourly to Lichfield, with a limited Sunday service at half this frequency. Day returns to Birmingham were 1/4d (7p) from Four Oaks, 1/7d (8p) from Sutton and a dizzy 2/11d (14.5p) from Lichfield. The new trains were clean, fast and reliable, sporting a dark green livery with yellow whiskers over the buffers in the days before yellow end warning panels. During 1958 the number of passenger journeys rose to 2.5 million, a round average of 48,100 per week, or 6,850 per day, not allowing for smaller numbers on Sundays.

Brian Clarke, a fireman at Monument Lane in 1956, recalled the atmosphere when the diesel service began and the new trains were allocated to the former carriage shed there:-

> "We thought that the diesel shed was very modern then, but it was primitive compared to today. There

Table 69

BIRMINGHAM, SUTTON COLDFIELD AND LICHFIELD

(First extract — summer 1953)

WEEKDAYS

Stations (with mileage): 0 BIRMINGHAM (New Street) dep. · 1¼ Vauxhall and Duddeston · 2¼ Aston · 4 Gravelly Hill · 5 Erdington · 5¼ Chester Road · 6¼ Wylde Green · 7¼ SUTTON COLDFIELD · 8¼ Four Oaks · 10¼ Blake Street · 13¼ Shenstone · 16¼ LICHFIELD (City) arr. · 17½ 72 LICHFIELD (Trent Valley) arr.

Train	Birm	Vaux	Aston	Grav Hill	Erd	Chester Rd	Wylde	Sutton	Four Oaks	Blake	Shenstone	Lich City	Lich TV
a.m.	6 22	6 25	6 29	6 33	6B42	6 45	6 48	6 53	6 58	7 3	7 8	7 15	7 38
a.m.	7 50	7 53	7 57	8 1	8 5	8 8	8 11	8 16	8 20	8 25	8 30	8 37	8 53
a.m.	8 50	8 54	8 58	9 2	9 6	9 9	9 12	9 17	9 22	9 27	9 32	9 39	9 43
a.m.	9 45	9 48	9 53	…	…	…	…	…	…	…	…	10 52	10 56
Via Walsall (Table 72)													
12 10 pm	12 10	12 13	12 17	12 21	12 25	12 28	12 31	12 36	12 41	…	…	…	…
12 25 pm SX	12 25	12 28	12 32	12 36	12 40	12 43	12 46	12 52	12 56	1 1	1 6	1 13	1 44
12 45 pm SO	12 45	12 48	12 52	12 56	1 0	1 3	1 6	1 11	1 15	1 20	1 25	1 32	…
1 15 pm SO	1 15	1 18	1 22	1 26	1 30	1 33	1 36	1 40	1 45	…	…	…	…
1 20 pm SO	1 20	1 23	1 27	…	…	…	…	…	…	…	…	…	…
2 24 pm	2 24	2 27	2 31	2 34	2 39	2 42	2 45	2 49	2 53	2 58	3 3	3 10	3G28
Via Walsall (Table 72)												2 21	2 25
4 12 pm	4 12	4 15	4 19	…	…	…	…	…	…	…	…	…	…
4 18 pm SO	4 18	4 21	4 25	4 29	4 33	4 36	4 39	4 43	4 47	4 52	4 57	5 4	5 19
4 48 pm	4 48	4 51	4 55	4 59	5 3	5 6	5 9	5 14	5 18	5 23	5 28	5 35	5 19
5 17 pm SO	5 17	…	…	…	…	…	5 30	5 35	5 40	5 45	5 50	5 57	…
5 27 pm SX	5 27	5 30	5 34	5 38	5 42	5 45	5 48	5 52	5 56	6 1	6 6	6 13	…
5 42 pm SX	5 42	5 46	5 51	5 56	6 0	6 3	6 7	6 12	6 17	…	…	…	…
6 2 pm	6 2	6 5	6 11	6 15	6 19	6 22	6 26	6 30	6 34	6 39	6 44	6 51	6 54
6 35 pm SX (Via Walsall, Table 72)	6 35	6 38	6 42	…	…	…	…	…	…	…	…	7 41	…

WEEKDAYS — continued

Train	Birm	Vaux	Aston	Grav Hill	Erd	Chester Rd	Wylde	Sutton	Four Oaks	Blake	Shenstone	Lich City	Lich TV
6 45 pm SX	6 45	6 48	6 52	6 56	7 0	7 3	7 6	7 10	7 15	…	…	…	…
7 33 pm	7 33	7 36	7 40	7 44	7 48	7 51	7 54	7 59	8 3	8 8	8 13	8 20	…
8 37 pm (Via Walsall, Table 72)	8 37	8 40	8 44	…	…	…	…	…	8	…	8 18?	9 42	8 56
9 20 pm	9 20	9 23	9 27	9 31	9 35	9 38	9 41	9 45	9 50	…	…	…	9 45
10 0 pm SX	10 0	10 3	10 7	10 11	10 15	10 18	10 21	10 26	10 30	10 2?	…	10 43	10 56
10 30 pm SO	10 30	10 33	10 37	10 41	10 45	10 48	10 51	10 56	11 0	11 5	11 10	11 17	10 56

SUNDAYS

Train	Birm	Vaux	Aston	Grav Hill	Erd	Chester Rd	Wylde	Sutton	Four Oaks	Blake	Shenstone	Lich City	Lich TV
9 25 am (Via Walsall, Table 72)	9 25	9 28	9 32	…	…	…	…	…	…	…	…	10 19	…
11 55 am	11 55	11 58	12 2	…	12 8	12 11	12 14	12 19	12 24	…	…	12 37	…
2 25 pm	2 25	2 28	2 32	…	2 38	2 41	2 44	2 49	2 53	…	…	3 6	…
2 55 pm	2 55	2 58	…	…	3 8	3 11	3 14	3 19	3 24	…	…	…	…
3 25 pm	3 25	3 28	3 32	…	3 38	3 41	3 44	3 49	3 54	…	…	4 7	…
4 55 pm (Via Walsall, Table 72)	4 55	4 58	5 2	…	5 8	5 11	5 14	5 19	5 24	…	…	4 7	…
6 55 pm	6 55	…	…	…	7 4	7 7	7 10	7 14	7 19	…	…	…	…
7 40 pm (Via Walsall, Table 72)	7 40	7 43	7 47	…	…	…	…	…	…	…	…	8 46	…
8 55 pm	8 55	…	…	…	9 4	9 7	9 10	9 14	9 19	…	…	…	…
10 55 pm	10 55	…	…	…	11 4	11 7	11 10	11 14	11 19	…	…	…	…

Table 69

BIRMINGHAM, SUTTON COLDFIELD AND LICHFIELD

(Second extract — regular interval diesel service from March 1956)

WEEKDAYS

Birmingham (New Street) departures: 6 30, 7 0, 7 41, 8 0, 8 33, 9 3, 9 30, 9 45, 10 0, 10 30, 11 0, 11 33, 12 10 (SX), 12 12 (SO), 12 33 (SX), 12 43 (SO), 1 0, 1 20 (SO), 1 30, 2 0, 2 25, 3 0, 3 30, 4 0, 4 17 (SX), 4 33 (SO), 4 55 a.m./p.m.

Lichfield (City) arrivals for the above: 7 15, …, 8 24, 8 49, 9 16, …, 10 13, 10 52, …, 12 16, 12 53, 1 16, 1 26, 1 43, …, 2 21, 2 13, …
Lichfield (Trent Valley) arrivals: 7 38, …, 8 56, 9 45, …, 10 56, 10 56, …, 12804?, 1 9, …, 2 25, …, 3G32, …, 5 24, 5 24

WEEKDAYS — continued

Birmingham (New Street) departures: 5 17 (SX), 5 27 (SX), 5 42, 6 0, …, 6 30, 6 38, …, 7 0, 7 30, 8 0, 8 40, 9 0, 9 30, 10 0, …, 10 30 …
Lichfield (City) arrivals: 5 52, 6 10, …, 6 43, …, 7 13, 7 42, …, 8 13, …, 9 30, …, 10 13, …, 11 13
Lichfield (Trent Valley): 6 49 …

SUNDAYS

Birmingham (New Street) departures: 8 0, 9 0, 10 0, 12 (noon), 12 0, 2 0, 3 0, 4 0, 5 0, 6 0, 7 0, 7 40, 8 0, 9 0, 10 30 (a.m./p.m.)
Lichfield (City) arrivals: 8 37, 10 15, 10 37, 12 37, 2 37, 3 37, …, 4 37, …, 6 37, …, 8 32, 8 40

A—Arrives 4 minutes earlier.
B—Arrives 5 minutes earlier.
C—Arrives 6 minutes earlier.
D—Arrives 7 minutes earlier.
F—On Fridays departs Lichfield (T.V.) 9.1 p.m., Lichfield (City) 9.8 p.m.
G—On Saturdays arrives Lichfield (T.V.) 3.36 p.m.
J—2 minutes later on Mondays to Fridays.
SO—Saturdays only.
SX—Saturdays excepted.

Two time-table extracts that say more than a thousand words about the transformation of the Sutton line service in the 1950s. The first shows the irregular and infrequent summer time-table for 1953. Notice the huge gaps in the off-peak service. There were, for example, no departures for the Sutton line from New Street between 08.50 and 12.10. The second extract is from the regular interval diesel service which began in March 1956. The service to Lichfield was still supplemented by a few steam workings via Walsall.

(courtesy of British Rail and John Hicks)

were no fork lifts, no facilities to change bogies or engines, they had to go away for all the heavy work and anything that required the unit to be lifted. They could change a cylinder head, gasket, radiator, fuel pump, that sort of thing. They were very much feeling their way, as Monument Lane was a pilot scheme. When it opened with about twenty-five units, all for the Sutton line, it was the largest diesel shed in the country!

When the diesels arrived they created some job opportunities at the shed at first because rosters formerly worked by Aston and Burton men were now dieselised. There was a lot of excitement when almost en block the senior hands were chosen to operate the diesels, and some of the junior hands were promoted to steam express work. In 1956 driving a new dmu was seen by many drivers as superior to driving a steam express.

There had even been excitement before the service began. When the diesels were first delivered the shed at Monument Lane was not fully ready and between driver training runs some of the units were stabled in the sidings at Four Oaks. Some passengers, when they saw the new trains, actually went to the booking office and asked for tickets specifically to ride in 'those new diesels', which of course they could not.

For the next few years there was no new uniform to match the new trains. The drivers wore overalls and the standard hat with a shiny top, just as though they were in a steam cab."

There was one small welcome addition to the diesel driver's uniform, a sturdy leather satchel to contain the control handle, reversing lever amd various keys, which became standard issue in 1957.

That same summer the Scout Jamboree, more correctly the "World Jubilee Jamboree of the Scout Movement" was held in Sutton Park between August 1st and 12th. This was the first and only time that a scouting event had been planned on such a scale, and 100,000 visitors were expected. (About 80,000 actually came.) Most of them would arrive by rail, so the handling of such numbers required careful groundwork. There were three stations convenient for the park - Sutton Coldfield, Sutton Park and Streetly. Sutton Coldfield had been enjoying its half hourly diesel service for over a year, but the other two stations, on the ex-Midland Sutton Park line, only had a minimal rush hour service, so they were given a brief lick of paint and then asked to bear the brunt of the influx of boys, small and not so small, who came from "87 parts of the world" as the plaque in the park records, on all sorts of special trains.

The normal signalling on the Sutton Park line was supplemented by special temporary signals controlled from equally temporary block posts at Streetly and Penns stations. The 'block posts' were small and basic signal cabins, which made it possible for trains to operate with just four minutes between them. The one at Penns was an asbestos lined lamp storage hut which would definitely not pass muster today.

The boys did not merely arrive by train and then stay put for the duration. Some stayed for a few days, others came on day excursions. August 6th was a special day for the Cubs, thirty thousand of them, two thirds of whom arrived on 23 special trains, the bulk of the remainder by road coach. Having made camp the boys were entertained by visits - most of them by train - to such places as Cadburys or Coventry, where the new cathedral was in the early stages of construction.

After the Jamboree the dispersal of so many boys over two days needed almost military precision. They were each given a boarding card showing their departure station. Those for Sutton Coldfield were coloured red, and Scouts were asked to be at the station an hour before departure time.

An immaculate but practically deserted Streetly station, on the Sutton Park line, receives an ordinary service train bound for Birmingham, at the time of the World Scout Jamboree, August 1957. The signal is temporary, and the temporary block post hut can be seen at the far end of platform 2. The leading coach is a motor driving brake third for push-pull working, and presumably the second vehicle is its normal partner. The only explanation for these two forming part of a four coach train, conventionally hauled by Ivatt 2-6-2T No.41224, is the necessity to make up longer trains to cope with the demands of the Jamboree.   (A.R.Spencer)

Trains came and went from all parts of the country, pulled by a wide variety of express steam locomotive types - 'Royal Scots', including 46169 "The Boy Scout"; 'Jubilees'; and BR Standard 'Britannias' including 70045 "Lord Rowallan" (the Chief Scout). The Jamboree was the last special occasion on which such a wide variety of steam locomotives could be seen in large numbers in the Midlands; absolute bliss for the train-spotters of the day, few of whom could have imagined that main line steam would be extinct on British Railways just eleven years later.

It may seem remarkable to some that as late as 1957 the railways were still carrying such a large total percentage of people to a unique event like this. Car ownership was growing inexorably but the railway was - and remains - well suited to move large numbers of people, even when they are not commuting. Consider:- in 1957, despite the growth in road traffic, more people travelled to their summer holidays in Devon and Cornwall by rail than in any other year before or since; today the International Motor Show at Birmingham's National Exhibition Centre could not function properly if the majority of its visitors did not arrive by rail.

The car was responsible for the next development at Sutton Coldfield, which was chosen as the Midland terminus of a new Car-Sleeper service to Stirling in 1958 (the term "Motorail" was not in common official use before 1967). It was convenient for motorists, with good road links even then. The former branch terminus was an ideal site for loading cars into the specially converted vans.

The Sutton service normally operated overnight. The train engine waited in the bay platform with the sleeping cars, alongside the car vans, as in the photograph. At departure the loco and sleeping cars reversed onto the main line, then drew forward into the down platform. A second engine pulled the car vans out of their siding, then pushed them forward to be attached to the main train, which proceeded on its way, running via Lichfield and Wichnor Junction. Motorail trains had to be routed carefully as the cars were driven in at one end of the rake of vans and out at the other. The front van at Sutton had to be the rear van at Stirling, facing the unloading ramp, so that cars could be driven off without having to reverse through the vans! At first there was accommodation for twenty cars and eighty-four passengers.

In 1958 the return fare for a car and driver was £14/10/- (£14.50), plus £5 for other adults and £3 for children. Trains ran north on Sundays and Wednesdays, returning on Mondays and Thursdays. By 1961 the service operated on three nights a week and the driver's fare had risen to £19.50. In later years drivers of longer vehicles were charged extra, and those travelling at the height of summer were subjected to a peak surcharge of £1/10/- per carload by 1964. During 1967 the combined Anglo-Scottish Motorail services carried 37,000 cars and 103,000 passengers.

Britannia class 4-6-2, No.70046 'Anzac', simmers gently at Sutton Coldfield while the car sleeper train is loaded in 1959. No.70046, along with No.70048 'The Territorial Army 1908-1958', were transferred from Holyhead to Aston at the start of the summer timetable, specifically to work these heavy trains.

(A.R.Spencer)

The Sutton Motorail survived until 1972, when it was used by four thousand cars and twelve thousand passengers, who could travel direct to Inverness, Newton Abbot and St.Austell, as well as Stirling. The carrying capacity of each train was forty-four cars. Departures and arrivals for that final busy summer were:-
Departures (May 22nd - September 16th)

SUNDAYS	23.15	Stirling
MONDAYS	23.15	Stirling and Inverness
WEDNESDAYS	13.10	Stirling
THURSDAYS	23.15	Stirling
FRIDAYS	23.15	Newton Abbot
SATURDAYS	23.15	St.Austell

Arrivals

SUNDAYS	18.25	St.Austell
MONDAYS	19.45	Stirling
WEDNESDAYS	05.50	Inverness and Stirling
THURSDAYS	05.50	Stirling
FRIDAYS	19.35	Stirling
SATURDAYS	19.00	Newton Abbot

After 1972 Sutton and Newton-le-Willows Motorail terminals were closed, as Crewe was to be developed in their place. Crewe itself now handles no Motorail traffic. Birmingham is the hub of both the motorway and rail networks, yet the Midlands has not been served by Motorail trains since 1972.

DECLINE

For a few years the Birmingham - Lichfield line had the best suburban service in the West Midlands.

Duddeston station was rebuilt in 1956 and the new road level booking hall, staircases and platform buildings, all of reinforced concrete, looked good for a while.

The following year Butlers Lane opened. The "Railway Magazine" reported in November:-

> "A temporary station, Butlers Lane, which has been experimentally installed by the LMR to meet the needs of a housing estate under development, was opened on September 30th. .... The new station consists of two platforms 250ft long, each with a small booking office and waiting shelter. There is a sloping pathway from the road to each platform."

The opening of a new station was an earth shattering event in the 1950s. There were new stations built in that decade, but most appeared on declining rural lines as last ditch attempts to attract extra traffic. They have all now vanished. Butlers Lane is the second oldest station built since the formation of British Railways in 1948 which remains open today. Originally known as Butlers Lane Halt, even though it has always been staffed, this temporary station was constructed entirely of wood. It lasted

Butlers Lane Halt under construction, 1957. *(A.R.Spencer)*

until October 1991, to be replaced by a permanent station on the same site, although the original booking office on the up platform remained until 1993.

Five years after they had started the dmus were still meeting with overwhelming public approval:-

"Over 96% of passengers using the diesel service between Birmingham and Lichfield like it, according to a poll conducted by the London Midland Region of British Railways. The main attractions in order of popularity are increased frequency and regularity, speed, comfort, cleanliness and better visibility. The poll was spread over three days and covered 200 passengers ranging in age from 19 to 74 and including all categories of people. Criticisms, which will be investigated from the point of view of making improvements, covered the heating system (either too hot or too cold) and the difficulty of getting seats at peak times. Young people asked for later trains from Birmingham, and many travellers favoured the introduction of a cheap day single ticket."

("Railway Magazine, June 1961)

A smart updated black uniform was issued to Monument Lane diesel drivers in 1965. It included shirts and ties and was made of the same material as police uniforms. There were three stars on the lapels, and a German style peaked cap in imitation leather, which the drivers refused to wear because rain water ran off it and straight down the back of the neck. One driver on the Four Oaks run was heard to call, "All aboard Von Ryan's Express!" to his passengers, for which he was officially reprimanded.

The service had been improved, passenger levels had risen dramatically, and then - nothing. There were no further developments to keep progress going, despite the continued movement of population to Sutton, where over 8,000 new owner occupied homes had been built during the 1950s. Gradually, almost unnoticed at first, a decline set in.

This was always a passenger line first and foremost, but there had been wagonload goods and parcels traffic. There were yards at Erdington, Chester Road, Sutton Coldfield and Four Oaks, a coal wharf at Blake Street and minimal sidings at Shenstone. As road competition increased traffic fell away. With the spread of smokeless zones the demand for coal fell. By the Beeching era, in the mid 1960s, the railway was actively discouraging such wagonload traffic as remained.

On 18th January 1965 the passenger service north of Lichfield City was withdrawn, as it was on the South Staffs line between Lichfield and Walsall. For the first time Lichfield was on the end of a branch line - the wrong end, with a dwindling service.

The Sunday trains were withdrawn in 1963 as an economy measure, after an attempt to run a reduced train, which was a two car dmu with just one engine running. 'Reduced' meant 'cheap and nasty', and as trains were only two-hourly north of Four Oaks this experiment was doomed to failure.

It had originally been proposed that the Lichfield line should be included in the Midlands' first electrification scheme, completed in 1967, but this was rejected on the grounds of cost. All the local electric trains in the area that were included in that scheme rode on the back of main line services, except for those to Walsall, which had a simple extension beyond newly electrified Bescot yard into just one of the platforms at the town station. Twenty-five years later the Cross City Line became the first passenger railway wholly within the Midlands to be electrified on its own merits.

Meanwhile the drift continued. No money could be found to replace the oil lamps at Blake Street and Shenstone; the service to Lichfield almost became two-hourly and plans were made to single the line north of Four Oaks.

During the early 1970s the stations at Wylde Green, Sutton, Erdington and Chester Road suffered bouts of vandalism and arson. (Erdington suffered a further arson attack on July 26th 1989.) Gravelly Hill became semi-derelict. As an economy measure very little track work was done. This led to a reduction in line speed, which beyond Four Oaks was cut from 60 to 50mph for considerable stretches. Trains still kept to time because of slack schedules and they managed to be faster than buses because the parallel roads and limited stop bus services had not yet been developed.

The original dmus were lightweight units - 57 tons for the two cars, top speed 62mph - and when they were withdrawn or transferred elsewhere they were replaced, for the most part, by ex-Western Region dmus based at Tyseley. These had begun their careers working local trains out of Snow Hill. They were sturdier but heavier and less sprightly than their predecessors, unable to cope with the gradients so well. The time-table had to be eased. Before electrification these three-car trains, mainly Class 116 units, took 23 minutes for the journey between Birmingham and Sutton, a whole two minutes faster than steam in 1862.

As a way of easing congestion at New Street it was decided to experiment by linking the Lichfield service with that to Kidderminster. At the time both places only had hourly trains, calling at all stations. Through running began in 1972 but was not shown clearly in the time-tables until the following year. (The Birmingham - Four Oaks workings continued to be self-contained.) This was a false dawn, and nobody was using the word "Cross City" to describe the service. The route did not follow a natural, established or desired traffic flow across Birmingham and the trains ran merely for operational convenience. Any through passengers were an incidental bonus which the railway had not won by its non-existent publicity or promotional material. Nevertheless a through route across the city did make sense, if only the right choice were made ....

CROSS CITY '78
(The Concept of a Line Across Birmingham : New Works : The Train Service)

THE CONCEPT OF A LINE ACROSS BIRMINGHAM

Official backing for the idea of an electric railway running through the centre of Birmingham dates back at least to the end of 1954. According to the "Railway Magazine" for February 1955:–

"Birmingham Corporation is to investigate the possibility of building a trans-city electric railway about 14 miles long, with a central section underground. In the open the line would use the central reservation of double-carriageway roads, such as the Bristol Road, which until the abandonment of the 3'6" gauge Birmingham tramways carried a reserved-track tramway in the centre. The underground section might have stations at the Horse Fair, New Street Station, Snow Hill Station, the Central Fire Station and Bagot Street".

Nothing came of this scheme, but it left an indirect landmark at Longbridge which is still there. When the Austin car plant

The school holidays have just started as a well-loaded train leaves New Street for Lichfield, July 1970, by which time dmus had been given all-over yellow ends which were much more prominent than the earlier whiskers. At this date the idea of a rail route across Birmingham was beginning to be taken seriously by some. *(P.J.Shoesmith)*

built a covered bridge linking two departments across the Bristol Road, near the junction with Longbridge Lane, it had sufficient clearance to allow for the passage of trains, which at this point would have been on an elevated section, in case the 1954 scheme were ever revised or updated.

During the 1960s Birmingham, along with the rest of the country, experienced a standard of living higher than ever before. People were enjoying a consumer spending boom as all sorts of goods, especially cars, became affordable. Much of the city's economy had been allied to car production since before the First World War and more cars meant more roads to accommodate them. The scheme to build the Inner Ring Road dated from 1943 from an idea first conceived in 1917 and, with no fundamental amendments to the plans, work began on 8th March 1957. The completed road opened on 4th January 1971. This and other projects built during that period – The Aston Expressway, the major underpasses at Five Ways and Birchfield and parts of the Middle Ring Road – meant the demolition of many buildings and banishment of pedestrians to dingy subways, 52 of them on the Inner Ring Road alone. It soon became apparent that the new roads were not solving the problem of traffic congestion, but the authorities were not yet seriously considering alternative forms of

transport. Local trains suffered from lack of investment, and many lines and stations closed in this period. Local buses were victims of congestion, declining use and frequent fare rises.

By 1970 the Lichfield line was attracting more passengers, a rise of 72% since 1966, thanks in part to road congestion but also to generous fare offers which undercut the buses, eg: two adults and two children could travel off peak return between Four Oaks and New St. and still have change from 10/- (50p). That summer Wylde Green became the first park and ride station on the line, which then received an annual grant from central government of £292,000. These were days when the support grant for each socially necessary railway was individually itemised.

South of the city the Redditch line seemed to be taking an unreasonably long time to die. The peak hour trains survived but were not promoted in any way.

During the late 1960s (and again twenty years later) the area around Five Ways experienced a boom in office and service industry accommodation. This was not matched by improved public transport or better parking facilities, resulting in chronic congestion. Many people employed near Five Ways had been relocated from the city centre and felt no longer able to make the journey by public transport.

The idea of a rail service across the city was resurrected around this time. The Railway Development Association published a scheme in September 1970 calling for a new line under the city from Gosta Green to Edgbaston, with stations at Gosta Green, the Law Courts, Colmore Row, Paradise Circus and the Civic Centre. It called for new rolling stock and electrification, the line to be in twin bore concrete tunnels. It was dubbed the 'briefcase special' by the "Evening Mail" (October 1st 1970), which thereby acknowledged its business commuter potential. The price tag of £12 million, even in 1970, was optimistic, and the lack of an interchange station for New St. was a fundamental flaw. Nevertheless it was an idea that could be pursued.

The city council recognised the potential of the A38 corridor (Sutton-Longbridge) through Birmingham where public transport could be developed as a way of easing road congestion. They were uncertain what to do, so called in a firm of consulting engineers – De Leuw, Chadwick, OhEocha – to carry out a rapid transit study. "Rapid Transit" was an exciting new phrase at the time, what would then be called 'trendy', and consultancy was a new growth industry. The scheme was presented to the General Purposes and Public Works Committee in June 1971 and called for a route from Longbridge to Four Oaks, with a new tunnel under the city centre and an elevated section alongside Aston Expressway. The rest of the line would use existing BR tracks. The price tag was £50 million and again there was no connection with New Street Station. This was all rather exotic and expensive. It was left to two letter writers to the "Birmingham Post" (18th June 1971), to add the voice of common sense to the debate. Mrs. Davies of Northfield noted:–

"Since all the tracks and stations are there for the journey from Redditch into the city, I am quite sure the general public would be content to have our old 'slow transit system' back, making the journey from Northfield into the city 15 minutes as opposed to 30 minutes on the bus – if one comes".

While C.K. Retallack of Edgbaston wrote prophetically:–

"I am appalled at the advice which has been given by expert consultants to spend £50 million on a rapid transit system from Four Oaks to Longbridge. It should be obvious to anyone who lives in the city that there is adequate railway track to cope with everything, apart from wasting money on tunnels. The only possible deviation would be a link to serve Longbridge, coupled, one would hope, with the reopening of Five Ways Station and a new station to serve the Queen Elizabeth Hospital and the university. Apart from that the existing track is more than adequate and I would certainly have thought that trains every three minutes is a ludicrous suggestion; something between five and ten minutes is more adequate".

Although the scheme was flawed the concept was good. The word "cross-city" entered the debate in a report by the Railway Development Association in 1972, the same summer as an £11 million elevated Edgbaston Expressway road was proposed along the course of the railway and canal, past the university via Bournville to link with the M5 at Quinton. Happily this monstrosity never left the drawing board.

In February 1973 the West Midlands Passenger Transport Executive (WMPTE) undertook a travel survey on the Redditch line. The letter accompanying the questionnaire announced the intention of upgrading the service, with improved bus interchange and new stations at Longbridge, University and Five Ways. "Car parks will be provided and local bus services will connect with trains at stations". The concept was now in writing in what amounted to a declaration of intent by WMPTE. The survey found that the number of expected daily users would be between 6,000 and 13,000. Even the lower figure had potential on which to build. The PTE Development Report of April 1973 agreed to new stations, modern rolling stock and a train every ten minutes. In the event, only the first of these good intentions proved possible, and no further progress was made for two years. Finally, in May 1975 the West Midlands County Council Passenger Transport Sub-Committee sanctioned improvements to services between Longbridge and Four Oaks, the core of the Redditch-Lichfield line lying within the West Midlands County.

NEW WORKS
The project sanctioned in May 1975 was costed at £5.2 million and was part of a larger £11 million package, which would have included the whole line, plus re-opening of a stub of the Halesowen line as far as Frankley, then being built up as a Birmingham overspill area.

Originally the Redditch branch had come within the West Midlands Passenger Transport Authority area, but the boundary had been re-drawn in 1974 so that it was, for transport financing purposes, within its geographical county of Hereford & Worcester. At that time members of that county council saw little merit, and even fewer votes, in financing rail schemes, and claimed that an improved service to Worcester via Bromsgrove was higher in their priorities than the Redditch line. They saw the Frankley branch, which also lay within their county, as a non-starter. Staffordshire, another classic shire county, adopted a similar attitude to the Lichfield end of the line.

The most visible new works were the stations at Five Ways, University and Longbridge. University attracted particular attention. Although there had never been a station on this site it was anticipated that it would be heavily used by the 11,000 students and staff at the university, together with staff and visitors to the adjacent 780-bed Queen Elizabeth Hospital, which is also next to the city's largest maternity hospital. These hospitals were especially poorly placed for public transport, with only one meandering infrequent bus service that originated in Harborne, not the city centre.

On 11th January 1976, Sidney Weighell, General Secretary of the NUR, dug the first sod for the new station. That same evening, in a live televised transport debate, he countered the arguments of the other panellists, who were pedalling the idea of more roads as the only solution to traffic problems, by telling them what he had done earlier in the day. They gave him the curious sideways glance people use when they think they see an oddball, not realising that they were the ones who were to become out of step with the changing times. Two years later University station was chosen as the site for the opening ceremony of the Cross City service.

Longbridge is a simple two platform station. When the train service began the down platform was finished, the up platform was complete along half its length and the rest of the work had hardly started.

On the quadruple track south of King's Norton the trains were to use the outer or slow lines, not the inner lines as formerly. The island platforms at King's Norton and Northfield became redundant, and there were minor difficulties at both stations. At King's Norton there had been access to the platforms direct from the Station Road bridge. This was to be sealed, a car park and new entrance provided alongside the down platform, with a bus bay on the road bridge. The centre of gravity was shifted, to suit

A Class 37 heads through Northfield with a scrap metal train. The new Cross City platforms are under construction, 12th January 1978. The lamp standards on the island platform are believed to be the only ones of their type on British Rail. *(P.J.Shoesmith)*

the vast majority of new users. This did not stop the existing commuters organising a successful campaign to retain the old entrance to the up platform during the morning peak.

The other stations south of Birmingham were all upgraded in the same materials as the three new ones by D.T.Bullock & Co. of Aldridge. From decaying unstaffed halts they were transformed into as-new fully staffed stations, in a uniform house style. Station staff were committed to the success of the service and many were full of youthful enthusiasm; the station manager at Selly Oak, for example, was only 21 when appointed.

The depot at Tyseley was extended at the cost of £1,163,000 to accommodate the extra three car units that were required. There were now 76 of them stabled here, and almost half (34) were required for the Cross City Line. Tyseley's loco-hauled carriages were dispersed to Oxley and Duddeston and four new servicing roads, one new fuelling road and an extra inspection pit were added to the depot. A stabling siding long enough for a nine-car train was built south of Longbridge, alongside the up main lines, and two stabling sidings were put in at Four Oaks.

Three new crossovers were installed within New Street to allow for more flexibility of working within an already congested station. Northbound Cross City trains were to use Platform 5, and southbound used Platform 12, which had previously been used mainly by parcels trains. A side effect of the Cross City service was increased use of all platforms at New Street,

including the bleak, remote escalatorless extremities, 1 and 12. The exit from the enclosed platform bridge to Station Street, a hole in the wall, was opened for peak commuters when the Cross City service began.

The junctions at Longbridge and south of King's Norton were modified to minimise the risk of conflicting movements between the new service and freight traffic at British Leyland's works and car terminal. Extra signals were installed between University and Proof House Junction, and also south of Four Oaks, to increase line capacity and minimise disruptions to the service.

The stations north of Birmingham required no fundamental alterations, except for Butlers Lane where the platforms were extended - in the same temporary wood as 1957 - to take six car dmus.

Another vital new work was provision of easy interchange with buses and cars, and this particularly affected the outer sections of the line. Bus bays were built, with shelters and clearly marked stops, existing car parks were resurfaced and extended and new ones provided. As a matter of policy all car parks were to be free. At this time all the local lines in the area benefitted from the easily affordable West Midland Travelcard (£3.40 per week, £10 for four weeks), valid on buses and trains. Within the WMPTE area rail journeys were priced on distance, at the same level as comparable bus journeys. All this was common sense, but such thinking was only just beginning to be taken seriously and backed with cash by planning authorities. The Cross City Line and the Tyne & Wear Metro (opened 1980) were pioneers in the integration of different transport modes.

A description of the interchange facilities available in 1978 will illustrate the point:-

LONGBRIDGE	: 1 connecting bus route
NORTHFIELD	: 3 connecting bus routes free parking for 106 cars (increased from 20)
KING'S NORTON	: 7 connecting bus routes free parking for 80 cars (completely new car park)
BOURNVILLE	: 1 connecting bus route
UNIVERSITY	: 1 connecting bus route
SELLY OAK	: 4 connecting bus routes small free car park
FIVE WAYS	: 2 connecting bus routes (many others within a short walk)
DUDDESTON	: 1 connecting bus route
ASTON	: 5 connecting bus routes
GRAVELLY HILL	: no connecting buses
ERDINGTON	: 2 connecting bus routes
CHESTER ROAD	: 4 connecting bus routes
WYLDE GREEN	: free parking for 45 cars
SUTTON COLDFIELD	: bus station a short walk away free parking for 100 cars (increased from 17)
FOUR OAKS	: 4 connecting bus routes free parking for 200 cars (increased from 60)

As the work progressed there were calls from some residents and the Railway Development Association for the existing pathetic service south of Birmingham to be improved in stages, particularly when, in the New Year of 1978, petrol rationing seemed likely for a while. The calls were resisted, rightly, as British Rail and WMPTE realised that they could extract maximum favourable publicity from a big bang rather than a gradual whimper. Everything was ready - more or less - for the opening on Monday 8th May 1978.

THE TRAIN SERVICE

Monday May 8th 1978 dawned grey and cool. A handful of rail enthusiasts arrived at Longbridge in good time for the first train at 6.35am, keen to be at the start of the most significant local rail development in the Midlands since the war. I was the first passenger booked to Five Ways, for which the duty railman on the building site that would soon become Longbridge station issued me with ticket number 00000. There were a few others, like myself, out for the ride, but most people were commuters. The vast majority could not have been seasoned rail commuters, yet they behaved as such, and the atmosphere was curiously matter-of-fact and routine.

The first train ran without ceremony, as the line was officially opened later the same day at University station by William Rogers, Secretary of State for Transport, who later became one of the 'Gang of Four' founder members of the Social Democratic Party. His message is now more relevant than ever:-

> "I particularly welcome the fact that this is a development of an existing line. On the one hand the disruption to the local environment is minimal.
>
> On the other hand, it will provide a large increase in transport capacity in a corridor where it would be extremely difficult and costly to meet present and future needs for travel by building new roads.
>
> I am sure that this new rail service will be of real benefit to many people who find that road congestion within the conurbation is making their local journeys more and more of a burden.
>
> Birmingham is the centre of the car industry, but to rely on motor transport alone is not possible, even here, if we are to have a life really worth living."

People living near the stations south of New Street were issued with vouchers enabling them to enjoy half price rail travel for the first week.

There were four trains an hour between Longbridge and Four Oaks, from around 06.30 to 23.00 (half-hourly north of New Street after 19.00), and a half-hourly service all day on Sundays, the first local Sunday trains on any line in the Birmingham area for over ten years. Many Cross City dmus even sported the smart

Table 55 **Mondays to Saturdays**

Birmingham and Redditch

Service suspended on Bank Holidays 6 June, 7 June, 29 August, 2 January, 27 March and 1 May

Second Class only unless otherwise shown

Miles				A		B SO		SO		SX		C SX		C SO			
0	**Birmingham New Street**	d	..	06 47	..	07 05	..	12 55	..	17 18	..	17 35	..	17 35	..	17 45	..
3¼	Selly Oak	d		06 55		07 13		13 03		17 26		17 43				17 53	
4½	Bournville	d	..	06 58	..	07 16	..	13 06	..	17 29	..	17 46	..	..	..	17 56	..
5½	King's Norton	d		07 01		07 19		13 09		17 32				17 46		17 59	
7	Northfield	d	..	07 05	..	07 23	..	13 13	..	17 36	..	17 52	..	17 50	..	18 03	..
10½	Barnt Green	d		07 12		07 30		13 20		17 43		17 58		17 57		18 10	
12¼	Alvechurch	d	..	07 18	..	07 36	..	13 26	..	17 49	..	..	..	..	..	18 16	..
15¼	**Redditch**	a		07 25		07 43		13 33		17 56						18 23	

Miles			D SO	E				SX		SO							
0	**Redditch**	d	..	..	..	07 58	..	08 15	..	13 40	..	18 35	..	..	..	..	..
3	Alvechurch	d				08 06		08 23		13 48		18 43					
4¾	Barnt Green	d	08 02	08 04	..	08 12	..	08 29	..	13 54	..	18 49	..	..	..	..	..
8¼	Northfield	d	08 08	08 12		08 18		08 35		14 00		18 55					
9¾	King's Norton	d	08 11	08 15	..	08 21	..	08 38	..	14 03	..	18 58	..	..	..	..	..
10¾	Bournville	d	08 14	08 18		08 24		08 41		14 06		19 01					
12	Selly Oak	d			..	08 27	..	08 44	..	14 09	..	19 04	..	..	..	..	..
15¼	**Birmingham New Street**	a	08 25	08 30		08 37		08 54		14 19		19 14					

For general notes see pages 2-4

A Not Saturdays 7 May to 1 October

B Until 1 October

C To Hereford arr. 19 19 (Table 67). First and Second Class

D From 8 October. From Worcester Shrub Hill dep. 07 29 (Table 67)

E Mondays to Fridays throughout, also Saturdays until 1 October. From Gloucester dep. 06 55 to Leeds arr. 11 18 (Table 51). First and Second Class

No Sunday service

Things could only get better. The complete Birmingham-Redditch time-table for 1977-78, prior to the start of the Cross City service in May 1978.

(courtesy of British Rail)

New Travellers make friends with FARE FOR TWO to Birmingham New Street

This day return bargain is just the rail ticket for two adults (or one adult and up to two children) who are travelling to Birmingham New Street and returning together. So don't keep the shops and entertainments to yourself – take a friend, or the kids, with a Fare for Two ticket on the Cross-City Line.

From		
Longbridge **50p**		Four Oaks **60p**
Northfield **40p**		Sutton Coldfield **50p**
King's Norton **35p**		Wylde Green **40p**
Bournville **35p**		Chester Road **35p**
Selly Oak **30p**		Erdington **35p**
University **30p**		Gravelly Hill **30p**
		Aston **30p**

Available on any train after 09.30 Mondays to Fridays and on any train Saturdays, Sundays and Bank Holidays. Return on any train the same day.

Promoting the Cross City Line with a Fare for Two, May 1978
(courtesy of British Rail)

new WMPTE livery of all-over white with a dark blue waist band. This was a brave try but thoroughly impractical, as most children could have told them, and was soon abandoned in favour of something that showed the dirt less. Originally the all-white scheme was to have included an apple green roof colouring!

The service was up and running, the term "Cross City" was entering the vocabulary and people were soon wondering how on earth they had managed without it. Even casual observation at New Street showed healthy numbers of passengers remaining in their seats on journeys through that station - office workers from Four Oaks to Five Ways, people with homes in the north of the city who worked at Cadburys or British Leyland, nurses, students and hospital visitors commuting to University - and there were some unexpected new traffic flows, one very short and very noticeable. Brian Clarke remembered that:-

> "Particularly in fine weather there would be a mid-
> day surge of use between Five Ways and New
> Street as office workers used their season tickets to
> nip into the city centre for a bite to eat, a spot of
> shopping or just to sunbathe in the cathedral
> gardens."

It would be a mistake to think that, after its launch, the Cross City Line had a trouble free existence. There were many problems between May 1978 and the end of the diesel service, most of which were caused by inadequate resources and the need to expand.

Even before the service began concern was being expressed about the time-table. Difficulties with line capacity between King's Norton and New Street meant that InterCity and mail trains had priority and the far more numerous Cross City trains had to be fitted round their schedules. The regular interval service pattern could not be followed exactly. Worse was the layover time in New Street, sometimes as much as eight minutes, and the omission of stops, often Bournville, whenever a train needed to be speeded up slightly because of an InterCity running on its tail. This took two years to cure but, as more than one driver has told me, the skipping of station stops was more of a nuisance on paper than in practice because, "We realised it would be a problem for the passengers, so most of us used to call at all stations anyway".

The line opened at a time when other local services were carrying large increases in passengers, 37% overall since the 1974 introduction of travelcards and greater integration with bus routes. Initial expectations were for 15,000 daily users on Cross City South, an increase of almost 14,000, and 9,000 on CrossCity North, which had 7,000 prior to May 1978.

On the first weekend after the launch there was a rather pathetic jibe in the "Sunday Mercury" from an anonymous staff reporter:-

> "Birmingham's new traffic revolution, the Cross-
> City rail line, has got off to a quiet start with many
> trains little more than half full."

He/she omitted to say that the vast majority of cars choking the city's roads were little more than a quarter full, even during the rush hour.

By July 22,000 people were using the service every day, rising to 30,000 by year's end, and the following March passenger number 7,500,000, hospital worker Mrs.Katherine Green, was officially toasted in champagne at University.

The success all along the core of the route caused an inevitable restlessness amongst the natives of Lichfield, with an hourly service, and Redditch, with three trains per day. Councillors in the shire counties were not so sure. Co-operation and financial support between local authorities and British Rail was a new concept alien to them, in which they could see little merit. Early

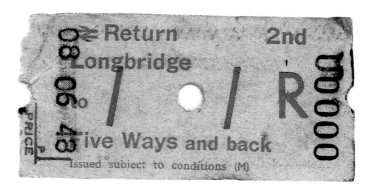

Ticket to Ride, May 8th 1978. Longbridge had a short-lived station, open between 1840 and 1849. The first station at Five Ways did not open until 1885, so it was not possible to travel on an ordinary train between these two places until the Cross City service began. The second Longbridge station (1919-1964), on the Halesowen branch, was only ever served by workmen's trains.

WMPTE experience seemed to confirm their thoughts, as when the line needed £1million in support from various sources during its first year, and later when the Sunday morning trains were axed and the evening service south of Birmingham halved as economy measures in 1981. They could not see it as good value for money, even when compared with the huge annual expenditures on road improvements within their own counties that would benefit fewer daily commuters and blight the lives of many.

This policy delayed developments at the outer ends of the line for several years and numerous discussions between West Midlands County Council, WMPTE, British Rail, Staffordshire and Hereford & Worcester bore no fruit at first. Gradually attitudes changed until the service developed to its present level. Hereford & Worcester County Council and Redditch Development Corporation decided to support an hourly service to Redditch from May 1980. As usual there were financial hiccups, with the estimated cost of their support rising from £168 000 to £216 000 per annum. The Chairman of the Council, Sir John Cotterell, was quoted as saying that as the county had already spent a fortune on road building this scheme ought to be scrapped and the money spent on improving Bromsgrove rail services instead, on the grounds that the Bromsgrove scheme would cost less and be easier to implement, according to information supplied to the county by British Rail. The Redditch service did go ahead, but was supported by the county on a short term basis, renewed every six months. Support was not established on a more permanent basis until May 1983, and only then did BR feel confident enough to include the trains in its all-line time-table. Further improvements gradually filtered through to Redditch over the next few years.

North of Birmingham, WMPTE decided to extend half the Four Oaks trains to its boundary at Blake Street, partly to offer a better service to the edge of the conurbation and partly in the hope of shaming Staffordshire into action. The absence of a crossover at Blake Street meant that trains terminating there would have to run empty to Lichfield just to change track. Blake Street station lies almost on the county boundary and any crossover installed north of the platforms would be in Staffordshire. To navigate round this bureaucracy a crossover was inserted south of the station, at a cost of £100 000, with a down fixed colour light home signal showing permanent red on the up line at the north end of the platform. Blake Street saw half-hourly off-peak trains from May 1984, but just two years later they were continued through to Lichfield, so the crossover became redundant except for the occasional peak working. It last saw intensive use in 1990 when the service was disrupted following the IRA shooting of two soldiers while they were waiting for a train at Lichfield City.

By the middle of the 1980s the dmus were feeling their age, reliability was becoming a problem and the local media were quick to reach for the emotive word "notorious" whenever they mentioned the line. In the autumn of 1986 the off-peak expresses began, a bold experiment which showed both the local management's determination to improve the service and the sort of things that can happen with chronic underfunding. A fifth train every hour was grafted onto the existing service, running non-stop between New Street and Sutton or King's Norton. No single train was an express both north and south of New Street, timings were almost impossibly tight, and the expresses did not stop at University, Five Ways or Erdington - three of the busiest stations. The train indicator blinds were not modified, Tyseley merely provided hand written "Express" signs for cab display. These were often mislaid, expresses were sometimes unannounced at New Street and confusion reigned for passengers. Any speed advantage was neutralised when an express was caught behind the preceeding stopping train, suffering a series of signal checks. Sadly, one disabled man fell to his death attempting to alight from a slow moving express as it passed through Wylde Green station. The expresses were discontinued in May 1989, but at the same time the service at the outer stations was improved, to counter bus competition.

A summary of the main developments and changes in services during the diesel era is given below:-

MAY 1980 Hourly service to Redditch during the day, plus one evening train, dep. New St. 22.48.

JUN 1981 Sunday morning trains withdrawn; weekday evening trains south of Birmingham reduced to half-hourly.

MAY 1984 Half-hourly service extended to Blake St.

MAY 1986 Half-hourly service extended to Lichfield

SEP 1986 Express service commenced; hourly evening trains began on the Redditch branch.

MAY 1987 Sunday morning trains restored; Sunday service extended to Barnt Green and Lichfield.

NOV 1988 Lichfield Trent Valley High Level platforms re-opened.

MAY 1989 Express service discontinued; all trains north of Birmingham extended to Lichfield City, alternate ones worked through to Trent Valley; Redditch service doubled to half hourly throughout the day; Sunday service extended to Redditch.

When electrification was sanctioned, in February 1990, the line had had less than a year to enjoy a full all-day service at all stations, seven days a week.

Station																	A								
Lichfield City d	0931			1006		1031				1106		1131			1206			1231			1306		1331		
Shenstone d	0936			1011		1036				1111		1136			1211			1236			1311		1336		
Blake Street d	0941		1001	1016		1041			1101	1116		1141		1201	1216			1241		1301	1316		1341		
Butlers Lane d	0944		1004	1019		1044			1104	1119		1144		1204	1219			1244		1304	1319		1344		
Four Oaks d	0947	0952	1007	1022	1037	1047	1052		1107	1122	1137	1147	1152	1207	1222		1237	1247	1252	1307	1322	1337	1347		1352
Sutton Coldfield d	0950	0955	1010	1025	1040	1050	1055		1110	1125	1140	1150	1155	1210	1225		1240	1250	1255	1310	1325	1340	1350		1355
Wylde Green d		0958	1013	1028	1043		1058		1113	1128	1143		1158	1213	1228		1243		1258	1313	1328	1343			1358
Chester Road d		1001	1016	1031	1046		1101		1116	1131	1146		1201	1216	1231		1246		1301	1316	1331	1346			1401
Erdington d		1003	1018	1033	1048		1103		1118	1133	1148		1203	1218	1233		1248		1303	1318	1333	1348			1403
Gravelly Hill 70 d		1006	1021	1036	1051		1106		1121	1136	1151		1206	1221	1236		1251		1306	1321	1336	1351			1406
Aston 70 d		1009	1024	1039	1054		1109		1124	1139	1154		1209	1224	1239		1254		1309	1324	1339	1354			1409
Duddeston d		1012	1027	1042	1057		1112		1127	1142	1157		1212	1227	1242		1257		1312	1327	1342	1357			1412
Birmingham New Street 70 a	1005	1018	1033	1048	1103	1105	1118		1133	1148	1203	1205	1218	1233	1248		1303	1305	1318	1333	1348	1403	1405		1418
d	1006	1021	1036	1051	1103	1106	1121		1136	1151	1203	1206	1221	1236	1251		1303	1306	1321	1336	1351	1403	1406		1421
Five Ways d	1009	1024	1039	1054		1109	1124		1139	1154		1209	1224	1239	1254			1309	1324	1339	1354		1409		1424
University d	1013	1028	1043	1058		1113	1128		1143	1158		1213	1228	1243	1258			1313	1328	1343	1358		1413		1428
Selly Oak d	1016	1031	1046	1101		1116	1131		1146	1201		1216	1231	1246	1301			1316	1331	1346	1401		1416		1431
Bournville d	1017	1033	1048	1103		1118	1133		1148	1203		1218	1233	1248	1303			1318	1333	1348	1403		1418		1433
King's Norton d	1026	1036	1051	1106	1113	1121	1136		1151	1206	1213	1221	1236	1251	1306		1313	1321	1336	1351	1406	1413	1421		1436
Northfield d	1029	1039	1054	1109	1116	1124	1139		1154	1209	1216	1224	1239	1254	1309		1316	1324	1339	1354	1409	1416	1424		1439
Longbridge d	1029a	1043a	1058a	1113a	1120	1129a	1143a		1158a	1213a	1220	1229a	1243a	1258a	1313a		1320	1329a	1343a	1358a	1413	1420	1429a		1443a
Barnt Green d					1125						1225						1325				1419	1425			
Alvechurch d					1130						1230						1330					1430			
Redditch a					1138						1238						1338					1438			

This extract from the ill-fated express time-table highlights the difficulties of operating such a service. It can be seen that timing was tight, to put it mildly. Lack of spare line capacity meant that expresses could not operate during the peak hours, just at the times when they would have been most attractive to the weary outer suburban commuter. When they did operate they omitted to call at some of the busiest stations.

(courtesy of British Rail)

90

In common with much of Britain the Cross City line suffered severe disruption due to the blizzards of Friday 8th January 1982. Train services were suspended and not resumed until the Sunday of that weekend. This picture shows what is believed to be the first northbound train, a Class 116 dmu, around 11.00am, as it heads towards Bournville past Lifford Curve.   *(P.J.Shoesmith)*

CHAPTER THREE: UNDER THE WIRES

(Why Electrify? : Into the Black Hole :
A Diary of Events : Possible Future Developments)

WHY ELECTRIFY?

Official Attitudes to Rail Modernisation in the 1980s : The National Background to the Cross City Electrification Scheme

Given the ground rules in existence at the time of the submission, British Rail and the West Midlands Passenger Transport Authority knew that the case for electrification was going to be difficult to justify. Apologists for the government of the day frequently point out that during the 1980s more money was spent on railways and more route miles were electrified than in any previous comparable period. This is correct, but it masks some unavoidable truths, four of which stand out like sore thumbs.

First, the money spent on British Rail had already been generated by British Rail, chiefly in the form of fares, freight revenue, property rentals and the sale of redundant assets; the railway was merely being permitted to spend its own money. In addition, the interest paid on money previously borrowed from the government was a continuing millstone around the railways' neck. Rubbing salt into the wound, any rail improvement scheme lucky enough to attract an £X million grant from the European Community meant that £X million was deducted by the Treasury from the national grant payable to BR. This was the notorious "additionality" rule. Worse than the politics of the madhouse, it was the politics of petty spite.

Second, the narrow criteria applied to freight traffic were based on every single tonne carried being able to generate a profit, with no margin for loss leaders or fluctuations in traffic levels. No other transport haulier is expected to operate like this. Consequently, just when it should have been increasing in volume, valuable freight traffic continued to be lost to the roads when their environmental impact was becoming ever more intolerable. Throughout the 1980s, whenever politicians were questioned about the wisdom of such a trend, most threw up their hands in despair and mouthed the standard catch-phrase, "But rail only carries about 10% of this country's total freight traffic". They had been hypnotised into confusing what was happening with what should have been happening. They failed to mention the strategic nature of many rail-borne goods, particularly chemicals, minerals, roadstone, nuclear waste and bulk fertiliser, or to see any merit in increasing rail's share of the total market.

Third, the replacement of 1950s diesel trains with 1980s diesel trains - the Sprinter series that began regular service in 1985 - was superficially beneficial, but hardly forward thinking. Unfortunately the government bound the railway's hands behind its back; they normally sanctioned the replacement of old three-car diesel multiple units on any given route with new two-car trains. Whilst it is true that two-car Sprinters have roughly the same seating capacity as old three-car sets, this does not allow for growth in traffic which almost always follows improvements in a train service. Any extra third car had to be purchased, justified and wrangled over after the new trains entered service.

Fourthly, a rolling programme of electrification failed to materialise, despite a pledge from the government as long ago as 1981 that there was to be one for the rest of that decade and beyond. During those years it was never possible for designers, engineers and construction gangs to finish one scheme knowing that there would be another in the pipeline. Teams were disbanded and had to be re-formed whenever the next scheme was sanctioned, an unnecessary dissipation of time, skill and money. Without a rolling programme there could be no continuity, and the sectorisation of British Rail - in effect an attempt to run it as mutually dependent but separate businesses - only hindered this even further.

Most 1980s electrification schemes were small scale, all were long overdue and very cost effective, and none were directly aimed at increasing rail's share of freight traffic. Extensions of electric mileage around Glasgow and in the Liverpool/Manchester area were of local significance, though hardly major pieces in the national rail jig-saw. In third-rail territory, south of London, the extension to Weymouth should have been incorporated when electric trains to Bournemouth replaced steam in 1967. Another opportunity was missed in the 1970s when the 125mph High Speed Trains took over the East Coast Main Line. In the final analysis they are beautiful trains in which to travel, but expensive to operate, environmentally unsound and technologically backward when set alongside even 1970s electric traction. A further decade was wasted before electrification of this main line began.

Extensions to the existing electric network, such as Edinburgh-Aberdeen, Bedford-Sheffield, Crewe-Holyhead and Manchester-Blackpool, were suggested in vain and ad nauseam by many transport analysts and local authorities quick to see the 'sparks effect' benefits a modern electric railway brings in its wake. It aids all-round economic development and encourages a rise in property values, as anyone living in Peterborough, Bedford or even Diss will know.

Finally, at the turn of the decade, in March 1990, the then Transport Secretary had the gall to attend ceremonies marking the completion of electrification between Portsmouth and Southampton. This diesel island in an electric sea had been an anomaly ever since 1967, adding considerably to difficulties of operation and cost. Eventual electrification was no thanks to government flair and initiative, nor to their generosity with investment cash. It would probably have been more fitting to open this link without ceremony. The Transport Secretary's presence was rather like a smiling burglar handing some of the stolen goods back to his victim many years after the robbery; unfortunately such behaviour with regard to rail is perceived as so normal that the victim was grateful.

Scales Weighted Against Electrification

Such was the unpromising national climate in which the scheme for the Cross City Line was submitted. Those responsible at BR and the passenger transport authority were well aware of the likely difficulties that lay ahead.

The passenger transport authority (Centro) had consistently advocated electrification of the Cross City Line since the beginning of the 1980s, although at first British Rail considered replacing the vintage stock by Sprinters, largely on the grounds of fuel costs. At the time a diesel multiple unit was cheaper to run, mile for mile, than an electric equivalent, thanks to deflated oil prices caused by a prolonged glut on the world crude market. On the other hand BR, unlike any domestic consumer, pays a premium rate for all the electricity it draws from the National Grid because it is costed to them at the level used when they have peak demand for it. This coincides with peak demand from other users, therefore the maximum tarrif is charged, even outside the limited hours of maximum demand.

In 1989 the Department of Transport's "Seven Per Cent Rule" was still in force, by which British Rail had to 'guarantee' a 7% rate of return on investment before any improvement scheme costing over £1 million could be sanctioned. This rule dates back to 1981. On February 11th of that year the final report of a BR/Department of Transport review was published which supported a major rolling programme of electrification. One of its conclusions was that:-

> "it would take an unlikely combination of adverse
> factors to undermine entirely the prospect that a
> programme of main line electrification would earn
> a return of at least 7%".

The rolling programme was stillborn, but the Seven Per Cent Rule stuck. Of course, no such cast-iron guarantee can ever be given before the event, although it had been the case for many years that forecasts of passenger numbers following any major improvement to a service were almost invariably an underestimate. Bitter experience meant that the Department of Transport was only ever approached, and then only hesitatingly, with the most water-tight proposals.

Soon after the Cross City scheme had been submitted the Seven Per Cent Rule, without prior warning, became the Eight Per Cent Rule, a small increase on the surface, and one above which the scheme was well able to rise, but it brought into even sharper focus the double-thinking that was endemic at the Department of Transport. How?

The growth in traffic was expected to be achieved at first without any increase in rolling stock capacity. The number of new electric trains was to be the same as existing diesel trains on a service that was already overcrowded.

Neither was the British Railways Board permitted, in any way whatsoever, to support its case for electrification by stating that an increase in rail traffic would lead to a corresponding decrease in the level and cost of parallel commuter car traffic, accidents, pollution, etc., despite overwhelming evidence to this effect, for example, during London's brief "Fare's Fair" experiment of the early 1980s.

There was even a technical hitch with the northern tip of the route between Lichfield City and Lichfield Trent Valley. This valuable link was re-opened in 1988 under the terms of the "Speller Amendment" legislation, named after its creator, Tony Speller (Conservative M.P. for North Devon), whereby a station or line could be re-opened to passengers more easily than formerly on an experimental basis. This enlightened provision has resulted in many re-openings, including the line to Hednesford in 1989. Unfortunately such services can also close again without the normal statutory procedure, and there is as yet no standard definition as to how long they remain experimental. Because the line between Lichfield City and Trent Valley was re-opened on this basis there was no legal device for its inclusion in the original scheme. However in the autumn of 1990 British Rail Provincial (now Regional Railways) decided to fund electrification of this 1.3 mile stretch of line, at an estimated cost of £0.75 million.

To summarise, where did all this leave the Cross City Line? The civil engineering, particularly the signalling on the southern section, would be costly; electric multiple units carried a price tag of around £1.5 million each and were more expensive to run than comparable diesels (1989 prices); the trains were expected to increase passenger revenue by at least 8% but there could be no provision for increased overall capacity; any environmental benefits the scheme might bring could not be accounted in its favour; the northern terminus had to be excluded from the original scheme because of a technicality.

Arriving at a Viable Scheme

Given all the above it will come as no surprise to learn that the scheme had to be pared to the bone before it could hope to succeed. Three main factors had to be considered - the density of traffic, the new trains and the alterations to signalling, stations, etc. that would be necessary.

There is no dispute that the Cross City Line was the busiest diesel commuter service in the country, if not the world, with six trains per hour each way in the peak periods, four in the off-peak, carrying over 30,000 passengers per day in 1989. Sixteen trains arrived in New Street from the Sutton direction alone during the morning peak. The service had become expensive and unreliable. It was worked entirely by life-expired multiple units based at Tyseley, which were only kept going at all thanks to the skills and dedication of that depot's staff. By 1990 every unit had run more than three million miles and some spare parts with which they were being fitted had not been manufactured since 1959.

Assessing the cost of electric rolling stock was not the only consideration. New diesels would not need expensive overhead wiring, substations, immunisation of signalling, improved clearances under bridges, etc.. However, electric trains score over diesel equivalents once they are up and running because of their much lower maintenance costs. The more miles they run the greater their advantage, and nowhere is there better scope for this than on the Cross City Line.

Modern electric multiple units, including the Cross City's fleet of Class 323s, bring further cost benefits with their regenerative braking system; in effect the surplus energy generated whenever the brakes are applied is re-cycled back into the power supply system, so that it can be used again. The 323s return up to 30% more energy to source than older units. They are very efficient and simple machines. With few moving parts, there are few things to go wrong and few to maintain. They can easily run four hundred miles per day - six round trips between Lichfield and Redditch - and still only need attention at roughly ten week intervals.

The Cross City Line required sufficient new trains to operate a full electric service, especially during the peak hours. By implication this meant that some trains would be surplus to requirements most of the time, so they could be used to improve the quality of off-peak travel on other routes in the West Midlands. This in turn meant some of the older less efficient electric multiple units would be confined to peak-hour use, and a few of these only for the more intensive morning peak. Careful planning meant that the twelve-hour inspection needed by each

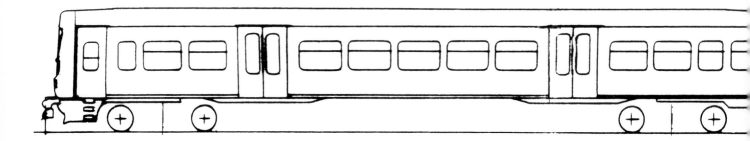

323 unit every ten weeks could be carried out without disruption to regular train diagramming.

The scheme cast a wider net in the search for economies. With electrification the workload of the diesel-only depot at Tyseley was to be halved, but it would make economic nonsense to have this expensive installation working at half capacity as a result. Originally it was proposed that Cross City electric units should be based there but, in fact, they can all be accommodated elsewhere. Most are stabled at Soho depot, along with the area's other emus. All are maintained at Longsight depot, Manchester. This has removed the need to electrify and immunise over three miles of double track to Tyseley.

Work was to be brought in to Tyseley from smaller diesel depots, at least one of which could be closed. Chester was selected. A cold economic decision perhaps, which would bring no cheer to railwaymen and their families in that city, but one which was taken knowing the harsh scrutiny any scheme of railway development is subjected to by the Department of Transport and the Treasury.

In an ideal world the Camp Hill line would be energised as a strategic diversionary route; this was briefly considered but soon rejected. It was agreed that all four tracks between King's Norton and Barnt Green ought to be electrified, but this was rejected by InterCity, prime user of the fast lines, on the grounds of cost without benefit. It can be argued that this was a false economy. If there is a train failure, a minor mishap, or even routine maintenance, Cross City trains cannot weave between slow and fast lines, as is standard practice on quadruple track elsewhere in the country.

Keeping electric trains out of Tyseley and off the fast lines shaved £4 million from the cost of the total scheme, which was beginning to look viable.

By happy chance the cost of some improvements could be excluded from the scheme because, although they were necessary for a modern high quality electric service, they would have happened anyway. Chief among these was the replacement of the semaphore signalling between Aston and Lichfield, part of a rolling programme financed by Centro which was timetabled to start as electrification work proper was beginning in earnest, during the winter of 1990/91. (An earlier beneficiary of Centro-sponsored improved signalling had been the Stourbridge line, where headway between trains had been reduced from ten to five minutes, a valuable saving at peak times.) A programme of station improvements not dependent upon electrification and not confined to the Cross City Line, but again financially supported by Centro, also took place at the same time. For example, the wooden platforms at Aston were replaced, Butler's Lane was

rebuilt and platforms at Shenstone, Bournville and Sutton Coldfield were lengthened and upgraded. Ramps or lifts for disabled travellers were installed at most stations. None of these added one penny to the cost of electrification, but the benefits they brought were considerable.

In a nutshell the scheme, as eventually sanctioned by the Department of Transport, was for electrification south from New Street to Redditch and north from Aston to Lichfield; a total of 33 route miles, or 60 track miles. The line was to be operated by new emus. Upgrading and immunisation of signalling south of Birmingham was included, as were all necessary earthworks. These consisted mainly of lowering about seven miles of track to provide sufficient clearance under bridges for the catenary, cutting back lineside trees and shrubs - particularly on the Redditch branch - and adapting or removing platform canopies at certain stations. Only two bridges, at Lichfield City and Shenstone station, would require rebuilding.

The scheme was submitted - or was it? - to the Department of Transport early in 1989, following authorisation by the West Midlands Passenger Transport Authority at their meeting on January 24th. Hopes were high for an early favourable reply, but for over a year nothing definite was to be heard; the scheme had disappeared into a void.

INTO THE BLACK HOLE

The British Railways Board had agreed on a scheme in November 1988, and the PTA ratified it two months later. They immediately made a joint approach to the Department of Transport and outside observers presumed, not unreasonably, that this equalled a formal submission. Not a bit of it!

When nothing more was heard for several months questions were asked, even in the House of Commons, but the D.of T. denied ever receiving a submission. Whilst this proved to be technically correct it was treading very close to the margins of deceit.

This double-speak is a device used when the Department is stalling non-road building schemes for which it can see no obvious merit. It is successful all too frequently and, to those on the receiving end, is a refined form of Chinese water torture. In this case the D.of T. was 'discussing' the scheme with British Rail and the PTA, telling them which parts would be unacceptable should they wish to submit it. A few dates and quotations will illustrate the confusion.

"... I can assure you that no formal investment proposals has"(sic)"yet been put forward by British

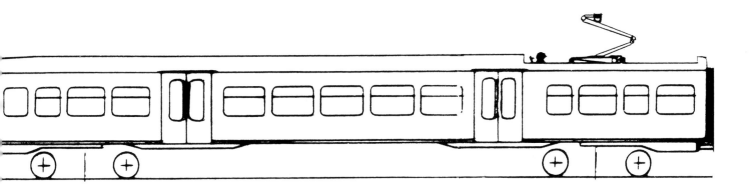

Rail to the Department. I understand that BR are carrying out further studies, then if, a formal proposal is put forward, the Secretary of State would be happy to approve it provided that it offers good value for money."

reply to myself from D.of T., relating to an enquiry while preparing an article under preparation for "Modern Railways", 13th April 1989

".....the submission will be made to the government in the next few days."

Cyril Bleasdale, General Manager, British Rail's Midland Region, speaking on Central Television, 16th June 1989

".....the submission is imminent."

a British Rail spokesman, 22nd September

"The proposals for electrification were passed to the Department of Transport two weeks ago."

a B.R. spokesman, 4th October

"The scheme should be submitted to the Department very shortly"

The B.R.Chairman, 26th October

"...the plans are sitting on the Transport Secretary's desk and he will be dealing with them very quickly."

Michael Portillo, Minister for Public Transport, speaking in the House of Commons on 30th October.

And three days later ....

"I am afraid I cannot give immediate approval to the electrification of this line, although I hope to do so in due course. I can see that, on central assumptions, the case for electrification is made. However we cannot be absolutely certain that electrification is the most cost-effective solution until the new year when the rolling stock tenders have been evaluated. I accept that there seems to be a low risk that the cost of the new electric trains relative to new diesel trains would be so great as to overturn the case. But the risk remains and I do not feel justified in giving my approval before the outcome of the evaluation is known."

Cecil Parkinson, in a letter to the P.T.A. and British Railways Board, 2nd November.

Other tactics were employed throughout this sorry saga. There were a dozen or so meetings that took place during 1989 at the behest of the D.of T. specifically to discuss this scheme. Without exception every meeting was postponed at short notice, sometimes for weeks and some more than once. One rail official directly involved at the time ruefully described the thwarted efforts to make progress as "attempting to wrestle with a blancmange". No credible reason was ever offered for such chaotic mis-management of the Department's appointments diary. There were even conflicting messages from different parts of the Department of Transport, the Railways Division and Metropolitan Division openly contradicting each other. (The latter is responsible for funding transport schemes in the former metropolitan counties and the P.T.A. areas.) On one occasion their contradiction was so obvious that they were embarassed into an apology! Sir Robert Reid (mark 1) wrote in despair to the Secretary of State for Transport, stating that the process by which such vital schemes were dealt with by his department needed to be looked at to prevent such heavy delay in future. (At the time of writing no improvements have been made.)

Why the all-embracing awkwardness at the Department? The answer is political. For many years industries that have continued in public ownership have suffered the dead hand of political dogma. As seen from the D.of T. and H.M.Treasury a successful nationalised railway industry would contradict received political wisdom. It is in their narrow interests to ensure that as much potential success as possible is strangled at birth. The fact that a successful rail industry - no longer a political football and allowed to compete on equal terms with other forms of transport - would be in the wider interests of the country as a whole is something they appear unwilling to accept or incapable of grasping. Every railwayman of whatever background with whom I have raised this point while preparing my book has privately agreed that this is the root cause of the ills that beset the industry.

For at least thirty years the funding of transport schemes has not been based on their merits but on perceived political advantage. The Humber Bridge was sanctioned while the government of the day was looking over its shoulder at an approaching by-election in the area; the Tyne & Wear Metro was delayed because there was no obvious political gain in agreeing to construction; a fear of voters in some marginal Kent constituencies has unduly influenced the routing and severely delayed a proper national rail link with Europe until well after completion of the Channel Tunnel. These are just three examples of many. The bid to electrify the Cross City Line looked like becoming another victim of this twisted way of thinking.

The death of the M.P. for Mid-Staffordshire in the autumn of 1989 caused a by-election. This sprawling constituency is centred on Lichfield and Rugeley, extending south to the county boundary at Blake Street station. The late John Heddle (Conservative) had increased his majority at the 1987 election to a healthy 14 654, but by the time of his death the government's popularity was in decline, due in part to the newly introduced poll tax. Opinion polls indicated that it might lose the seat.

On February 7th 1990 the Transport Secretary suddenly gave approval for electrification of the line. The announcement, during a by-election campaign which was rapidly becoming the focus of national media attention, may have been mere coincidence. Conversely, those with little charity to spare for the government's woes might interpret it as a cynical bribe to the constituency's many rail commuters. Be that as it may the Labour Party candidate, Sylvia Heal, was returned to Parliament with a majority of 9,449. Although the seat subsequently returned a Conservative member in the 1992 General Election, if the Cross City Line *was* used as a political football in this by-election the Department of Transport managed to score an own goal.

A DIARY OF EVENTS

1990
Initial Engineering Work at Northfield
Sunday May 27th

In the small hours of Sunday May 27th 1990, and on into a glorious early summer morning, an army of gangers, aided by a tamping machine, removed ballast from almost a quarter of a mile of the up slow line just outside Northfield station, on either side of the bridge carrying a narrow offshoot of Norman Road. The track was lowered by about five inches to obtain sufficient clearance for the overhead.

The sight of thirty or so men, tamping machine and mechanical digger, plus two Class 47-hauled ballast trains in attendance - all for the sake of those essential five inches - put the term "heavy engineering" into a new perspective.

Contract for Class 323 Electric Trains Signed
Tuesday June 26th

The contract for building the Class 323 electric multiple units was won by Hunslet Transportation Projects Ltd., of Birmingham, in stiff competition with six other European manufacturers. The new trains would not be solely for the Cross City Line, and the success of Hunslet was considered a remarkable coup by some.

Thirty-seven 323s were ordered, of which eighteen would be needed by Cross City. The remainder were destined to replace old electric trains operating in the Greater Manchester area. The contract also contained an option for a further fourteen units.

The story of the intrigue and rivalry between the bidders for the contract is told clearly and in depth by Roger Ford in his 'Informed Sources' column in "Modern Railways" for August 1990.

Appointment of first Schools Liaison Officer for British Transport Police, Birmingham
Monday October 1st

Whilst the force has always maintained close links with communities living near the railway, especially with children, P.C.Gary Read was the first of four officers appointed specifically to work with schools and children on a full time basis. He was to have special responsiblities for schools near the Cross City Line during electrification. He was helped by Stan Watson, a retired train driver.

They had the huge task of visiting all schools near the railway, from nursery units up to sixth form colleges. On the Cross City Line, *excluding* the twelve route miles in Staffordshire and Hereford & Worcester, there are over ninety such schools within a mile and a half of the tracks.

Community Policing at Aston Tower Primary School, Birmingham 19
Wednesday December 5th

P.C.Gary Read was at work near the start of the rail safety campaign, and he quickly established an excellent rapport with sixty lively eight year olds.

He began by saying that he was no ordinary policeman, but a member of the British Transport Police, "and for that you need to be 5'10" tall, under 30 years old and handsome, so they took one look at me and said I could join; I didn't even have to fill in a form!"

He told a few jokes and spun a few yarns, before showing the video "Robbie", about a boy who was badly injured when trespassing on an electrified railway. A glimpse of his horrific burns changed the audience's mood and helped to reinforce the message, but the visit could not really end on such a sombre note. One girl decided that she would like to join the railway police, and there followed an amusing few minutes while she was kitted out with P.C.Read's jacket, helmet, handcuffs, etc., before the children were reminded again of the dangers of playing on the railway and sent home with badges saying "Trains are for travel, not play!".

This particular visit took place near Aston station, where the line was electrified in 1967, and over five months before the first masts were planted on the Cross City Line itself, but it was no less relevant for that.

Sadly, a 13 year old Lichfield boy died in May 1993 when dangling a length of kitchen foil from a bridge onto the wires below, the first such tragedy on the Cross City Line.

First Public Forum at Sutton Coldfield Station
Tuesday October 2nd

This was the first of a series of informal public meetings held along the line, entitled "You Can Have Your Say". BR and Centro officials were in attendance, literature was available, and members of the public came and went at will over a period of two hours. No real conflict of views emerged, as people welcomed the coming electrification; "It should have been done years ago" was a commonly expressed opinion. They recognised that disruption to services and the lineside environment would be minimal. Some people wondered whether they would have a mast at the bottom of the garden, and even in this respect B.R. was often able to help by minor re-siting at the planning stage, although at least two masts in the Sutton area were moved after planting.

This was a well run public relations exercise. The stress level experienced by officials in attendance was low!

When mast planting began the following spring there were a few unfortunate incidents on location, such as the time when a mast foundation team was verbally abused for twenty solid minutes by an irate commuter at Four Oaks. Their crime? They had had the temerity to park their vehicle in his parking space. He would not be persuaded that they were there to improve his railway and he also chose not to notice that the car park was three-quarters empty!

Construction Contract Awarded
Monday January 7th

Pirelli Construction, of Eastleigh, Hampshire, was awarded the contract for installing masts and overhead wiring. Together with commissioning and testing by British Rail engineers this contract was worth £4 million. A total of 1,700 masts would be required and the Pirelli team was based at the King's Norton depot.

New Signalling System on Cross City North
Wednesday January 30th

The contract for installing a new £2.8 million signalling system between Aston and Lichfield Trent Valley (15 miles) was awarded to EB Signal (UK) of Plymouth. The fifty-eight signals and associated cabling were to replace all existing signalling. The semaphore signals were condemned and the boxes at Erdington, Four Oaks and Lichfield City were to be closed and demolished. The new signals would be controlled from the renovated 1950s box at Duddeston. They would be better spaced, increasing track capacity and enabling trains to run closer together - only three minutes apart south of Blake Street, five minutes apart between Blake Street and Trent Valley - useful in the event of late running and at peak periods. The work was due for completion in the spring of 1992, with commissioning the following autumn.

More Buses Brought In
Monday February 4th

From this date evening trains were replaced by buses to allow greater track possession by the engineers. There were no trains at all on Sundays. From October 1990 buses had replaced trains between New Street and Redditch on Saturday evenings and all day on Sundays.

Centro erected special stops at stations, for the exclusive use of buses.

It would be tedious to catalogue every alteration, but at various times during electrification evening and weekend trains were restored whenever possible, then replaced by buses on a planned basis whenever engineering made it necessary.

Taking a first bite
Wednesday February 20th

Councillor Phil Bateman, Chairman of WMPTA at the time, operated a mechanical digger for the first mast foundation, at King's Norton Electrification Depot. Ceremony apart, foundation work had actually begun ten days earlier, near Blake Street.

Class 323 Preview
Friday May 17th

This took place in Coventry at Tickford Rail Limited, a company specialising in design and styling for urban and mass transit rail systems. The preview consisted of a full scale wooden mock-up of a Class 323 car, composite so as to include features normally distributed thoughout the three cars of a complete train.

The plans show a well designed train, the technical data for which is as follows:-

Number ordered	37 3-car units with an option on a further 14
* Construction	welded aluminium extrusions
Length	23 metres per car
Seating	284 + 5 tip-up seats, 3+2 layout
* Passenger doors	twin leaf sliding plug design, one third and two thirds along the body side
Gangways	between vehicles within each 3-car unit
Toilets	one per unit
Wheelchair space	one per unit
* Destination indicators.	electronic, external only
* Traction	alternating current, 3 phase drives, 8 motors per unit with regenerative braking.
Unit end coupling	Tightlock auto-coupler
Driver-shore radio	fitted as standard
* On-train monitoring and recording equipment	fitted as standard
* Windows	double-glazed, with opening hopper for ventilation
* Seating bays	in line with windows
Convertible area with tip-up seats	for wheelchair-bound passengers, parcels, parents with prams

Notes on the technical data (* above) -

Aluminium construction ensures corrosion resistance for the whole life of the vehicle.

At 1.28 metres the door openings are wider than on a Class 321 unit, further helping swift movement of passengers at busy stations. The doors plug the gap on closing, rather than merely sliding across it. The system operating the doors is electric, which is smoother and more reliable than a comparable pneumatic system.

The indicators are dot matrix, with each letter/numeral composed of a series of dots, as on a computer screen.

The traction units were manufactured by Holec, a Dutch based company. There are 4 motors under each end car and running costs are minimal, thanks to the few moving parts and regenerative braking.

On-train monitoring equipment doubles as a kind of tachograph, checking that speed limits are being observed, and a black box in the event of mishap.

At last, after a gap of twenty long years, here were some new trains in which the seating bays matched the windows!

The Class 323 units were to be constructed and fitted out at Hunslet's Leeds works. At the time of the preview the first one was due for delivery on June 27th 1992.

Terry Jeffries of Hunslet TPL claimed that the 323 would set new standards for electric vehicles in this country. Councillor Dick Worrall of WMPTE confirmed this, adding:-

> "When the public get to use these things they will die of culture shock. It's great to see something tangible. I look forward to the time when all local lines are electrified, and beyond the boundary into the shire counties."

There was sufficient comfortable room for my 6'2" frame in even the most confined seat - an acid test. The seating arrangements near the doors and gangways, where 3 x 2 became 2 x 2, would seem to aid easy movement at peak times.

The interior was bright and light, despite the drab grey austere decor. The pint-sized toilet was only for the small or the desperate, but these were minor blemishes which could be improved during manufacture.

The driver's cab was functional and comfortable, all instruments easy to see and reach, with two emergency brake plungers, two phones (one internal, one to shore) and a standard speedometer which could register 150mph, but not on this line or unit. Centro has a no smoking policy for all its bus and train passengers but each 323 driving cab comes complete with an ashtray.

The train starts to leave the drawing board. At the Birmingham offices of Hunslet TPL a designer, working with computer-generated plans of the Class 323 emu, is able to assess all aspects of the design by using high quality, full colour, three-dimensional computer graphics.
(courtesy of Hunslet TPL and Darley Communications)

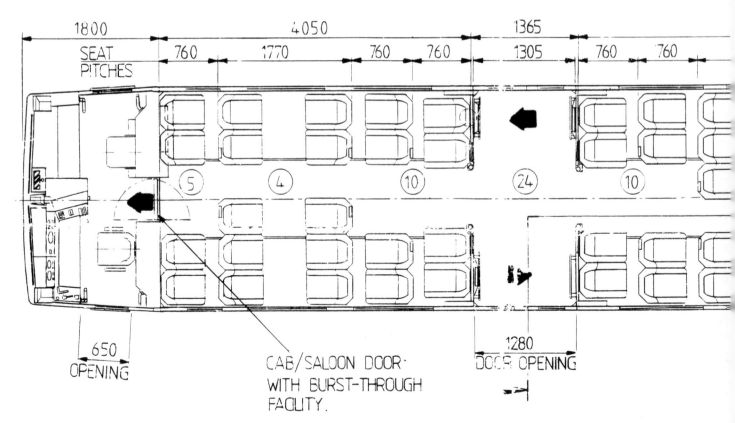

The business end of a 323 electric unit, showing driver's cab and part of the passenger accommodation. Figures in circles indicate the number of standing passengers in each area under crush loading conditions.

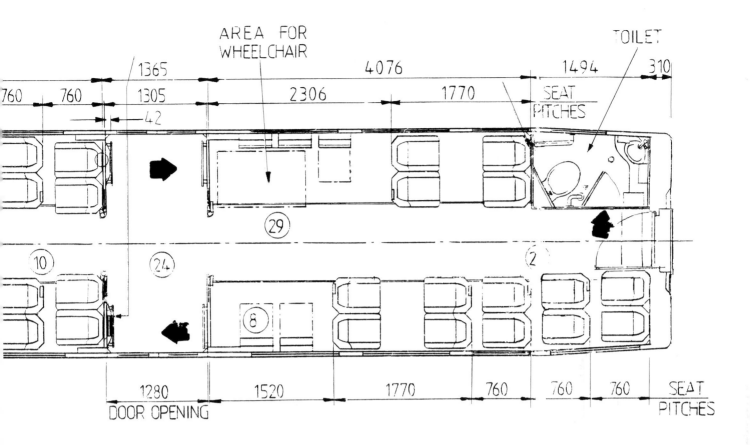

One end of a 323 centre car, showing the toilet and wheelchair areas. There are five wall-mounted tip-up seats. All measurements are in millimetres.

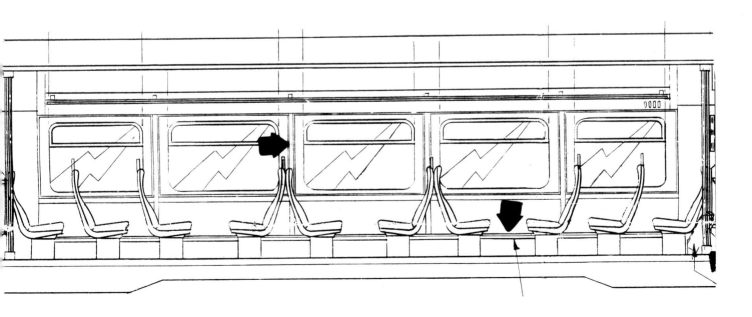

This section of the elevation of a 323 centre car shows how well the pitch of the seating matches the windows.

The ability of the 323s to accelerate rapidly from station stops would help to speed up the time-table. Provisional timings issued in 1991 anticipated a journey time of 34 minutes between Birmingham and Redditch, as against 43 minutes by diesel, and 37 minutes between Birmingham and Lichfield (45 minutes by diesel).

First Mast Planted
Monday May 20th

The first mast was planted, without ceremony, near Erdington station.

Safety Campaign Launched
Wednesday May 22nd

Some pupils from The Arthur Terry High School, Sutton Coldfield, had designed rail safety badges for the electrification. At the launch on New Street Station it was announced that 24,000 badges would be made by the older pupils, some of whom were using the experience as part of a GCSE design course. The badges would be given away to children living near the line. Each design, one of which included the TV puppet Edd the Duck, bore a slogan, Edd's choice being "Quack, quack, stay off the track".

Mast Milestone at Sutton
Tuesday July 16th

The Lord Mayor of Birmingham, Councillor Bill Turner, planted the 500th mast, complete with ceremonial plaque, at Sutton station.

At this date the work was on schedule and almost a third of the masts had been planted, all between Aston and Shenstone.

On September 24th the thousandth mast was planted behind the buffers at Redditch, four weeks ahead of schedule.

Replacement of Butler's Lane
Sunday October 20th

The 1957 station was closed from this date and the platforms were demolished, to be replaced by new ones on the same site. They would have been rebuilt in any event, but work coincided with lowering of the track under the road bridge. It was easier to provide a bus link to Blake Street than erect a temporary station on this difficult site, which is in a cutting and has a narrow road approach. The new station was completed in March 1992.

Wiring up begins
Tuesday November 12th

Wiring began on Cross City North in October and I was invited to spend the first part of the night shift aboard the wiring train on November 12th, a day noted over most of Britain for wild windy weather and heavy rain, so we were fortunate to have cold but moderate winds under a clear sky. The train, which our party boarded at Shenstone, consisted of a Class 31 loco, four flat topped vans - tools, mess, store, etc. - and four bogie flat wagons for the drums of wire. Power for the lighting and winches came from the 240v generator, re-charged between trips at King's Norton depot.

The crew of eight men employed by the contractors, Pirelli, were under the direction of British Rail's Jimmy Edgar, Senior Overhead Line Construction Inspector. Most of the men were Scots and some had been moving around with the work for some time. Jimmy Edgar himself worked on the Ayshire Coast scheme in 1985, moving on to the Scottish section of the East Coast Main Line and the Edinburgh-Carstairs route before reaching Cross City.

To the interested layman the workings of an electric railway might mean little more than a jumble of overhead wires from which the trains somehow derive energy. Let me, in basic terms, clarify this. In essence, each running line must have three overheads - contact, catenary and return.

Rail safety stickers designed in 1991 by Adam Timbrell and Dan Poyner, students at Arthur Terry High School, Sutton Coldfield.
(by permission of Mr.A.D.Sayers, Head of Art & Design, Arthur Terry High School)

The aluminium return wire is mounted on the masts but insulated from them. Electric trains are supplied with energy at 25Kv not because they need all of that amount, but in the interests of efficient working. The surplus energy is returned to the feeder station (ie; re-cycled) initially via the train wheels and track and then into the return wire via booster transformers which are mounted on the masts at roughly 3 kilometre intervals. These transformers boost the power supply when it is some distance from source, as well as minimising interference to nearby electronic circuits, such as telephones, etc.

The catenary wire hangs from the cantilever supporting frame, attached by hinges to the mast. The main components of the frame are three steel tubes with a 42mm bore. One of the tubes is inclined, the other two are horizontal. The bracket is fitted with standard porcelain insulators. The catenary consists of seven-ply twisted wire, five strands of aluminium and two of aluminium-coated steel. The steel provides sufficient tensile strength because the catenary dips slightly but precisely and in tension between masts, so as to counteract the uplift from a train's pantograph, which is also in tension.

The contact wire, which is reckoned to have a life expectancy of sixty years, is suspended from the catenary by stainless steel wires, know as 'droppers'. As the contact wire does not dip, but is at a fixed height above the track, the length of each dropper is computer calculated, to be assembled and packaged in order before the train leaves the depot. There is nothing random about this or any of the other equipment in the tool van. As Jimmy Edgar remarked, "It may look like a large jumbled Meccano set, but each piece has its own location and it won't fit anywhere else".

The solid copper contact wire has two continuous grooves which are gripped by pincers, known as 'noddy clips' attached to each dropper. This to me was the most interesting revelation of the evening; the BR 25Kv electric network, parts of which are used by trains travelling at up to 140mph (Cross City maximum 90mph) depends ultimately on copper wire of only 12mm diameter held in place by noddy clips!

Each section of contact wire is, on average, about 1.5 kilometres long, depending on the constraints of the location. At a point about 2km south of Shenstone one end of the contact was anchored, with a system of weights and pulleys fixed to a mast. This done the train began to move at a brisk walking pace, and for the first fifty metres, between adjacent masts, the new contact wire paralleled some that had been installed previously. Such overlapping is standard practice. As the wire played out men stood in line on the van roofs, adding noddy clips and fixing the contact wire loosely into place. Once this process was complete the other end of the wire was anchored, weighted and subjected to the necessary tension of 1.25 tonnes, read from a meter slightly larger than a phone handset. This was basic initial installation, as fine tuning and adjustment of both contact and catenary would follow later.

The vertical array of anchor weights at the side of a mast, necessary wherever wires end, is always accompanied by a system of pulleys. This is an overhead high-tech equivalent of jointed rail, allowing the wire to expand or contract with the temperature whilst keeping the tension constant. Mean temperature is reckoned at 10 degrees Celsius.

At this time wiring was complete from Gravelly Hill almost to Shenstone, apart from a gap at Butlers Lane. There are no electricity feeder stations on the line itself, but new ones at Galton Bridge and Winson Green allow for the increased needs of the enlarged West Midlands electric network as a whole.

The wiring train in Shenstone station, having completed installation of a length of contact wire, November 12th 1991.

(courtesy of Fastline Promotions Limited)

Butlers Lane being demolished, to make way for a permanent station and lowering of track under the bridge, October 20th 1991.

(A.D.Sayers)

1992

The year began with a flurry of trackwork. Weekends in January were occupied with track lowering at Blake Street, removal of redundant points at Four Oaks and installation of new ones at Wylde Green.

King's Norton Depot
Sunday January 12th

An interesting afternoon at the depot, courtesy of Senior Overhead Line Construction Inspector Jimmy Edgar, learning more about the nuts and bolts of the electrification process. The accommodation and administration areas consisted of Portakabins. Some offices were located in standard containers, known as green security cabinets, without windows and fitted with secure locks.

To the rear of the site a compound housed crates and pallets for an assortment of small and medium components, the bits of the Meccano set referred to earlier. There was a stack of about twenty high speed insulators, waiting to be inserted in the contact wire wherever a break in current was required, mainly for loops, sidings, and crossovers.

Forty-kilo cast iron ballast weights, for anchoring lengths of wire, were neatly stacked, each with a pattern for locking into its neighbour. Porcelain insulators have been easy targets for stone throwers in the past. The latest type consists of a cylindrical porcelain core with a thick ribbed outer coating of white rubber. The look remains the same, apart from the colour, but stones merely bounce off. More traditional insulators are now made in single segments, so only damaged segments need be replaced.

The compound housing the drums of overhead wire was the most secure part of the site, with the full benefit of high fencing topped with razor wire, flood-lighting, and gates protected by a seriously robust padlock.

There were only a few masts on site, as most had long since been installed. Some lattice girder arms remained, for use at awkward locations to span two tracks from a single mast.

There was a wide variety of rolling stock in evidence, owned by BR but operated by Pirelli. The younger of the two cranes was a 1987 Plasser GPC 38, weighing 44 tonnes, capable of lifting 4 tonnes and with a telescopic jib ideal for mast erection. The other crane, dating from 1964, was capable of lifting 6.5 tonnes. In outward appearance it differed little from the steam cranes of earlier years.

The Atlas EPV 360 (EPV = excavating purpose vehicle) with hinged arm, was used for digging holes for mast foundations. It could be fitted with three sizes of bucket or, in tough territory, a hydraulic hammer for breaking rock. The arm of this 42 tonne machine could be 'locked on' for working in confined spaces, allowing digging to proceed while trains continued to run on track alongside. Most earlier machines had cabs which rotated with the jib, fouling adjacent running lines and disrupting the train service. The Atlas had its own engine, being able to travel to site without the expense of a locomotive.

This was also true of smaller machines, even down to the four-wheel short wheelbase 5-tonne Permaquip Trolley, used for fine tuning and inspection of overhead equipment. Its platform could be raised to 5.8m above track level and, even though its fully enclosed cab had room for a five man crew, it still looked rather like a high-tech version of the hand pumped trolleys which feature in so many silent films.

The northern boundary of the site was the four-track main line and concrete mast foundations (average depth 1.3m) were much in evidence here. The process of mast erection is in two stages. When each mast hole is excavated a polystyrene plug with the same profile as the mast is inserted into the middle of the hole. Vertical steel reinforcing rods, horizontal wrap-around binder rods, and vertical steel bolts are positioned around the plug. The hole is then filled with concrete, just the tops of the bolts protruding. After a fortnight the polystyrene is burnt out with xylene, a volatile solvent also used in the manufacture of dyes, insecticides and resins. The mast is then planted, the bolts matching the position of the bolt holes on its base.

Last Mast Planted
Thursday January 16th

Patrick Lichfield, photographer cousin to the Queen, planted the so-called last mast in a ceremony at Lichfield City station, although a few short stretches of line south of New Street remained mastless.

Signalling Contract for Cross City South
Monday February 3rd

The contract to modify and upgrade signalling between Birmingham and Redditch was awarded to ABB Signal Ltd., of Plymouth. It was worth £2.5 million, only £0.3 million less than for the installation of a completely new system between Aston and Lichfield, a sign that modification can be more difficult than building from scratch. The same firm won both contracts, with a change of name in the meantime (see January 30th 1991). Work was due for completion in March 1993.

Chairman inspects 323 replica
Monday 2nd March

Sir Bob Reid, Chairman of British Rail, unveiled a full-sized wooden replica of the 323 emu at a ceremony for invited guests in a marquee at Stanier House.

Barnt Green Facelift
Monday 27th April
Work began on improving the environment of Barnt Green station, at a cost of £125,000. The package included raising the height and increasing the length of the branch platforms, installing new lighting and improving the entrance from the car park.

Duddeston signal box is prepared for action
Sunday 7th June
A new signalling console - eighteen feet long, weighing one tonne, and looking like a giant piano under wraps - was lifted into Duddeston box at about 9.30am. This box renamed 'Aston Signalling Centre' now controls train movement between Aston and Lichfield by means of 54 colour light signals along the route, replacing three manual boxes of LNWR vintage at Erdington, Four Oaks and Lichfield City.

New platform at Lichfield Trent Valley
Tuesday 1st September
The new platform at Lichfield Trent Valley High Level was opened by Michael Fabricant the new Conservative MP for Mid-Staffordshire.

New station at Redditch
Monday 5th October
Work began on Redditch's fourth station. The existing platform was to be retained but other facilities were to be improved.

Visit to Class 323 Driver Simulator at Stafford
Tuesday 22nd October
Most people are aware that airline pilots receive much of their training on a flight simulator; not many realise that rail drivers can now be trained in the same way. The £1 million simulator at Stafford is housed in a high security container and used exclusively for training railmen to drive the Class 323 electric multiple units.

Late delivery of Cross City 323 electrics
November
Problems with the first 323 to emerge from Hunslet's Leeds works resulted in late delivery. The first three-car unit, 323 201, suffered gearbox problems and severe vibrations during test running in November and was promptly grounded at Bletchley. Its gearbox was sent away for investigation. To prevent any possible repeat performances the only other unit which had been delivered was not run, on advice from Hunslet. This second unit was later shipped to Vienna, to undergo rigorous testing of its insulation, to find out if it was fully proofed against severe weather. Austrian Railways have the most sophisticated plant in Europe for this type of test. The visit of 323 202 to Vienna was routine and planned, unconnected in any way with the faults found in the first unit. It was not intended to deliver or test any further unit until the nature of 323 201's gearbox fault had been discovered, neither would British Rail accept any from the manufacturer. The next five units, 323 203 - 323 207, were securely stored at the MOD railway depot at Kineton in Warwickshire.

Electric service begins on Cross City North
Monday 30th November
This had been the target date for an all-new electric service for over a year but the late delivery of the 323s meant that it was operated by three sets of Class 310 emus, supplemented by the

heritage diesels. The first electric train left Lichfield Trent Valley at 06.34 without ceremony or incident. The Class 310 sets were built in the mid 1960s and used for local and semi-fast services. These three units were brought out of store in Manchester and worked successive trains on the first day. The increased reliability and capacity of the new signalling and the ability of the emus to make up for lost time when running late were two important benefits felt immediately.

The very first public electric train - unplanned - was the 17.28 from New Street to Blake Street, which ran four days earlier on Thursday November 26th. It was formed of emu unit 304 043. This train had often been top of the list for cancellation whenever there were stock/staff shortages but on this occasion the spare Soho emu was commandeered at short notice instead. It was unannounced, almost a public proving run, and spotted rather by chance by the local press. "We were putting our toe in the water" was the wry comment of Robin Etherington, Cross City Line Public Relations Officer.

1993

New station at Alvechurch
Saturday 9th January
Work began on the new station on a site nearer the road. A new platform, shelter and lighting were provided, together with a proper surface for the small car park and a vehicle turning area. The cost was £232 000 and took two months. The original station, which suffered serious vandalism in recent years because of its isolated position screened from nearby houses, was demolished.

Further Delays to Electric Service
Monday 1st February
British Rail announced further delays today. Vandalism and arson had destroyed signalling equipment at Soho on December 28th, severely disrupting services on the Birmingham-Wolverhampton line for six weeks. Signalling technicians were transferred away from the Cross City Line to help with this emergency. Although others were drafted to Cross City from York, Hull, Stafford and Worcester, the overall disruption and continuing problems with the 323s meant that a full electric time-table could not be introduced until the summer. July 12th was the new target date.

Signalling Marathon to complete the job
May 14th-16th & May29th-June 1st
These two weekends saw closure of much of the line south of New Street as the final large piece of the electrification jig-saw was fitted into place. This was the £5million installation of new signalling and track circuiting between New Street and Redditch, and along the Camp Hill line. Planned with military precision, it meant two weekends of severe but brief disruption to the train service. A team of 150 signalling engineers, many from as far afield as Hull, Leeds and Norwich, was involved in replacing 55 signals, 115 track circuits and 53 points motors.

The system was symbolically switched on by Dame Jill Knight, MP for Birmingham Edgbaston, in an informal ceremony inside Saltley Power Box on Thursday 3rd June. The displays appear on two monitor screens above the main panel.

The overhead between New Street and Redditch became live at 00.01 hours on Sunday 6th June.

A Double First
Thursday 24th June
Electric unit 310 106 formed the 16.15 departure from New Street to Redditch, the first public electric train on the southern half of the Cross City Line. Unannounced beforehand, this train ran seventeen days early. Following arrival at Longbridge, it formed the 16.50 service to Four Oaks, thus becoming the first Cross City electric *through* New Street. It was intended to operate more such trains before July 12th whenever possible. Problems with the 323s had been resolved during the summer. The first units were expected to be phased in during the autumn, and an all-323 time-table starting in May 1994 would mean further reductions in journey times.

At Last!
Monday 12th July
An all-electric service began on the full length of the Cross City Line this day.

FUTURE DEVELOPMENTS
The Total Cost of the Cross City Electrification Scheme is reckoned to be £64.5 million, 70% of which is funded by Centro, the remaining 30% by the Regional Railways sector of British Rail.

Completion of the scheme must not be seen as some kind of ending; it is only a landmark along the way. The train service must be allowed to develop, otherwise it will eventually stagnate, just as the Birmingham-Lichfield diesel service once did. Possibilities are already being discussed.

First, the spur to the West Coast Main Line at Lichfield Trent Valley should be electrified. The cost will be very small when set against the advantage of the link for diversions, emergencies or empty stock movement. The spur will never be used by regular electric service trains; it should merely act as an inexpensive strategic link. In the autumn of 1991 it was said that the expense, likely to be shared between Regional Railways and InterCity, could not be justified. By the time this book appears there may have been a change of heart.

The idea of reviving the Frankley end of the former Halesowen Railway has been around since the 1970s; its time has now come. "Keeping The West Midlands Moving", the 20 year strategy document issued by Centro in 1992, says:-

> "Over the next few years Centro will investigate other opportunities that will exist to improve the local rail network, particularly in the early years of the next decade. These include .. reinstatement of a passenger service on the former branch line from Longbridge to Frankley."

The same document outlines plans for seven new stations on the Cross City Line, already referred to in Chapter One.

The few InterCity trains that call at Lichfield Trent Valley en route to Euston or the North West merit more vigorous promotion on the Cross City Line, so that potential passengers from the Sutton area are aware that they can go to Manchester, for example, without the need to travel to New Street first.

After the aluminium Class 323 bodyshells are shotblasted and primed, fillers are applied and flatted off to remove surface imperfections, before a final prime coat.
(courtesy of Hunslet TPL and Darley Communications)

A new express service over at least part of the line deserves serious consideration. North of the city an hourly diesel Sprinter could run non-stop to Sutton Coldfield, going forward to Four Oaks, both Lichfield stations, Alrewas, Barton-under-Needwood (both re-opened), Burton and Derby. This would improve Sutton and Lichfield area journey opportunities to Yorkshire, North-East England and Scotland, by substituting a simple change at Derby for an initial journey in the wrong direction.

South of the city, a Barnt Green call by at least some of the existing Regional Railways express dmus to Cardiff would increase the attraction of southbound travel - none of it in the wrong direction - for passengers from every Cross City station south of New Street.

The Camp Hill Line has been without a regular passenger service for over fifty years. Traffic congestion, especially in King's Heath and Moseley, is chronic for much of the day, particularly since the opening of the M40 has had a knock-on effect over much of south Birmingham. A restored passenger service would be welcomed by those who live near the line and need to commute to the city centre. If only life were that simple.

Many awkward questions need to be answered first. How would the trains be fitted into an already overcrowded New Street? Would they start from Frankley, Bromsgrove, King's Norton? Would they integrate with Cross City trains and would the line be considered for electrification? The Centro strategy document makes no direct mention of passenger services for this line, neither are there plans for a Metro to serve the area. There can be no easy answers, but there are many people living in King's Heath, Moseley and Balsall Heath who would like to see some answer, easy or not. This line passes over the Snow Hill-Leamington line just south of Bordesley station. A short south-west spur linking the two (a north-east spur already exists) would provide for direct running between the Camp Hill line and Moor Street/Snow Hill. The Camp Hill trains could be integrated with others serving Snow Hill, including the Centro-proposed electric service between Walsall and Earlswood, which would use its own new spur at Soho.

Whatever happens in future years, the electrification of the Birmingham Cross City Line marks the beginning of an exciting new chapter in its long and eventful history.

ACKNOWLEDGEMENTS

Many people have readily offered help, advice, assistance, use of facilities, photographs, documents, etc. in the preparation of this book. Without them it would not have been possible. Particular thanks are due to the following:-

Richard Abbott	- Local Studies Department, Birmingham Central Library
Paul Adams	- BR Planning Office, Birmingham
Alan Bevan	- Railway Development Society
Anne-Marie Boynton	- for constructive criticism and limitless patience
Roger Carpenter	- for photographs
Brian Clarke	- BR Area Traction Inspector, for information and acting as my escort on cab rides over the line
Helen Davies	- Cadbury's Library and Archive Dept
John Dawson	- British Rail
Jimmy Edgar	- Senior Overhead Line Construction Inspector
Robin Etherington	- British Rail Cross City Line Public Relations Officer, for generous general help, arranging site visits, cab rides, use of library, etc.
Neil Harvey	- Hunslet Transportation Projects, for information about the Class 323 emu
A.Holme-Barnett	- for photographs
Fred Jenkins	- retired railwayman, ex-Midland Railway, LMS and British Rail
Graham Kendrick	- Secretary, West Midlands TUCC
David King	- Director, Hunslet TPL, for permission to use plans of the Class 323 emu
M.A.King	- for photographs
Stewart King	- Rail Services Manager, Centro
Tom King	- retired railwayman, ex-Midland Railway, LMS and British Rail
Steve Knight	- "Rail" magazine
David McIntosh	- British Rail Regional Railways Manager, East & West Midlands
Ian McLean	- BR, for Motorail archive material
Chris Mew	- British Rail, Cross City
David R.Morgan	- for Redditch information
Chris Needham	- British Rail Traction Officer
Ian Pardoe	- Superintendent, Kineton Military Rly
Don Powell	- for memories and photographs
P.C.Gary Read	- British Transport Police
A.D.Sayers	- Head of Art & Design Arthur Terry High School, Sutton Coldfield
P.J.Shoesmith	- for photographs
A.R.Spencer	- for photographs
Colin Smalley	- for photographs
David Voice	- tramway author
Steve Young	- BR Information Services Assistant

The author wishes to state that although he received much valuable assistance from BR staff and others working in an official capacity, any unattributable opinions expressed in the text of this book are entirely his own.

AN OUTLINE CHRONOLOGY : 1836 - 1993

1836
April 22nd
An Act of Parliament included provisions for the Birmingham & Gloucester Railway to have a junction with the London & Birmingham Railway "at or near the Garrison in the parish of Aston", and gave it the right to use the L&B station "or any future terminus of that company in or near Birmingham". The act also required the line to pass by Moseley Church in a tunnel, not a cutting.

1837
July 4th
Grand Junction Railway reached Birmingham from Warrington with temporary station at Vauxhall.

1838
January 6th
World's first Post Office sorting carriage began running between Vauxhall and Liverpool.

1839
January
GJ terminus at Curzon Street opened, replacing temporary terminus at Vauxhall.

1841
August 17th
B&G passenger services extended into Curzon Street; goods traffic commenced in October.

1846
August 7th
Act of Parliament provided for construction of station at New Street, to be for passengers only with a public footbridge across the station in lieu of King Street, which was to be obliterated.

1849
May
King's Norton station opened.
June
Lichfield (City) opened on Walsall-Lichfield section of South Staffordshire Railway. Passenger services extended to Lichfield Trent Valley, then known as 'Trent Valley Junction', in August.

1854
June 1st
Birmingham New Street opened fully to LNWR trains.
July 1st
Birmingham New Street opened to Midland trains and Curzon Street closed to regular passenger trains.
November
Aston station opened.

1859
September 19th
The Redditch Railway, operated by the Midland, opened to passengers - and to goods on 1st October.

1862
June 2nd
Sutton Coldfield railway opened, with stations at Gravelly Hill, Erdington, Wylde Green, Sutton Coldfield.

1863
December 1st
Chester Road station opened.

1868
May 4th
Redditch ceased to be terminus, when line to Alcester opened. Original Redditch station replaced by second one, quarter of a mile south.

1869
March 1st
Vauxhall opened on present site; Bloomsbury & Nechels (a quarter of a mile to the north) closed.

1870
September 1st
Northfield opened.

1871
July 3rd
At Lichfield the original Trent Valley stations closed; replaced by station on present site.
July 31st
Act of Parliament authorised construction of Birmingham West Suburban Railway, a single track branch to be worked by Midland Railway.

1876
April 3rd
Birmingham West Suburban Railway opened, with stations at Stirchley Street, Selly Oak, Somerset Road, Church Road and Birmingham Granville Street. The station at Lifford opened on June 1st.

1880
June 29th
An Act authorising construction of a line from Sutton to Lichfield was passed.

1883
September 10th
The Halesowen branch opened, with intermediate stations at Rubery and Hunnington. Goods traffic was exchanged at Northfield and passenger trains ran to/from King's Norton.

1884
September 1st
The line between Sutton and Lichfield opened for goods and to passengers on December 15th.

1885
February 8th
Midland platforms brought into use at New Street.
July 1st
West Suburban extension into New Street opened; Five Ways opened; Granville Street closed.
September 26th
Deviation between King's Norton and Bournville opened, original line converted into loop siding; Lifford (BWS) closed and replaced by new station on Camp Hill line.

1892
July 1st
Lifford Curve opened and Circle passenger service began,

New Street to New Street via West Suburban Line, Lifford Curve and Camp Hill Line. Quadruple track brought into use between King's Norton and Halesowen Junction.

1893
May 7th

Viaduct carrying Sutton and Walsall lines clear of tracks into Curzon Street opened, relieving a notorious bottleneck.

May 22nd

The last day Curzon Street was used by any type of passenger train - an excursion to Sutton Coldfield.

1925
January 1st

Church Road station closed.

During this year King's Norton was rebuilt as quadruple track was extended through the station.

1928
May 11th

Part of Cofton Tunnel collapsed, killing four workmen.

1929
January 26th-28th

Demolition of Cofton Tunnel completed.

1930
May

Last vestiges of Cofton Tunnel removed, the final act in completion of quadrupling between King's Norton and Barnt Green.

July 28th

Somerset Road station closed.

1939
May

Running revised on four track section between King's Norton and Halesowen Junction, in time for summer Saturdays. The outer lines, used by freight, upgraded and used by local passenger trains in order to ease the passage of holiday expresses through this bottleneck. Signalling altered and new crossovers installed at Northfield, which still had a single island platform.

1940
September 30th

Lifford closed as wartime economy.

19th-21st November

New Street Station closed by enemy action.

1941
January 27th

Circle service via Lifford Curve withdrawn and all stations on Camp Hill line closed to passengers as a wartime economy. Closure made permanent, November 27th 1946.

10th-18th April

West Suburban Line tunnels closed by enemy action.

1944
October 2nd

Five Ways closed as wartime economy. Closure made permanent (or so they thought!) in November 1950.

1955
January 23rd

Seventeen lives lost in Sutton Coldfield disaster.

1956
March 5th

Birmingham-Lichfield service converted entirely to regular interval diesel operation.

1957
August 1st-12th

World Scout Jamboree held in Sutton Park.

September 30th

Butlers Lane Halt opened.

1958
June 1st

First Motorail train from Sutton Coldfield to Stirling.

1960
April

Hourly diesel service began between Birmingham and Redditch.

1965
9th August

Closure consent for the Redditch branch refused.

1978
8th May

Cross City service began, between Four Oaks and Longbridge. New stations opened at Five Ways, University and Longbridge.

1990
7th February

Electrification of Cross City Line, between Redditch and Lichfield City, approved by Secretary of State for Transport, Cecil Parkinson.

27th May

First engineering work in preparation for electrification takes place.

1991
20th May

First electrification mast planted at Erdington.

1992
30th November

Electric service begins - Birmingham-Lichfield.

1993
6th June

Whole Cross City line energised, Lichfield to Redditch

12th July

Electric train service begins over the whole route.

BIBLIOGRAPHY

"A REGIONAL HISTORY OF THE RAILWAYS OF GREAT BRITAIN, volume 7, THE WEST MIDLANDS"
  Rex Christiansen
  David & Charles
  1973
  ISBN 0 7153 6093 0

"BIRMINGHAM NEW STREET, THE STORY OF A GREAT STATION"
  (volumes one & two)
  Richard Foster
  Wild Swan Publications Ltd.
  1990
  ISBN 0 906867 78 9 (vol 1)
  ISBN 0 906867 7 97 7

"BIRMINGHAM RAILWAY SCENE"
  compiled by C.C.Dorman
  Town & Country Press ltd.
  1971

"BRITAIN'S FIRST TRUNK LINE, THE GRAND JUNCTION RAILWAY"
  Norman W.Webster
  Adams & Dart
  1972
  SBN 239 00105 2

"CROSS CITY CONNECTIONS"
  John Bassett
  Brewin Books
  1990
  ISBN 0 947731 78 4

"FORGOTTEN RAILWAYS, volume 10, THE WEST MIDLANDS"
  Rex Christiansen
  David & Charles
  1985
  ISBN 0 946537 01 1

"KING'S NORTON"
  Roger Carpenter
  Article and photographs outlining redevlopment in 1920s
  in "British Railways Journal" for Christmas 1990

"LMS ENGINE SHEDS" Vol.1 & 2.
  Chris Hawkins and George Reeve
  Wild Swan
  1981
  ISBN 0 906867 02 9
  ISBN 0 906867 05 3

"PRE-GROUPING IN THE WEST MIDLANDS"
  P.B.Whitehouse
  Oxford Publishing Company
  1984
  ISBN 0 86093 328 8

"RAILWAYS OF THE WEST MIDLANDS, A CHRONOLOGY, 1808-1954"
  Ed.C.R.Clinker
  The Stephenson Locomotive Society
  1954

"REDDITCH RAILWAYS RE-VISITED"
  David R.Morgan, editor
  University of Birmingham, Department of Extramural Studies
  1983
  ISBN 0 7044 0688 8

"STEAMING UP TO SUTTON"
  Roger Lea
  Westwood Press Publications
  1984
  ISBN 0 9502636 8 0

"THE BIRMINGHAM AND GLOUCESTER RAILWAY"
  P.J.Long & Rev.W.V.Awdry
  Alan Sutton Publishing
  1987
  ISBN 0 86299 329 6

"THE LMS IN THE WEST MIDLANDS"
  P.B.Whitehouse
  Oxford Publishing Company
  1984
  ISBN 0 86093 259 1

"THE LOST RAILWAYS OF BIRMINGHAM"
  Keith Turner
  Brewin Books
  1991
  ISBN 0 947731 89 X

"THE RAILWAY HISTORY OF BROMSGROVE AND THE LICKEY INCLINE"
  Roger Harris
  on behalf of the Bromsgrove Steam Enthusiasts Club

"THE REDDITCH RAILWAYS, 1859-1979"
  David R.Morgan, editor
  Redditch College Department of Education
  1980

"THE STORY OF NEW STREET"
  F.W.Grocott
  British Railways (London Midland Region),
  1954

Various editions of "Railway Magazine" and relevant newspapers and documents, all acknowledged in the text.

FOUR LAST PORTRAITS OF THE CROSS CITY LINE,
as seen through the discerning lens of Peter J. Shoesmith

Blake Street opened on a green fields site in 1884. Very little had changed almost a century later when this picture was taken on 17th March 1972. A Class 101 dmu pauses en route to Lichfield. The area around the station has since been developed, but only as far as the county boundary just north of the station, beyond which the fields are still green. *(P.J.Shoesmith)*

On the eve of the Beeching era steam was widespread and freight still played a significant role. A local passenger train from Redditch, comprised of four LMS period III corridor coaches and hauled by Ivatt 2-6-0 No.43122, heads north towards Bournville, while a freight bound for Cadbury's, hauled by ex-Midland 4F 0-6-0 No.44226, waits to come off Lifford Curve at Lifford West Junction, 2nd August 1963. Although modernised with an upper quadrant arm, the signal controlling the exit from the branch still retains its wooden Midland post.

(P.J.Shoesmith)

Branch platforms at Barnt Green, as BR Standard 2-6-2T No.80063, then in the first flush of its youth, arrives from Redditch with a set of LMS coaches in BR 'blood and custard' livery, 31st July 1954

(P.J.Shoesmith)

The essence of the power and grace of steam. An ex-LMS Stanier 'Black Five', No.44859, heads south into the sunset from King's Norton, 28th March 1963.

(P.J.Shoesmith)

ELEVATION NEXT APPROACH ROAD

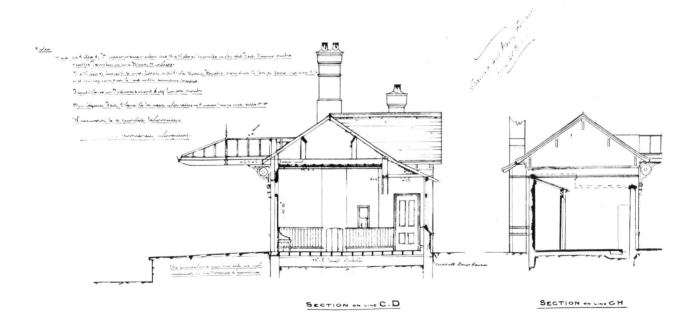

SECTION ON LINE C.D

SECTION ON LINE G.H

Beautifully executed plans from the Architects Office, Derby, dated July 7th 1885 and showing Midland Railway improvements to the station buildings at Selly Oak.

(by permission of British Rail)

" RAILS ACROSS
THE CITY "

New Class 323 electric multiple units for the Cross City Line, in Centro livery, at Kineton Military Railway, April 15th, 1993. Seen here are 323 307 (left) and 323 303.

(John Boynton, courtesy of Kineton MR)

ISBN 0-9522248-0-1

MID ENGLAND BOOKS
£9.95 net

9 780952 224808